DATE DUE

W9-AVG-299

The Nature
of the
Resurrection Body

The Nature
of the
Resurrection Body

A Study of the Biblical Data

by

J. A. SCHEP

Professor of New Testament at
The Reformed Theological College
Geelong, Victoria, Australia

WM. B. EERDMANS PUBLISHING COMPANY
GRAND RAPIDS, MICHIGAN

TO MY WIFE

ACKNOWLEDGMENTS

I remember with gratitude my teachers at my Alma Mater, the Free University, Amsterdam, where I had the privilege of studying for the Candidate of Theology degree under such eminent Professors as Dr. G. C. Aalders, Dr. H. Bavinck, Dr. F. W. Grosheide and others, and where I obtained the Master of Theology degree, specializing in New Testament studies, under the guidance of the Reverend Professor Dr. R. Schippers.

I express my sincere thanks to the Senate and Theological Faculty of Potchefstroom University for Christian Higher Education, for graciously granting me the opportunity of submitting the present book in manuscript form in satisfaction of the requirements for the degree of Theologiae Doctor, *in absentia.*

I am grateful also to my esteemed Promoter, the Reverend Professor Dr. J. W. Snyman, Dean of the Theological Faculty, for his kind assistance in several respects; and to all those who have assisted me in preparing this study, in particular to my friend and colleague the Reverend Principal A. Barkley, M.A., of the Reformed Theological College, Geelong, who read and re-read the manuscript and offered valuable suggestions, especially with a view to English idiom.

Geelong, Victoria, Australia

—J.A.S.

CONTENTS

7

LIST OF ABBREVIATIONS

A-G	*Greek-English Lexicon of the New Testament,* by W. F. Arndt and F. W. Gingrich
ANF	*The Ante-Nicene Fathers,* ed. A. Roberts, J. Donaldson, A. C. Coxe
ASV	American Standard Version
BAT	*Die Botschaft des Alten Testaments*
BDB	*Hebrew and English Lexicon of the Old Testament,* by F. Brown, S. R. Driver, and C. A. Briggs
BV	Berkeley Version
CBSC	*Cambridge Bible for Schools and Colleges*
CD	*Church Dogmatics,* by Karl Barth
CNT	*Commentaar op het Nieuwe Testament*
COT	*Commentaar op het Oude Testament*
DSB	*Daily Study Bible,* ed. W. Barclay
Erl.	*Erläuterungen,* by A. Schlatter
ERV	English Revised Version
ExT	*Expository Times*
IB	*Interpreter's Bible,* ed. G. Buttrick
ICC	*International Critical Commentary*
KB	*A Hebrew and English Lexicon of the Old Testament,* by L. Koehler and W. Baumgartner
KD	Keil and Delitzsch
KJV	King James (Authorized) Version
KNT	*Kommentaar op het Nieuwe Testament*
KV	*Korte Verklaring der Heilige Schrift*
LXX	Septuagint
MNTC	*Moffatt's New Testament Commentary*
MT	Masoretic Text
NBG	*Nieuwe Vertaling Nederlands Bijbelgenootschap*
NEB	The New English Bible, New Testament
NIC	*The New International Commentary on the New Testament,* ed. N. Stonehouse, F. F. Bruce
NLC	*The New London Commentary* on the New Testament
NPNF	*The Nicene and Post-Nicene Fathers,* ed. P. Schaff, H. Wace

NTC	*New Testament Commentary,* by W. Hendriksen
NTD	*Das Neue Testament Deutsch*
NTS	*New Testament Studies*
PNT	*De Prediking van het Nieuwe Testament*
RSV	Revised Standard Version
SB	*Kommentar zum Neuen Testament,* by H. L. Strack and P. Billerbeck
TBC	*Torch Bible Commentaries*
TNT	*Tyndale New Testament Commentaries,* ed. R. V. G. Tasker
THNT	*Theology of the New Testament,* by R. Bultmann
TU	*Tekst en Uitleg*
TWNT	*Theologisches Wörterbuch zum Neuen Testament,* ed. G. Kittel, G. Friedrich
ZK	*Kommentar zum Neuen Testament,* by Th. Zahn

INTRODUCTION

One of the most controversial matters in the field of biblical theology today is the nature of the resurrection-body.

Many theologians reject the idea that Scripture warrants any real hope for the present human body of flesh. They appeal to the alleged biblical distinction between body and flesh, and argue that there can be no resurrection of a *fleshly* body. They point also to certain definite statements in Scripture which seem to deny resurrection to the flesh, e.g., Mark 12:25, "For when they shall rise from the dead, they . . . are as angels in heaven"[1]; I Corinthians 15:44, "it is raised a spiritual body"; I Corinthians 15:50, "flesh and blood cannot inherit the kingdom of God"; and other passages.

Among those who deny that the resurrection-body will consist of flesh two groups can be distinguished. There are, first, several theologians who believe in a complete spiritualization of man after death. In their opinion the resurrection-body will be absolutely immaterial.[2] There is also a second group consisting of scholars who hold that the resurrection-body, though not a body of flesh, will yet be composed of some other "substance," some different kind of matter.[3]

---

[1] Unless stated otherwise, quotations from Scripture will be from ASV.

[2] These include R. Bultmann, *Theology of the New Testament*, I, 198-99; E. Brunner, *Das Ewige als Zukunft und Gegenwart*, pp. 164ff.; A. J. Ebbutt, *The Life, the Question and the Answer*, p. 125; H. E. Fosdick, *A Guide to Understanding the Bible*, p. 286; H. J. Heering, *De Opstanding van Christus*, p. 163; A. M. Hunter, *Interpreting Paul's Gospel*, p. 133; Kirsopp Lake, *The Historical Evidence for the Resurrection of Jesus Christ*, p. 226; Chas. E. Raven, *St. Paul and the Gospel of Jesus*, pp. 73, 81; J. A. T. Robinson, *In the End God . . .* , p. 66; *The Body*, p. 32; E. Teichmann, *Die paulinischen Vorstellungen von Auferstehung und Gericht*, pp. 65ff., as quoted by J. Jeremias, NTS, Feb. 1956, p. 158; and Leslie Weatherhead, *After Death*, pp. 48-49.

[3] E. g., P. Althaus, *Die letzten Dinge*, pp. 124ff.; *Die christliche Wahrheit*, pp. 475-81; S. Barton Babbage, in *Reformed Theological Review*, IX, No. 4, pp. 22ff.; H. Bavinck, *Gereformeerde Dogmatiek*, IV, 775; W. Bieder, "Auferstehung des Fleisches oder des Leibes," *Theologische Zeitschrift*, Aug. 1945, pp. 105ff.; O. Cullmann, *Christ and Time*, p. 240; *Immortality of the Soul or Resurrection of the Dead?*, pp. 39, 45; C. H. Dodd, *The Meaning of Paul for Today*, p. 58; *The Epistle to the Romans*, p. 110; K. Dyk, in

The second group is by no means homogeneous. The opinions of some members differ very little from those of the first group, whereas others, especially H. Bavinck and K. Dyk, are essentially in agreement with the doctrine of the resurrection of the flesh. The latter think the term "flesh" to be less correct, but believe firmly that the resurrection-body will consist of visible matter and that it will essentially be the same as this present body of flesh.

Finally, a smaller number of theologians are convinced that the resurrection of the flesh is taught by Scripture. The resurrection-body, according to them, will be a body of flesh; as far as the believers are concerned it will be a body of glorified flesh.[4]

Most of those who deny that the resurrection-body will consist of flesh base their opinion on the contrast between body and flesh as they claim to find it in Scripture, particularly in Paul's writings. Whereas the body is good, the flesh is regarded as intrinsically evil, or at least inferior to the body. Consequently there can be no hope for the flesh; the body to be raised will consist of some other "substance."

Cullmann's view on this point is especially extreme. He says that *body* (Greek *soma*) is good in itself, as appears from the Genesis record which speaks of man's body and soul as God's creation. Here Christianity differs from Greek thought. But *flesh* (Greek *sarx*) is pictured in the New Testament as the transcendent power of sin and death, which entered man's body and soul from without after Adam sinned. Hence man's body and soul must be delivered from flesh, and the resurrection-body will consist not of flesh but of Spirit.[5]

Het Dogma der Kerk, ed. G. C. Berkouwer and G. Toornvliet, p. 592; Over de Laatste Dingen, III, 106; and H. A. Guy, The New Testament Doctrine of the Last Things, p. 115.

[4] Cf. G. C. Berkouwer, De Wederkomst van Christus, I, Ch. 4; R. C. H. Lenski, Commentary on Second Corinthians, pp. 730ff.; K. J. Popma, De Vrijheid der Exegese, p. 168; Eerst de Jood maar ook de Griek, p. 131; Inleiding in de Wijsbegeerte, p. 87; H. Sasse, This Is My Body, pp. 388-89; Erich Sauer, The Triumph of the Crucified, p. 182; Wilhelm Schlatter, Biblische Menschkunde, pp. 74ff.; and K. Schilder, Wat is de Hemel?, pp. 147-49.

[5] Immortality . . ., pp. 30-37, 45-47; Christ and Time, pp. 239ff. Apart from the question whether Cullmann's conception of the flesh is scriptural, a question that will be discussed later, it may be observed here that Cullmann's argumentation seems rather inconsistent. If man was created good in body and soul, then the flesh as matter cannot possibly be evil, for the body Adam received from God was a body of flesh. Accordingly the "flesh" which is said to have invaded Adam's body and soul after the Fall

Others do not go so far as Cullmann, but nevertheless hold that the biblical and particularly the Pauline concepts of *soma* and *sarx* show an essential difference between the two.

Even such a conservative scholar as Dr. William Milligan at the end of the last century held this view. According to him there exists no necessary relation between *soma* and *sarx*. There is even an intrinsic difference: the *soma* is "for the Lord; and the Lord for the body" (I Cor. 6:13); it is the temple of the Holy Spirit in believers (I Cor. 6:19) and can be holy and presented to God as a living sacrifice (Rom. 12:1), but the *sarx* can never be holy.[6]

In recent times J. A. T. Robinson has expressed himself in much the same way,[7] as do most authors who deny the resurrection of the flesh. To the names already mentioned might be added E. Käsemann,[8] H. Wheeler Robinson,[9] and W. David Stacey.[10]

General agreement in this respect does by no means imply, however, that all the respective definitions of "body" and "flesh" are identical. Käsemann, for example, rejects Cullmann's definition of "flesh,"[11] John A. T. Robinson disagrees with the opinions of C. H. Dodd and R. Bultmann regarding the "body,"[12] and W. David Stacey contests the views of Otto Pfleiderer as to the distinction between "body" and "flesh."[13]

Among the theologians referred to in this Introduction, the name of one of the most prominent scholars of our day is not yet mentioned, that of Karl Barth. This is due to the ambiguity of his statements on the matters under discussion.

On the one hand Barth uses the traditional and scriptural language and speaks of the flesh of the risen Christ;[14] he calls Jesus' resurrection "a new beginning of this flesh,"[15] states that our flesh

---

as a transcendent evil power cannot have been "flesh-matter" but some spiritual power — the more so because according to Cullmann the flesh invaded also Adam's *soul*. Consequently this "invasion" of the "flesh" cannot reasonably be regarded as a ground why the resurrection-body should not consist of flesh.

6 *The Resurrection of the Dead*, pp. 147ff.
7 *The Body*, pp. 31ff.
8 *Leib und Leib Christi*, pp. 120ff.
9 *The Christian Doctrine of Man*, pp. 130ff.
10 *The Pauline View of Man*, pp. 186ff.
11 E. Käsemann, *op. cit.*, p. 121, n. 4.
12 *The Body*, pp. 12, 13, n. 1.
13 *Op. cit.*, p. 185.
14 *Credo*, p. 169.
15 *Ibid.*, p. 102.

is already in heaven in Christ[16] and uses more than once the expression "the resurrection of the flesh."[17]

In his *Church Dogmatics,* on the other hand, we find views which seem to deny the resurrection of the flesh altogether, at least if we understand the words "resurrection" and "flesh" in any traditional sense and as objective realities.[18]   The impression is given by Barth that man will have no real, objective existence after death since he lives only between the creation and the End: he did not yet exist before the creation and will no longer exist after the End. There will be continuation only in the sense that man will forever stand before God in the same manner as he was with God before the creation.   The only difference will be that after the End man will be "with God" as one who has been perfected and "eternalized."[19]

Among those who have given an analysis and criticism of these views from the Calvinistic viewpoint, we may particularly mention G. C. Berkouwer[20] and K. Runia.[21]

In the light of so many divergent opinions on the nature of the resurrection-body and the relation between body and flesh, which is fundamental to the problem under consideration, there can be no doubt that further study in this segment of biblical theology is required.

The procedure to be followed in this study is outlined in the Contents.   It will be noticed that much attention is paid to the scriptural data concerning the resurrection-body of Christ, since this is the pattern of the body which the believer will receive.[22] The fundamental distinction, made by some, between Jesus' resurrection-body of the great forty days and that of the glorified Christ after the Ascension (which is sometimes identified with the Resurrection), will be discussed in a special chapter.

---

[16] *Dogmatik im Grundrisz,* p. 183.

[17] *The Faith of the Church,* pp. 162, 165, 171.

[18] Especially III/2, 698ff. and III/3, 99ff., 257ff.

[19] A quite different impression, again, is created by statements like these: "We shall have eyes to see our life 'unveiled,' " and "human life will meet its final destination visibly. . . ." (*The Faith of the Church,* pp. 171-72).   Such expressions can hardly make sense unless Barth believes in an objective, real, and visible continuation of human life in eternity.

[20] *The Triumph of Grace in the Theology of Karl Barth,* Chapters 6 and 12.

[21] *De Theologische Tijd bij Karl Barth,* especially pp. 23ff. and 193ff.

[22] 1 Cor. 15:49; Phil. 3:21; 1 John 3:2.

From this outline it is evident that our study will be confined to the scriptural data concerning the resurrection-body of *Christ* and the *believer*. The resurrection-body of the unbeliever is a subject that would demand separate treatment.

CHAPTER ONE

FLESH AND BODY IN THE OLD TESTAMENT

1. FLESH AND BODY BEFORE THE FALL

As we have seen, Cullmann distinguishes between man's body as God created it and the flesh as the evil power which invaded man's body and soul when Adam fell into sin. One need not agree with Cullmann's conception of the flesh to appreciate the fact that here he takes into account Adam's fall into sin as a most important incision in the history of mankind, with far-reaching implications for man's nature.

Many theologians disagree on this point. To them the Genesis records of Creation and Fall are myths, legends, or sagas: there was no Fall in history, at least not as it is described in Scripture.[1] Especially on the ground of the evolutionary hypothesis, often combined with existential philosophy, they deny the trustworthiness of the Genesis accounts.[2]

It cannot be denied that in the exegesis of the first chapters of the Bible one faces many intricate problems. But it is equally obvious that philosophical, evolutionary theories about the origin of world, man, evil, and death meet with problems no less involved, as is evidenced by the numerous and profound differences of opinion existing in this field. In either case, the decision rests upon faith as "the terminal function of human existence." By faith one either accepts God's revelation in Scripture as the inspired infallible rule of doctrine and conduct, or he rejects it as such;

---

[1] Thus, for example, W. Barclay in ExT, March 1959, p. 175; K. Barth, CD, IV/I, 508ff.; E. Jacob, *Theology of the Old Testament*, p. 299; J. J. Jeremias, TWNT, *s.v.* "Adam," I, 141; J. Wren Lewis in ExT, Oct. 1960, pp. 4ff.; H. W. Robinson, *The Christian Doctrine of Man*, p. 59.

[2] E.g., P. Althaus, *Die Christliche Wahrheit*, II, 145ff.; R. Bultmann, "New Testament and Theology," in *Kerygma and Myth*, ed. H. W. Bartsch, p. 7; A. Richardson, *A Theological Wordbook of the Bible*, *s.v.* "Adam," pp. 14, 15; J. A. T. Robinson, *In the End, God . . .* , pp. 34, 64.

17

he may believe either the Scriptures or the presuppositions and postulates of human reason.[3]

For those who believe the testimony of Jesus and the apostles concerning the Old Testament[4] there can be no doubt as to the historicity and reality of the facts revealed in it, including the fact of the Fall as it is described in the Genesis record.[5]

In describing what happened before the Fall, the Genesis record employs the word "flesh" (Hebr. *basar,* LXX *sarx*) several times in narrating the creation of Eve (2:21-24). Leaving aside matters of source criticism[6] and various exegetical details which are irrelevant to our subject, the following remarks may suffice.

In verse 21 we read that God, having taken a rib from Adam's body, "closed up its place with flesh" (RSV). Here the word "flesh" doubtless denotes "the physical substance" of Adam's body, a usage of the word "which was always primary."[7]

When Adam, receiving his wife with joy, calls her in poetical exultation "bone of my bones, and flesh of my flesh" (vs. 23), then the words "flesh" and "bones" together denote the physical body.[8]

In verse 24 we find the word "flesh" again, when it is declared of husband and wife that "they shall be one flesh." With most Protestant commentators we regard verse 24 as not spoken by

[3] Cf. H. Dooyeweerd, *A New Critique of Theoretical Thought,* II, 298ff. Noteworthy is Bultmann's remark that "modern science does not *believe* that the course of nature can be interrupted . . . by supernatural powers" (*Jesus Christ and Mythology,* p. 15. Italics added).

[4] E.g., Luke 16:17, 29; John 10:35; II Tim. 3:16; II Pet. 1:19-21.

[5] For an evaluation of Barth's conception of the Genesis narratives as "sagas" see K. Runia, *Karl Barth's Doctrine of Holy Scripture,* pp. 92-103.

[6] This author would agree with G. Ch. Aalders' view on this matter in his study *A Short Introduction to the Pentateuch.*

[7] W. D. Stacey, *The Pauline View of Man,* p. 92. See also Koehler-Baumgartner, *A Hebrew and English Lexicon of the Old Testament, s.v. Basar.* Stacey (like many others) uses the word "substance" in its popular sense, a practice also followed in this study.

[8] Cf. E. Schweizer, TWNT, VII, 105. J. Skinner explains the expression as originating "in the primitive notion of kinship as resting on participation in a common mass of flesh, blood, and bones, so that all the members of a kindred group are parts of the same substance." This explanation does no justice to the fact that in Gen. 2:21ff. God reveals how he created Eve, using in a unique, creative act part of Adam's body as a substratum for that of Eve. Adam, to whom God must have revealed how he created Eve, recognized her *on that basis* as "part of the substance of his own flesh" (J. Calvin), and therefore "the completion of his being" (H. Frey, *Das Buch der Anfange* in BAT).

Adam but as "a concluding, summarizing word of the narrator."[9]
The indicative rendering, "therefore a man leaves his father and
his mother and cleaves . . . etc." (RSV, F.M.Th. Böhl, J. Skinner,
C. A. Simpson in IB, *et al.*), though grammatically correct, seems
inappropriate. Not only does it make the whole statement rather
dull, but it is excluded by the fact that our Lord appeals to this
verse as a divine *ordinance* in Matthew 19:5.[10] Though the words
"they shall become one flesh" may not refer exclusively to sexual
intercourse, the latter is undoubtedly implied, so that here we have
"an affirmation that sexual desire is part of the divinely ordered
nature of things" (IB).

This the Genesis record, speaking of our first parents in their
unfallen state (their sex life included) uses the word "flesh" several
times. It is as creatures of *flesh,* destined to be "one flesh" in
marriage, that they came forth out of the hand of God and were
therefore "very good" (Gen. 1:31). As such creatures of flesh,
"male and female," they even were the "image of God," as Genesis 1:27 declares. It may be true that Kittel goes too far when
he writes that especially in his *body* man showed that he was of
heavenly descent,[11] yet there can be no doubt that in his body of
flesh, too, man was God's image and a "very good" image as well.[12]

This appears also from the statement in Genesis 2:25 that man

<hr />

[9] G. von Rad, *ad loc.*

[10] Cf. G. Ch. Aalders, *Genesis,* KV. This does not imply that according
to our Lord the words of Gen. 2:24 were spoken directly by God. It certainly follows, however, that according to Christ the narrator's statement is
a revelation of God containing a divine ordinance (cf. KD, H. Frey, *op. cit.*)
and not merely a human explanation of "the true meaning of the sexual
desire of man" (J. Skinner). Nor is it a later addition to the text in which
v. 23 is criticized (C. A. Simpson, IB).

[11] TWNT, *s.v. eikon,* II, 389. The New Testament data concerning the
believer's renewal as God's image (Col. 3:10; Eph. 4:24) place more emphasis on the spiritual side.

[12] *Dichotomy* in the Greek and Rabbinical senses of the word is rightly
rejected in modern theological works, which emphasize that man is a uni-
fied, psychosomatic being (for example, P. Althaus, *Die letzten Dinge,* pp.
119ff.; R. Bultmann, TH.NT, I, 209; H. Dooyeweerd, *op. cit.,* II, 147; III,
87ff., 198ff., and numerous others). It is less correct to say that man does
not *have* a body but *is* his body, as many recent authors do (for example
R. Bultmann, TH.NT, I, 194; W. D. Jonker, *Mystieke Liggaam en Kerk in
die Nuwe Rooms-Katholieke Teologie,* p. 184; E. Käsemann, *Leib und Leib
Christi,* p. 119; J. A. T. Robinson, *The Body,* p. 14). The body as the
outward man must be distinguished from the *inner* man, the *heart,* "the
centre and radix of our humanity" (H. Dooyeweerd in *Philosophia Reformata,* 1960, p. 133). When this distinction is ignored, the initially legitimate reaction against dichotomy has gone too far.

and wife, though "they were both naked . . . were not ashamed."
In the light of 3:7, where the sense of shame is depicted as resulting from the consciousness of guilt, the absence of shame reveals
the state of sinlessness in which God created our first parents, a
sinlessness that also characterized their sexual relationship.[13]

All this is of paramount significance in connection with our subject.

In the *first* place, it shows that any theory which depreciates the
flesh and therefore considers it unworthy or incapable of resurrection finds no ground in God's revelation.   Although at present
there is a widespread recognition that the flesh is not intrinsically
and essentially evil,[14] yet despite this formal recognition the flesh
(understood as the "material" side of man) is often depicted as,
by its very nature, linked with sin and death.   Reference has already been made to Cullmann, who calls the flesh the "transcendent power of sin and death" and says that therefore it must be destroyed.   Others, who do not go so far, still maintain that the flesh
as such is in some way inseparably connected with sin and death.
P. Althaus, for instance, posits that the Fall (existentially understood) results from the fact that man as *homo sapiens* evolved from
an animal state.   That is why there never was a human being in
history who actually was without sin.   "The first sinful act in
history is not the Fall itself, but its appearance, its expression."[15]
R. Bultmann declares that according to Paul "in man — because
his substance is flesh — sin slumbers from the beginning.   Must
it necessarily awake?   Yes. . . ."[16]   According to C. H. Dodd,
Paul teaches that man's "visible substance is 'flesh,' material, and
inevitably subject to decay," quite different from his *reason* and
heart, which "partake of the nature of the invisible and eternal
world."[17]   F. J. Pop argues that because of the fact that man was

[13] Cf. G. Ch. Aalders, KD, H. C. Leupold, G. von Rad, and others.
[14] Thus, for example, W. Eichrodt, *Man in the Old Testament,* pp. 33, 70;
Kenneth Grayston in *Theological Word Book of the Bible,* ed. A. Richardson, *s.v. Flesh;* A. M. Hunter, *Interpreting Paul's Gospel,* p. 24; W. Kümmel,
Das Bild des Menschen im Neuen Testament, p. 12; E. Schweizer, TWNT.
VII, 135; C. Tresmontant, *Saint Paul and the Mysteries of Christ,* pp. 55ff.;
D. M. Baillie, *God Was in Christ,* p. 205.
[15] *Die Christliche Wahrheit,* II, 147-48. (All quotations in this study from
French, German, or Dutch works are given in the present author's translation.)
[16] TH.NT, I, 249.
[17] *The Meaning of Paul for Today,* p. 57.

created as "flesh," i.e., perishable in himself, he could be tempted to sin.[18]

All such theories are incompatible with the truth revealed in the opening chapters of Genesis. According to this revelation the *flesh,* which is nothing but man himself viewed from his "material" side, was created as the very good image of God. Therefore this flesh cannot possibly be regarded as "the source of sin," "the favorable ground for sin," "the power of sin and death," "by nature perishable and therefore an easy entrance for sin," or whatever disqualification may be used. There was *nothing wrong* with the flesh *as God created it.*

Even the fact that man as *flesh* was characterized by earthly finitude and creaturely weakness is not as such to be connected with evil.[19] Finitude and weakness, the latter denoting man's absolute dependency on God without whose sustaining power he cannot exist and live, did not only characterize man's flesh from the very beginning but also his "soul," the spiritual side of his person. And whatever resurrection-body man may have in eternity, he will always remain finite and weak in the sense just mentioned, for he can never cease to be a *creature* in both body and soul.[20]

For this reason there was nothing ethically wrong with man's flesh, viewed as finite and creaturely weak. Nor was this flesh inevitably subject to decay and death, as many claim.[21]

In Scripture, death is always exclusively connected with sin (Gen. 2:17; Matt. 10:28; Rom. 5:1; I Cor. 11:30-32; Heb. 9:27; etc.). Though mortality as a *possibility* was characteristic of human life before the Fall, as Genesis 2:17 shows, man's potential death became real and irrevocable (apart from grace) when he sinned.[22]

---

[18] *Bijbelse Woorden en Hun Geheim,* p. 349. For theories more or less similar to those mentioned above, see: W. Barclay, *The Mind of St. Paul,* p. 202; E. Jacob, *op. cit.,* p. 158; W. Morgan, *The Religion and Theology of Paul,* p. 17; J. Stafford Wright, *Man in the Process of Time,* p. 39.

[19] Cf. W. Eichrodt, *op. cit.,* p. 70.

[20] C. Tresmontant's conception of man as destined finally to reach a stage of "a supernatural order" and "to share with Christ in the trinitarian life of God" (*op. cit.,* p. 53) seems to imply a kind of deification of man which is foreign to Scripture. That II Pet. 1:4 gives no ground for such a conception is convincingly shown by many commentators (for example, S. Greydanus, KNT, XIII, 246; A. Schlatter, Erl. III, 102-3).

[21] To the adherents to this theory, already mentioned, may be added K. Barth, CD, III/2, 639 and E. Schweizer, TWNT, VII, 123.

[22] Cf. G. C. Berkouwer, *De Mens het Beeld Gods,* pp. 261ff.; R. Bultmann, TWNT, III, 14ff.; and E. Käsemann, *op. cit.,* pp. 8ff. The above

Neither is sin to be regarded as a transcendent, metaphysical power existing on its own. According to Scripture, sin is willful disobedience of God's creatures (men and angels) to their Maker (Rom. 5:19; I John 3:4). It is a guilty attitude or act of *persons*. Satan was the first to commit sin, followed by many angels who with him abandoned the "very good" state in which they, too, had been created (John 8:44; Jude 6; cf. I Tim. 3:6). Adam and Eve followed the tempter on the way of disobedience, doing what God "commanded them not to do" (Gen. 3:11, 17; Rom. 5:19), thus abandoning their very good original state.

Nobody will ever be able adequately to understand or explain how God's "very good" creature could become a disobedient and sinful one. But Scripture leaves no doubt that it was not man's nature as flesh which caused him to sin or made sinning easier for him. H. W. Robinson is right when he declares that "the essential source of evil is the evil will, sin being, in Scriptural language, rebellion against God."[23] This evil will is the will of what Scripture calls man's *heart*.[24] Here, in man's heart, and not in his flesh, we are facing the "source of sin."[25] It was in their hearts that Adam and Eve were tempted to disobedience and in which they made the evil decision to do what the Lord had commanded them not to do. It was here, in the human heart, that from the moment

---

scriptural teaching excludes Cullmann's conception of death as a transcendent power, opposed to God just as sin is, not reigning in this world by the will of God (*op. cit.,* pp. 28-9). The passages referred to show that *God* called death into existence as the punishment for man's sin. The qualification of death in I Cor. 15:26 ("the last enemy") only brings to expression the fact that "death stands in contrast to life as the essential being of God" (R. Bultmann, TWNT, III, 14).

[23] *The Christian Doctrine of Man,* p. 295.

[24] There is well-nigh complete agreement as to the central place of the heart (in its religious sense) in biblical anthropology and even in the teachings of the Rabbis (cf. W. D. Stacey, *op. cit.,* pp. 109ff.; and J. Behm, TWNT, III, 612-14). With only a slight difference of meaning between *leb* in the Old and *kardia* in the New Testament, both denote "the centre, the focus of man's inner, personal life" (O. R. Brandon, *Baker's Dictionary of Theology, s.v.* "Heart"), "our ego, our selfhood . . . the concentration point of all our cosmic functions" (Dooyeweerd, *op. cit.,* I, 3), "the seat of the intellectual functions and the source of planning and willing" (F. Baumgärtel and J. Behm in TWNT, III, 609ff.,) and "above all the one, central place in man, which God addresses, in which religion finds its root and which determines man's moral attitude" (J. Behm, *op. cit.,* III, 615) so that it can be said that "man is worth what his heart is worth" (E. Jacob, *op. cit.,* p. 166).

[25] Cf. J. M. Spier, *An Introduction to Christian Philosophy,* p. 16.

of the Fall sin was to have its permanent source and seat, as God says in Genesis 8:21, "the imagination of man's heart is evil from his youth," and as it is explicitly stated by our Lord, "from within, out of the heart of men, evil thoughts proceed, fornications, thefts . . . all these evil things proceed from within, and defile the man" (Mark 7:20ff.; cf. Luke 6:45).

When man fell into sin, his flesh was simply the ethically neutral instrument through which Satan approached his heart, and through which man revealed and worked out the evil desire and plan that he conceived in the depth of that heart.

Secondly, the Genesis record of man's origin seems to imply that the nature of man's resurrection-body will be *flesh.* The following tentative suggestions may be offered.

It is obvious from the narratives of Genesis 1 and 2 that being a creature of flesh belongs to the divinely planned and created structure of man. It was as a creature of flesh that man in Paradise was God's very good image.

Admittedly, man's condition before the Fall marks only a point of beginning. From several Scripture passages and particularly from Paul's teachings in I Corinthians 15:45ff., which will be discussed in detail later, we know that Christ as the last Adam leads the believers to a mode of existence which is infinitely more glorious than that of man before the Fall. The first Adam lived only at the origin of human history; he had wonderful possibilities in store for him, as is suggested by the fact that when he sinned he was forbidden to eat from the tree of life, the symbol and pledge of immortality.[26]

Nevertheless, we have learned that being a creature of flesh belongs to man's essence as the very good image of God. This leads us to infer plausibly that the final stage of man's development, as it will become real in the resurrection day for those that are Christ's, cannot mean the total abandonment of his flesh, since this would imply that man ceases to be man, or at least ceases to be a *complete* man. It would amount to the destruction forever of an essential aspect of man's humanity.

We read that Christ came to destroy the works of the devil (I John 3:8). Dare we suppose that he will also destroy man's flesh, God's very good creature, in which man was God's image?

According to Colossians 3:10 Christ renews the believer "after the image of him that created him." This means that *salvation*

[26] Cf. G. Ch. Aalders, *Genesis*, KV, *ad loc.*

is the continuation and perfection of *creation*. May we not expect, therefore, that the believer will be lifted up to the highest possible level that God has planned for him as a creature of *flesh?*

2. AFTER THE FALL

Most occurrences of "flesh" (Hebr. *basar*)[27] in the Old Testament from Genesis 4 and onwards have an ethically neutral sense. As such the word can denote: the flesh of men or beasts in its literal sense; the human or animal body; a living being (especially in the expression *kol basar*: all that lives, or all mankind); blood-relationship; the genitals; the entire outward existence of man; man in his creaturely frailty and powerlessness.[28]

For the purpose of this study it will suffice to pay attention to those few passages in which the word *basar* has or may have theological significance.

This is apparently the case in Genesis 6:3. "And Jehovah said, My Spirit shall not strive with man for ever, for that he also is flesh: yet shall his days be a hundred and twenty years."

The verse belongs to a passage of very controversial interpretation. We read of "the sons of God" who married the fair "daughters of men" in days when giants, "mighty men . . . men of renown," were living on earth (6:1-4).

According to some ancient Jewish writings[29] these "sons of God" were angels, whose sexual intercourse with human females constituted their fall as spirits.[30] The early Jewish commentators and the early Christian Fathers, too, regarded them as angelic beings or demigods, and so do many commentators of modern times.[31]

The scope of this study does not permit any thorough exegetical discussion of the passage concerned. The following remarks may suffice.

---

[27] The word *she-er* occurs very seldom and is never used with a theological connotation (BDB; F. Baumgärtel, TWNT, VII, 107). It may therefore be ignored here.

[28] Cf. BDB and TWNT, VII, 105-7.

[29] The Ethiopic Enoch (I, 6ff.), the Slavonic Enoch (18, 4ff.), the Book of Jubilees (4, 15), Josephus, *Ant.* I, 73.

[30] Cf. SB, III, 780-83; E. Schweizer, TWNT, VII, 118ff.

[31] To confine ourselves to a few of more recent commentators, we find this interpretation favoured by F. M. Böhl, (*Genesis*, TU); F. Delitzsch (*A New Commentary on Genesis*); H. Frey, *op. cit.;* C. A. Simpson (IB); A. Pieters (*Notes on Genesis*, I, 113ff.); G. von Rad; and J. Skinner.

As to the "sons of God," mentioned here, we would agree with those older and recent commentators who regard them not as angelic but as human beings. These men are called "sons of God" because they belonged to the line of Seth, the originally God-fearing section of mankind, in contrast to the "daughters of men," denoting the women born in Cain's line, the ungodly section of mankind in the period before the Flood.

The sin of the "sons of God" consisted in their marrying female descendants of Cain for the sole reason that they were beautiful, with complete disregard for the fear of the Lord as indispensable for the continuation of true piety in their offspring. In itself religious apostasy, this sinful behavior resulted in the general wickedness of all mankind in the days of Noah.[32]

Among the arguments in favor of this interpretation the following seem to be decisive.

1. The idea that angelic beings can actually live in marriage with human females and procreate children is contrary to all that we know about angels, particularly in view of our Lord's statement in Matthew 22:30.

2. To regard the passage as a record not of historical realities but of human traditions, springing from a mythological background, is incompatible with the New Testament teachings (especially our Lord's) concerning the Old Testament as the inspired and therefore trustworthy revelation of God.

3. The passage leaves no doubt that the "sons of God" were the sinners, who took the initiative. Their choice, their motives, their disregard for the will of God ("wives of all which they chose")[33] is described. If these "sons of God" were angelic beings, there is no satisfactory explanation for the fact that verse 3 speaks only of the Lord's anger against mankind. This difficulty is not removed by declaring that verse 3a is a *non sequitur* and verse 3b a gloss (IB); it only renders the whole passage more obscure.

---

[32] Thus (with some differences as regards details) G. Ch. Aalders; V. Hepp (*De Antichrist*, p. 110); A. Kuyper (*De Engelen Gods*, pp. 58ff.); C. F. Keil; H. C. Leupold; John Murray (*Principles of Conduct*, pp. 243ff.); W. H. Griffith Thomas (*Genesis*); to mention again only some of the more recent authors.

[33] H. Frey, *op. cit.*, who regards the "sons of God" as denoting (mythological) heavenly beings, interprets v. 3 as God's reply to the arrogance of the *flesh*, that tried to invade *heaven*. This seems very illogical, for according to him *"heaven"* invaded the flesh and should be punished.

If our interpretation is correct,[34] then verse 3 is a quite natural sequel to verses 1 and 2. Now that the holy line of Seth forsakes the fear of the Lord by mingling with the unholy line of Cain, resulting in the ever increasing general wickedness, the Lord announces his judgment: "My spirit shall not abide in man for ever, for he is flesh, but his days shall be a hundred and twenty years" (RSV).

The meaning of the verb *yadon* is uncertain.[35]   As best fitting the context we prefer the rendering "abide, dwell in," which already occurs in the LXX, Onkelos' Targum and other ancient versions. Verse 3 then says that the Lord will limit to 120 years the period that his spirit (here to be understood as the God-given breath of life in man) will dwell in man.   Whether this means that man's life span would be limited to 120 years, or that a delay of 120 years would be granted to mankind before the Flood destroyed life upon the earth, is controversial and can be left undecided here as irrelevant to our subject.

In this connection we find the reference to man being *flesh* (vs. 3b).   Again, rendering and interpretation are controversial.

Some regard the words as a causal clause, stating why the Lord's spirit will not abide in man forever: "because he is (also) flesh," or similarly in the plural (RSV, F.M.Th. Böhl, H. C. Leupold, *et al.*).   This rendering follows the Septuagint and other ancient versions.

Others, following the majority of the Hebrew manuscripts, render verse 3: "My spirit shall not abide in (or: strive with) man for ever in his going astray (i.e. because he goes astray).   He is flesh and his days shall be one hundred and twenty years" — or the plural: "they are flesh," etc. (G. Ch. Aalders, H. Frey, *et al.*).

According to the first rendering the fact that man is flesh constitutes the *sole* reason why the Lord's spirit will abandon man, whereas in the second translation it is *one* of the *two* reasons mentioned.   In either case one must explain why special reference is made to man's *flesh*.

If the first rendering is correct, then for the first time in the Old Testament the word "flesh" is being used in an ethically loaded sense. Since man was created in the image of God as man of flesh, the meaning cannot possibly be that because man has a body of flesh he must be punished.   Here the expression "for he is flesh"

---

[34] For additional and detailed argumentation reference may be made to the works mentioned earlier (note 32).

[35] For the great variety of renderings, see Skinner.

must mean "man is no longer sinful, as he has been right along since the Fall; the race has also as a whole practically sunk to the level of being 'flesh' (*basar*), just plain, ordinary, weak and sinful stock. . . ."[36]

In the second rendering the meaning is slightly different but points essentially in the same direction. Again the word "flesh" cannot possibly denote the substance of man's body. Since it stands in contrast to Yahweh's life-giving spirit, "flesh" will here signify in the first instance man's original and intrinsic weakness and dependency in his relation to God. But it will also signify in particular his frailty and mortality as *fallen* man, under the judgment of God, as he is depicted in Genesis 5 with its sad refrain, "and he died."[37]

In this case the explicit reference to the sinners of verse 1 and 2 as "flesh" emphasizes the severity of their apostasy in the eyes of God and the rightfulness of the judgment that is now announced: that men, who are flesh, absolutely dependent on God and living already under the judgment of death because of the Fall, dare so consistently disobey and dishonor their Creator makes their sinning utterly objectionable in God's sight and deserving of the most severe punishment.

This interpretation is probably to be preferred to the first one, which has not only insufficient support in the Hebrew text but seems to press the word "flesh" too much.

Whatever rendering and interpretation one chooses, however, any disqualification of the flesh as the substance of man's body is out of the question.

In dealing with the theological significance of *basar* we must also pay attention to circumcision. In Genesis 17:11 the Lord says to Abraham: "And ye shall be circumcised in the flesh of your foreskin; and it shall be a token of a covenant betwixt me and you."

Obviously the word "flesh" must be taken in its primary, neutral sense as the substance of the body. The question arises, however, why precisely circumcision in the flesh of the foreskin was to be the sign of the covenant between the Lord on the one hand and Abraham and his offspring on the other.

---

[36] H. C. Leupold, p. 255. Similarly John Calvin, F. Delitzsch, and others.
[37] Cf. G. Ch. Aalders, *ad loc*. This is the meaning of the word "flesh" in many Old Testament passages, as, for example, Ps. 56:5; 78:39; Isa. 13:3; 40:6ff. In this special sense man can be called "flesh" only after the Fall, "flesh" denoting the whole man, body and soul.

G. von Rad writes in his commentary that in Genesis 17 "circumcision is understood quite formally, i.e., without significant reference to the procedure itself, as a sign of the covenant, as an act of confession and an appropriation of the divine revealed will." Apart from the fact that here the emphasis is onesidedly on the meaning of circumcision from the human side, one can admit that in Genesis 17 there is no significant reference to the procedure of circumcision itself. On the other hand, there must be some reason why God chose *this* sign rather than another.

According to F. M. Th. Böhl (TU) the sacrifice of part of the organ of procreation to the Lord symbolized the dedication of the offspring to God. Within the framework of Genesis 17 this seems true enough and Abraham may certainly have been aware of it. Nevertheless, this explanation can be only part of the truth. Even in Genesis 17 not man's dedication to God, but God's gracious act in establishing the covenant, with its far-reaching promises, is in the foreground. Böhl's statement should therefore be preceded by one along these lines: the divine claim on part of the organ of procreation signified in the first instance God's gracious acceptance of Abraham and his offspring as his people, whom he would abundantly bless as their God. W. R. Bowie (IB) rightly remarks that in their flesh Abraham and his descendants bore "God's own sign and seal that Israel was a chosen people."

Even so, however, the cutting away of "the flesh of the foreskin" is not fully explained. In the light of other Scripture passages we may add that circumcision promised a gracious deliverance from *sin,* and demanded of the circumcised a life of repentance and faith and of abandoning sin; circumcision of the flesh was symbolic of and must be accompanied by that of the heart and life in all its expressions.[38]

From this it follows that "the flesh of the foreskin" is in some way closely connected with sin, more than any other part of the human body.

When we ask in what way, the answer cannot possibly be that the *flesh as such* or *sexual life as such* are to be considered sinful. For circumcision was a *sign* of the deliverance of sin, not its actual removal. Moreover, it was administered to the male members of the covenant only; if the flesh as such was considered evil the female members could not have been exempted. Furthermore, from the biblical teaching that physical circumcision is of no value

---

[38] See, e.g., Deut. 10:16; 30:6; Jer. 4:4; 6:10; 9:26; Ezek. 44:7; Acts 7:51; Rom. 2:25ff.

without circumcision of the heart it follows that it is not the flesh as substance which is viewed as sinful. Finally, the fact that circumcision pointed to Christ's death on the cross (Col. 2:11) shows that no depreciation of the flesh-substance or of sex is involved.

Yet the fact that deliverance from sin had to be signified by circumcision in "the flesh of the foreskin" indicates clearly that in God's sight there is a close relationship between man's flesh and his sinfulness, particularly between his sexual life and sin.

Here we would agree with H. Bavinck when he writes: "In human beings sin bears the character of *sarx*; it reveals itself through the flesh and works in the flesh, especially in the organs of generation and shows its power there. Circumcision clearly demonstrates that. . . ."[39] Or as C. F. Keil expresses it: "Circumcision . . . was based upon the religious view that the sin and moral impurity which the Fall of Adam had introduced into the nature of man had concentrated itself in the sexual organs, because it is in sexual life that it generally manifests itself with peculiar force. . . ." (KD).[40]

All this means that in circumcision the flesh and sexual life function as not evil in themselves and not as the source of sin, but as the *instruments* through which man's sinful and corrupt *heart* reveals its evil desires and purposes. We have already arrived at a similar conclusion in another connection.

There are only a few more passages in the Old Testament where the word "flesh" has theological significance.

Ecclesiastes 5:6 states a direct connection between flesh and sin: "Suffer not thy mouth to cause thy flesh to sin." Most commentators agree that this verse is to be taken together with the two preceding verses, and that it warns against trying to avoid the fulfillment of a rash vow by specious excuses. This is "sinning with the mouth."[41]

We must now ask why the *flesh* is mentioned here as the subject of sinning. G. G. Atkins (IB) writes that here (as in 4:5) flesh means no more than self or person, and translates, "Let not your mouth lead you into sin." This is satisfactory if "self" or "person"

---

[39] *Gereformeerde Dogmatiek,* IV, 576.
[40] Similar interpretations are given by J. Calvin, H. C. Leupold, and others.
[41] Some commentators interpret vs. 6 as a new warning against sinful speech in general (e.g. H. Lamparter, *Das Buch der Weisheit,* in BAT). Even if this is true it does not affect the point in question here.

is taken for the whole man of flesh, with special emphasis on the physical side. This is clear from 4:5, where it is stated of the lazy fool that he "eateth his own flesh," which apparently means that he ruins himself completely by being "reduced to poverty" (Atkins, IB), which is particularly hard on the flesh.

Lamparter seems to give the most satisfactory explanation: sinning with the mouth concerns the *whole body* and defiles it (cf. Matt. 6:22ff.), so that the whole man becomes guilty before God.[42]

This verse does not in the least indicate the sinfulness of man's flesh as such, since the person addressed is warned and held responsible for causing his flesh to sin. It is his *heart* which speaks through his mouth and which reveals his inner thoughts through his flesh.

Nevertheless, as *instrument* of the sinful heart, man's flesh is said here to sin. Therefore we may regard the reference to *basar* in this verse as one of the Old Testament points of departure for Paul's conception of the flesh, so far as he gives it a distinctly ethical connotation.[43]

There are several remarkable statements in the Old Testament which show conclusively that evil is not inherent in flesh. We will cite two of these from the Psalms.

In Psalm 63:1 the poet says to Yahweh: "My soul thirsteth for thee, my flesh longeth for thee." J. J. Valeton regards "soul" and "flesh" here as both denoting the whole man, with no distinction between the inner and outer aspects (*De Psalmen*). Even if this were the correct interpretation, the statement of the Psalm would imply that the poet *with his whole existence,* his flesh included, is "love-sick for God" (F. Delitzsch, KD).[44] We agree with various other commentators, however, who consider "soul" and "flesh" to denote respectively the inner life and the physical existence of the poet. That the flesh takes part in man's inner emotions is a quite common conception in the Psalms (16:9; 84:2).[45]

Particularly in Psalm 84:2b, where "heart and flesh" are mentioned in one breath and where they cannot occur in *parallelism membrorum,* it is obvious that the heart denotes the soul, and

---

[42] Cf. Jas. 3:2, where we find the converse statement.

[43] Cf. G. Ch. Aalders, *ad loc.;* H. W. Robinson, *op. cit.,* p. 25.

[44] Cf. C. A. and E. Briggs (ICC): "the whole man." F. Baumgärtel's claim that *basar* in our verse is used in a metaphorical sense, expressing the inward attitude, cannot be substantiated (TWNT, VII, 106).

[45] Cf. J. Ridderbos, *De Psalmen,* II, COT, on Ps. 84:2.

the flesh the body.   As Briggs points out, the words "heart" and "flesh," being "emphatic in position, denote the inner and outer man, cf. 16:9, the body sympathizing with the soul in worship." Compare also A. Noordtzij: "Even his body experiences the influence of that intensive longing" (*De Psalmen*, KV).

From both Psalm passages it is clear that the body, far from being evil or inferior, is the God-given, ethically neutral instrument which man very often uses in the service of sin, but which he can use as well to express and experience the closest fellowship with his God.

This is also evident from two nearly identical passages in the book of Ezekiel, 11:19 and 36:26, where the Lord promises that he will take the stony heart out of the flesh of his people and give them a heart of flesh.

It is generally agreed that the "stony heart" is the heart in its natural condition, hard as stone, insusceptible to the impressions of God's Word and the drawing of divine grace (Keil), while the "heart of flesh" denotes a heart that is spiritually alive, susceptible to the Word of God and prepared to do his will (F. Baumgärtel, TWNT, VII, 107).   Now since the "stony heart" will be taken "out of the *flesh*" of the people, the "heart of flesh," which replaces it, must also be located in the people's *flesh*.

Again we see that the whole man, his flesh as well as his soul, participates in divine grace.   The flesh is the place where, and the instrument by which, the sanctified heart exerts its influence.

We may conclude our analysis of *basar* in the Old Testament with the words of E. de Witt Burton: "Of any corrupting power of either body or flesh to drag down the soul, there is no trace in the Old Testament."[46]

There is, indeed, nothing wrong with the flesh as such, according to the Old Testament, either before or after the Fall.   The flesh is ethically neutral.   When it is involved in sin, it is man himself who sins in and through it.   It can as easily participate in heartfelt love toward God.   Its attitude is determined by the condition of man's heart.   If the flesh can have no eternal future because since the Fall it is involved in sin, then *man himself* can have no eternal future: *he* is the real culprit, not his flesh as such, which is only an aspect of man's undivided personality.

---

[46] E. De Witt Burton, *Spirit, Soul, and Flesh*, p. 73, quoted by J. T. Darragh, *The Resurrection of the Flesh*, p. 278.

APPENDIX

FLESH AND BODY IN THE SEPTUAGINT
AND IN JUDAISM

1. THE SEPTUAGINT

In Hebrew there is no special word to distinguish the flesh, as the "substance" of man's body, from the body, as man's outward aspect in its totality; the word *basar* covers both concepts.

In the Greek Old Testament, however, we see the distinction emerging. Here *basar,* when it denotes *human* flesh, is mostly rendered *sarx* (145 times), but on 23 occasions the word *soma* is used.[47]

One passage, Proverbs 5:11, makes this distinction most evident. There we read the warning that going to "the strange woman" will lead to physical misery: "thy flesh and thy body are consumed." Here the Hebrew has "your *basar* and your *she-er.*" The former denotes the flesh in general; the latter noun may originally have denoted "the inner flesh, full of blood, next to the bones," whereas in Proverbs 5:11 it may have the figurative meaning of "physical power."[48] Here the Septuagint has the remarkable rendering *sarkes somatos,* literally "the fleshes of the (your) body." In view of the context there can be no doubt that *sarx* and *soma* denote here the two sides of man's physical existence, respectively the flesh-substance and the outward man in his totality. But neither here, nor anywhere else in the Septuagint, is there any trace of an *ethical* distinction between the *sarx* and the *soma.*

2. JUDAISM

a. *The Dead Sea Scrolls*

Here the word "flesh" is used first of all in its various Old Testament "neutral" meanings, denoting (a) the flesh-substance (e.g., *Manual of Discipline,* 9:4); (b) man's body, or man in his total human existence (e.g., *Man. of Disc.,* 3:8); (c) mankind, or "everyone" (e.g., *Man. of Disc.,* 11:7); (d) man in his finiteness, his nothingness, his absolute dependence on his Creator (e.g., *Psalms of Thanksgiving,* 15:21).

---

[47] Cf. F. Baumgärtel, TWNT, VII, 107.
[48] Cf. BDB, *s.v. she-er.*

In some other passages "flesh" is used in the closest connection with sin. According to K. G. Kuhn here "flesh is not only contrasted to the spirit of God but to the 'spirit of truth' which the believer possesses . . . ; flesh becomes almost synonymous with evil . . . . Man is flesh because and in as much as he sins."[49] W. D. Davies, though differing from Kuhn as to the meaning of certain passages, agrees that in some cases "the association of the flesh with evil becomes so close that it seems to denote the morally lower nature of man."[50] In evidence these authors quote from the Qumran texts expressions like "The fist of war falls from God on all *flesh of evil*" (*War Scroll*, 4:3)[51]; "But I belong to the mankind of perversion and to the *company of the flesh of evil*" (*Man. of Disc.*, 11:9), and others.

R. Meyer, however, disagreeing particularly with K. G. Kuhn, claims rightly that in these and similar passages the word "flesh" is not used in a specifically anthropological, dualistic sense, but denotes man in his totality. Since man is a sinner, "flesh" can denote *man* in his *sinfulness*.[52]

It is significant that Kuhn, Davies, and Meyer, though differing on certain points, agree fully that nowhere in the scrolls is "flesh" regarded as intrinsically evil in the Hellenistic or Gnostic sense, which contrasts *flesh* as "matter" (and therefore evil) with *spirit* (and therefore of a higher order).[53]

Body is distinguished from flesh but never contrasted with it. Remarkable in this respect is the expression "the body of flesh" in the *Habakkuk Commentary*, 9:2. There it is said of the "wicked priest" that acts of vengeance were performed against his *body of flesh*. The expression obviously implies no condemnation either of body or flesh, and neither does it contrast them. Rather, "body" and "flesh" together simply refer to man's physical nature.[54]

---

[49] In his article "Temptation, Sin and Flesh" in *The Scrolls and the New Testament*, ed. K. Stendahl, pp. 101-2.

[50] W. D. Davies, "Paul on Flesh and Spirit," in Stendahl, *op. cit.*, p. 161.

[51] Th. H. Gaster, *The Scriptures of the Dead Sea Sect in English Translation*, renders this passage: "From God comes the power of battle against all sinful flesh" (p. 266).

[52] TWNT, VII, 111-2.

[53] W. D. Davies, *op. cit.*, p. 162; K. G. Kuhn, *op. cit.*, p. 104; R. Meyer, *op. cit.*, p. 113. F. F. Bruce also denies Gnostic influences in the Qumran documents (*Second Thoughts on the Dead Sea Scrolls*, p. 104).

[54] K. G. Kuhn, *op. cit.*, p. 107.

b. *The Targums*

In the Targums, the older elements of which probably date from pre-Christian times,[55] the conception of "flesh" is much the same as that of the Old Testament and the Dead Sea Scrolls. Flesh and sin sometimes seem to be identical, as for example in Isaiah 40:6, where the Targum on the Prophets renders the original "All flesh is grass" as "All ungodly are as grass." Since "ungodly" is taken here as equivalent to "flesh," the latter obviously does not denote part of man but man in his totality.[56]

The Targums express no depreciation of the flesh-substance as over against man's spirit, nor do they regard man's flesh as such to be the special domain of evil.[57]

c. *Talmud and Midrash*

Here we find the word "flesh" employed with the same connotations as in the Old Testament, the Dead Sea Scrolls, and the Targums. The Rabbis suggested no ethically loaded conception of "flesh" such as we find in Paul's writings. They concentrated, rather, on the concepts of *yetzer harang*, the evil impulse, and *yetzer tob,* the good impulse. They located the evil impulse in man's *guph* (body, or person) or in his *leb* (heart).[58]

Furthermore, in the Rabbinic literature the Old Testament concept of "flesh" as denoting the whole man developed into the anthropological dualistic dichotomy of *body* and *soul,* these being two essentially different parts of man. The body originates in the earth and is therefore inclined to ungodliness, while the soul comes from heaven and is therefore pure.[59]

This, however, does not imply that the Rabbis adhered to *Hellenistic* dualism, which regarded the body as essentially evil and therefore incapable and unworthy of an eternal future. According to Rabbinical theology body and soul, after they have been separated during the Intermediate State, are joined again in the day of judgment, when man is rewarded or punished for his deeds, in body and soul. Both have an eternal future, either in glory or damnation.[60]

---

[55] R. Meyer, TWNT, VII, 113.
[56] Cf. SB, III, 331.
[57] Cf. R. Meyer, *op. cit.,* p. 114.
[58] Cf. SB, III, 330. For *guph*, see R. Meyer, *op. cit.,* pp. 115-16.
[59] Cf. R. Meyer, *op. cit.,* p. 117; E. Sjöberg, TWNT, VI, 375-76.
[60] Cf. R. Meyer, *op. cit.,* pp. 117-18; SB, I, 580-81.

All this implies that in Rabbinical theology the flesh as such (or the body) was not regarded as essentially evil.

d. *Apocrypha and Pseudepigrapha*

Here, as in the Rabbinical writings, we find anthropological dualism. It is sometimes combined with a cosmic dualism, which regards the world of the flesh as far inferior to that of the spirits.

This view is particularly prominent in the interpretation given of Genesis 6:1-4, where we read of "the sons of God" who took them wives of the fair "daughters of men." The children born from these marriages were giants.

As we have seen already, according to the Ethiopic Enoch (I, 6ff.), the Slavonic Enoch (18, 4ff.), and the Book of Jubilees (4, 15), these "sons of God" were angels. Though created as holy spirits, destined to have immortal, spiritual, celestial life, they polluted themselves by entering into a sexual relationship with earthly women. Thus defiling themselves with "the blood of the flesh," they procreated "flesh and blood." For this reason they are eternally lost.[61] The cosmic dualism here is obvious, as is also the implied anthropological dualism, which easily leads to the depreciation of sexual life.

There are, however, only a few dualistic or ascetic passages in these writings. The prevailing conception of flesh is the same as in the Old Testament. The flesh occurs here and there in a very close connection with sin, but it is not regarded as necessarily evil. It is the *instrument* of sin. It can also be the instrument of *righteousness.*[62]

[61] Cf. SB, III, 780-83; E. Schweizer, TWNT, VII, 118ff.
[62] Cf. W. D. Stacey, *op. cit.*, pp. 96, 102.

CHAPTER TWO

THE RESURRECTION-BODY ACCORDING TO THE OLD TESTAMENT

In this chapter we will inquire whether the Old Testament provides any information concerning the nature of the resurrection-body.

With this limitation of subject matter, we will ignore here the teaching of the Old Testament concerning the afterlife in sheol.[1] Various aspects of the Old Testament problem of resurrection in general will also be passed over for the same reasons. Our study will be confined to those passages which directly or indirectly throw light on the nature of the resurrection-body, or are considered to do so.

1. THE TRANSLATIONS OF ENOCH AND ELIJAH

Genesis 5:22-24 and II Kings 2:11ff. describe the translations of Enoch and Elijah. Although we have no reference here to resurrection, the passages seem nevertheless significant for our subject.

As to Enoch, although the Genesis narrative does not state explicitly that he was spared death and removed to heaven, there can be no doubt concerning the former and hardly any doubt concerning the latter.

In Genesis 5 there is an obvious contrast between the monotonous "and he died," spoken of Adam and his offspring in general, and the surprising expression concerning the end of Enoch's career on earth: "God took him." It is natural to infer from this contrast that Enoch did *not* die — a conclusion which is rendered certain by Hebrews 11:5, where the expression "not see death" can only mean "not die."[2] Moreover, as we learn from Hebrews 11:5, 6, the *reason* that Enoch was spared

---

[1] For an excellent treatment of this subject from the conservative viewpoint see A. de Bondt, *Wat Leert het Oude Testament Aangaande het Leven na Dit Leven?*, Chapters 1-3.

[2] Cf. F. W. Grosheide (KNT), who refers to Luke 2:26 and John 3:36.

death was his life of faith: he pleased God, and was rewarded. Genesis 5:22-24 twice states that Enoch "walked with God," an expression which is also used of Noah (Gen. 6:9). The meaning, obviously, is that he lived exceptionally close to God in faith and obedience.[3]

Where God took Enoch is not explicitly stated either in Genesis 5:24 or in Hebrews 11:5, but the most natural interpretation is that God translated him to be with Himself in heaven. In the first place, what reward would there have been in being taken to some remote place on earth, far away from loved ones? Furthermore, in II Kings 2:3, 5 (cf. 2:1) Elijah's assumption into heaven is described with the same Hebrew verb (*laqach*) as is used in Genesis 5:24. G. Ch. Aalders (KV) remarks that this verb denotes a double action: "take away from" and "take to oneself." Therefore he translates "God took him to himself," i.e., into heaven. This in itself can hardly be considered conclusive, as one can take something to himself to bring it to a place where he himself will not be. In Enoch's case, however, Aalders is right, because in Genesis 5:24 the verb is used in an absolute sense, without the Hebrew preposition *min* ("away from," which would render the statement merely negative), or any indication as to where God brought Enoch. Here the only satisfactory interpretation, indeed, seems to be that God took Enoch to himself in heaven, as he later did Elijah.[4]

Concerning the second translation, that of Elijah as narrated in II Kings 2:11ff., it is explicitly stated that he "went up into heaven." Any other interpretation, such as supposing that Elijah was removed by God to some remote place on earth, does violence to this clear language.[5] In verse 16 we read that Elijah's disciples, with the exception of Elisha, tried to explain the prophet's disappearance along such lines. But the attitude of Elisha, who had been an eyewitness of his master's ascension, and the disappointing

---

[3] Cf. also Gen. 17:1; 24:40; Deut. 13:4. Particularly the explanatory expressions in the last verse show, as Leupold rightly remarks, that to walk with (or: before, or: after) God, denotes a life of faith and obedience. See also A. de Bondt, *op. cit.,* p. 143, where differing interpretations are discussed.

[4] R. Calkins (IB on II Kings 2:11) expresses the view, held by many, that "the truly reverent way is to leave the description of the assumption of Elijah in the realm of symbolism, of poetry, of the imagination." It is hard to understand how this can be a truly reverent way, since the description of Elijah's assumption is clearly presented in the Word of God as a historical fact.

[5] For examples we may refer to C. F. Keil, *ad loc.*

outcome of the search of the disciples, proves how much the latter were mistaken. Scripture leaves no doubt that Elijah went to heaven.[6]

Elijah's translation to heaven was generally recognized in Israel, as appears from the expectation of the Jews in Jesus' day that Elijah was to return bodily to the earth (Matt. 17:10; John 1:21). The claim that Malachi 4:5, "Behold, I will send you Elijah the prophet," was meant in a literal sense[7] cannot be substantiated. It is not required by the wording of this prophecy, which can be understood in a way similar to the eschatological Old Testament promises that the Lord will raise up to his people David their king and shepherd (Jer. 30:9; Ezek. 34:23; 37:24; Hos. 3:5). These passages speak of the Messiah as a king and shepherd *like* David, and Malachi's words may be understood similarly as referring to a prophet *like* Elijah. From Jesus' statements in Matthew 11:14, "this is Elijah, which is to come," and in Matthew 17:12, "Elijah has come already," we may conclude that Malachi's prophecy was at least primarily fulfilled in John the Baptist.[8] The interesting question whether Scripture provides any ground for the expectation of an additional, literal fulfillment of Malachi's prophecy we can pass over in silence because it is of no significance for our subject.

The translations of Enoch and Elijah have two significant implications. In the first place, these translations gave Israel the assurance that Yahweh's power with regard to Sheol and death is unlimited. He is able not only to *revive* those who have fallen a prey to these sinister powers, but also to prevent the latter from even *touching* one whom Yahweh wants to take to himself. Israel could know the Lord as a God who is *able* to do what (according to his promises in the New Testament) he *will* do to all believers who are alive when Jesus comes again; they will be taken up in glory, without seeing death (I Cor. 15:51ff.; I Thess. 4:15ff.). Since faith in such a powerful God existed in Israel, one cannot reasonably regard the later expression of faith in a glorious resurrection as a foreign element in Israel's religion.

A second implication, especially relevant to this study is that

---

[6] Thus, e.g., C. van Gelderen (KV) *et al.* As regards the objection based on II Chron. 21:12, we may refer to C. F. Keil's exegesis of this verse.

[7] This is the opinion of E. Jacob, *op. cit.*, p. 308, and many others. N. H. Snaith (IB) speaks of Mal. 4:5 as one of the "legends" around Elijah's translation.

[8] Cf. J. Ridderbos, KV.

the flesh is not considered incapable or unworthy of eternal life with God. Enoch and Elijah were granted eternal life as men of flesh, untouched by the destructive powers of death. No doubt they were changed to be fit for a life in the heavenly realm, but there is no ground to assume that they ceased to be men of flesh.

2. I SAMUEL 2:6

We turn now to the Old Testament passages that speak of resurrection, or are considered to speak of it; they will be discussed in order as they occur in the Old Testament.

In I Samuel 2:6 Hannah sings: Jehovah killeth, and maketh alive: He bringeth down to Sheol, and bringeth up."

With various older commentators C. J. Goslinga takes this literally, interpreting Yahweh's power to "make alive" and to "bring up" as his power to raise dead men from the grave. Sheol, he says, is here approximately equivalent to "grave."[9]

If this be correct, then we have here a strong statement concerning the resurrection of man in a body of flesh. For how can the making alive of a dead man, who was buried and is raised up from the grave, be envisaged apart from his resurrection in the body in which he had been buried?

Most modern commentators, however, attach a figurative meaning to our verse: the Lord hurls down into death and the danger of death, and (on the other hand) he is able to rescue and save a man whose life is endangered, so that he does not die. Here Sheol is taken as synonymous to "death," as is often the case in the Old Testament.[10]

A. de Bondt holds a similar view, but claims that Hannah is referring here to the birth of Samuel. As a childless woman she was virtually a dead woman in Israel, but the Lord delivered her from this death by granting her new life in Samuel.[11]

This latter interpretation seems rather farfetched. Hannah's psalm "goes in every respect beyond the scope of her own history,"[12] and with the exception (perhaps) of verse 5 the statements in verses 4-8 speak quite generally of Yahweh's power and doings.

---

[9] C. J. Goslinga, *Samuel,* I (KV).

[10] So, for example, G. B. Caird (IB), KD, and others.

[11] *Op. cit.,* pp. 127, 131.

[12] K. Gutbrod, *Das Buch vom König* (BAT). C. J. Goslinga shows conclusively that the wide perspectives in Hannah's psalm provide no ground for denying that she was the author.

G. B. Caird claims that the verb "bring up" in 6a must be understood as "give life," i.e., "give new life in granting a woman a a child," so that 6a simply refers to death and birth. This, however, is difficult to believe because of the *parallelism membrorum*. In Caird's interpretation the parallel is lost, for "killing and giving life to a child" do not run parallel to "bringing down to Sheol and bringing up (from Sheol)."

We prefer the figurative to the literal interpretation. Goslinga's argument, that the expressions "bring down to Sheol" and "bring up" show clearly that "Sheol" means the grave and the text therefore speaks of *resurrection* from the grave, is not convincing. Those who favor the figurative interpretation point rightly to statements such as Psalm 30:3: "O Jehovah, thou hast brought up my soul from Sheol; Thou hast kept me alive."[13] As to the verb "make alive" (Hebr. *chaiah*) at the end of verse 6a, it can denote "restore to life (the dead)," but also "preserve life, save life from death."[14] Hence from a linguistic point of view the figurative meaning has at least the same right as the literal.

Decisive, however, is the fact that I Samuel 2:6 does not occur in an eschatological context. Verses 4-8 give evidence of the wisdom and power of Yahweh, mentioned in verse 3. That evidence is taken from actual life, and all the statements of verses 4-8 are in the present tense; they declare what the Lord is doing here and now in this world. Within this framework, the literal interpretation makes Hannah declare that the Lord kills men here on earth but also reveals his power by raising men from the grave. Hannah, in other words, supposedly refers to actual historical cases of resurrection as evidences of God's providence. But such a statement would not be true. In the Old Testament we read of only three cases of resurrection from the dead,[15] and if Hannah composed the song of I Samuel, they took place after the words of our passage were spoken.

On the other hand, the figurative meaning fits very satisfactorily within the context. We may paraphrase that meaning as follows: The Lord is able to kill as well as to preserve life

---

13 Cf. also Ps. 86:13 and Isa. 38:17.

14 Cf. BDB.

15 They are: that of the widow's son in I Kings 17:17ff., that of the child of the Shunamite woman in II Kings 4:32ff., and that of the dead man who was cast into the sepulcher of Elisha and revived in II Kings 13:21. Since these are not cases of an eschatological resurrection to eternal life, but of a temporary restoration to earthly life, they will not be discussed further.

when death is nigh; he is able to bring down to Sheol (death) and to bring a man back from the gates of Sheol when his life is endangered.

We conclude that I Samuel 2:6 cannot be adduced as evidence of the Old Testament teaching that the dead are raised in a body of flesh.

3. JOB 19:25-27

This text was once a *locus classicus* in connection with our subject. It reads: "But as for me I know that my Redeemer liveth, And at the last he will stand up upon the earth: And after my skin even this body, is destroyed, Then without my flesh shall I see God; Whom I even I, shall see, on my side, . . . and not as a stranger."

In spite of appearances, however, most modern interpreters deny that Job is speaking here of his future resurrection in a body of flesh.

The Hebrew word *go-el,* which can denote a redeemer in the most general sense of the word, is in our passage best understood to mean "one who stands for the right of an oppressed person, of one who suffers wrong."[16] We might translate: my *vindicator* lives. For it is evident from the context that Job is not merely expecting deliverance from physical misery. He is addressing his friends, those who wrongly accuse him of gross sin, who say that God is punishing him justly (vv. 1-20; 28-29). What Job particularly desires, therefore, is that God may publicly justify and vindicate him, bringing to light his innocence. The Hebrew verb "to stand up" (25b) also points in this direction, since it is generally used to denote the action of a witness or judge, either human or divine (cf. Deut. 19:15; Ps. 27:12; 31:14; Isa. 2:19).[17]

In view of this context we cannot agree with P. Scherer (IB) and those others who deny that Job refers to God as his *go-el* for the reason that Job is constantly contending against God. In chapter 19 all the emphasis is on Job's defense against the accusations of his *friends,* and who but God can effectively defend Job against them? Job does complain more than once about God's attitude, but this is not a conclusive reason for

---

[16] For the various connotations of *go-el* see BDB; Koehler-Baumgartner; and R. B. Girdlestone, *Synonymns of the Old Testament,* pp. 117ff.

[17] Cf. S. Cox, *A Commentary on the Book of Job;* J. H. Kroeze, *Het Boek Job* (COT); and others.

Scherer's interpretation. In the experience of the believer such contrasting sentiments as complaining about God and nevertheless
placing one's hopes in God are often intermingled.[18]

But now — this is a controversial point — *when* does Job
expect God to justify him publicly? Before he dies (the *ante
mortem* interpretation) or after his death (the *post mortem*
interpretation)?

According to the *ante mortem* interpretation, Job surely
expects that God will restore his health, thus vindicating him
before the whole world.[19]   But this view is hardly consistent with
the fact that Job has lost all his expectation for this life and is
afraid that he will soon die (17:1, 11-16).   The logical line
of thought, therefore, seems to favor the *post mortem* interpretation,[20] which we also adopt: Job is certain that *after his death*
God will stand up as his *go-el* and vindicate him.

Here, however, another controversial point arises.   Will this
expected vindication by God include Job's resurrection in a body
of flesh?

Much depends on the rendering of the words *al-aphar* (ASV:
"upon the earth") at the end of verse 25, and of the expression
mibbesari (ASV: "from my flesh") at the beginning of verse 27.

Recent commentators[21] who favor an interpretation which implies Job's resurrection in a body of flesh take *al-aphar* as
"upon my dust, my dead body" or "my grave": the divine vindicator of Job's innocence will stand up over his body that has
returned unto dust, raising him up from the dead.[22]

This is going a little too far.   J. H. Kroeze remarks rightly

---

[18] Scherer finds it a reasonable conjecture that Job expects his defense
(against God) from some "heavenly being."   Referring to a passage from
the Ugarite literature, Scherer presupposes polytheistic influences in the expression of Job's hope.   This, however, is unacceptable; the inspiration of
Holy Scripture does not allow for polytheistic influences.

[19] Thus, among many others, L. H. K. Bleeker (TU); E. Jacob, *op. cit.,* p.
309; and H. H. Rowley, *The Faith of Israel.* Rowley, however, is very hesi-
tant on this point.

[20] Cf. F. Delitzsch (KD), who also points to the contrast which the *ante
mortem* interpretation creates between v. 25a and 25b; J. H. Kroeze, *op.
cit.;* G. von Rad, TWNT, II, 850.

[21] The traditional exegesis was largely based on Jerome's translation in the
Vulgate, "and in the last day I shall be raised from the dust," which "is now
generally regarded as a dogmatic correction of the Hebrew original" (H.
Lamparter, *Das Buch der Anfechtung* (BAT), p. 123, n. 5.).

[22] Thus, for example, A. de Bondt, *op. cit.,* p. 197, and C. van Gelderen,
De Hoofdpunten der Zielsgeschiedenis van Job, p. 40.

that the text simply and quite generally speaks of "dust" without the article or any suffix. He is of the opinion that here, as in 5:6 and 14:8, "dust" denotes all that is material, i.e., the earth. Job had confessed God as his witness in *heaven* (16:19), and now God will come down (eschatologically understood) to "dust," i.e., to the *earth,* to give his final judgment on what took place on earth.[23]

It is questionable, however, whether the word "dust" has within this context such a completely general sense. A. B. Davidson (CBSC) also favors the rendering "upon the earth," but he adds plausibly that within this context "dust" alludes to the earth "as that wherein Job shall have been laid before God shall appear for him." The whole passage, indeed, is thoroughly personal and it seems best, while retaining the general meaning of "dust," to understand it as denoting especially the *graves,* the burial-grounds.

If this interpretation be correct, then Job is saying in verse 25: After I die and am buried, my *go-el* (who will not die) will appear on the graves, my grave in particular, to vindicate me publicly. He is the final judge, and he will declare that men have misjudged me.

The question arises, Does this imply, although it is not explicitly stated, that God will raise Job out of the dust to which he has returned?

The answer depends on the interpretation of what follows. But here we are immediately facing a corrupt text in verse 26a, which makes the rendering very difficult. The many conjectures offered are more or less influenced by the exegetical position of the commentator with regard to the *ante* or *post mortem* interpretation.[24]

With a view to the parallelism in verses 25 and 26 we prefer the translation "after my skin has thus been destroyed" (BV, ERV, NBG, RSV), which in the *post mortem* interpretation may mean "after I have died of this horrible disease that is destroying my body," or "after my body has returned to dust." The difference is not essential.

Verse 26b states what will happen then: "Yet from my flesh shall I see God." Here the difficulty is that the Hebrew prepo-

---

[23] With Kroeze, K. H. Miskotte (*De Verborgene,* p. 57), Lamparter, and others, we regard Job's words as having an eschatological implication.
[24] J. H. Kroeze, *op. cit.,* gives an admirable survey of the various conjectures.

sition *min* in the word *mibbesari,* like the English "from," allows for two renderings. One can translate "away from (without) my flesh," or "from (out of, or, in) my flesh."

J. H. Kroeze (with others), though in favor of the *post mortem* interpretation and claiming that Job's statements have an eschatological meaning, prefers the translation "without my flesh." Job expects to see God as his vindicator, not with his physical eyes but in some way which it is impossible to define. It is not likely, Kroeze reasons, that in this early prophecy Job would already be thinking of *physical* life after death.

Readily admitting that any apodictic statement is to be avoided, we still question this argumentation. Kroeze accepts an eschatological interpretation and holds that Job is becoming more and more conscious of a life after death (14:14; 16:19; 19:26). He regards Job as gaining prophetic insight (though still in a vague way) into what later would become perfectly clear, e.g., in Daniel 12:2.

Here one wonders, if the Spirit of God gave Job so much prophetic, eschatological insight at this early stage in the history of revelation, why could He not have given Job the assurance of his resurrection, particularly since Job spoke these words while standing on an exceptionally high level of faith and hope?

Kroeze, admittedly, does not deny this as a possibility, but thinks it improbable. Without claiming any certainty, we are inclined to think it very likely, especially in view of what follows. Job declares there that when God comes to vindicate him, Job's eyes shall see him. Kroeze, like many others, takes the expression "my eyes" as denoting "I." Though it cannot be denied that this in itself is correct, it seems inconsistent with the view that Job does not expect his body to be raised. "I" and "my eyes" can be identical on this side of the grave because "I" see through my physical eyes. But why should Job use this expression while knowing that he will have no physical eyes at all? This seems especially difficult to understand when, with Kroeze, one rejects the interpretation that Job is speaking of seeing God while he (Job) is in Sheol. If Job, through the inspiration of the Spirit of God, has come to envisage a final judgment to be held *on earth,* and he declares that he himself with his eyes will see God there, vindicating him publicly, then it seems difficult to deny that Job envisages himself as present *on earth* and seeing what happens there with his physical eyes. This implies that he must have envisaged himself as risen from the dead in his body of flesh.

It is quite possible that Job had only a rather vague conception of this resurrection, and we have no ground to ascribe to him an insight as elaborate as that of Daniel 12. But we cannot escape the impression that Job implicitly speaks of his resurrection in a body of flesh. For this reason we would prefer rendering v. 26b: "Yet from out of my flesh (in my flesh) shall I see God."

If this interpretation, which we offer as no more than a humble opinion, is correct, then Job 19:25-26 still holds its place as a *locus classicus* for the resurrection of man in a body of flesh.

4. The Psalms

Of particular interest for this study is Psalm 16:9-11: "Therefore my heart is glad, and my glory rejoiceth: My flesh also shall dwell in safety. For thou wilt not leave my soul to Sheol; Neither wilt thou suffer thy holy one to see corruption. Thou wilt show me the path of life: In thy presence is fulness of joy; In thy right hand there are pleasures for evermore."

With various commentators we regard David as the author of this psalm. There is no convincing evidence that he cannot have been its author. On the contrary, in Acts 2:25ff. and 13:36 the authorship of David constitutes an integral element in the argumentation.[25]

Some commentators, though not all, believe that David composed this psalm while he was in a dangerous situation. H. C. Leupold says, rightly, that some have pressed the opening words "Preserve me" too much by concluding from them that the poet was in the greatest of peril.[26] On the other hand, H. H. Rowley is probably wrong when he claims that this psalm suggests no danger or distress for its author.[27] It is indeed possible to explain the opening words as asking for divine protection in general, without reference to any specific danger, and so might verses 8 and 10 be interpreted. But we would agree with F. W. Grosheide that this whole psalm presupposes some kind of emergency situation, in connection with which David takes his refuge to God (v. 1)

---

[25] Cf. J. Ridderbos, *De Psalmen* (COT), *ad loc.*

[26] *Exposition of the Psalms*, p. 148. Similarly H. Lamparter, *Das Buch der Psalmen* (BAT), *ad loc.*

[27] *Op. cit.,* p. 174. Cf. W. R. Taylor (IB) and others.

and rejoices in the assurance of God's help.[28] It is hard to decide whether this emergency already existed, or whether David, while enjoying a period of rest at the moment, saw it looming ahead. With a view to verse 6, which seems to speak of outwardly favorable circumstances, we are inclined with J. Ridderbos[29] to prefer the latter interpretation.

Facing distress and danger, then, David entrusts himself to the Lord, whom he knows as his God, his greatest good (vv. 2, 5), his counsellor (v. 7), who is "at his right hand" (v. 8), i.e. "present, near at hand, as close as possible to help,"[30] so that he will "not be moved," i.e. "shaken, or dislodged, or overthrown" (Leupold).

This sense of security, in fellowship with God and under His protection, moves David to express his joy in the opening sentence of our passage: "Therefore my heart is glad and my soul rejoices" (v. 9a). This exclamation is followed by the controversial statement concerning the safety of his flesh in connection with Sheol: "My flesh also shall dwell in safety" (v. 9b).

The first question is whether this safety of the flesh occurs after death, *in Sheol.*

Some scholars answer this question in the affirmative, arguing that verse 10 speaks either of God's comforting fellowship for the poet in death or of his resurrection from the dead.[31] With the great majority of commentators, however, we find no sound exegetical ground for this interpretation. The following reasons make it most unlikely:

1. It is at least *questionable* whether verse 10 refers to God's nearness and help after the author's death, and the interpretation of verse 10 depends partly on that of verse 9. It seems unwarranted, therefore, to interpret verse 9b in the light of verse 10 instead of determining first the meaning of verse 9b in the light of what precedes.

2. Verse 9 is construed as a *parallelism membrorum,* the first part speaking of joy because God gives saving help on this side of the grave. It is likely, therefore, that the second part also refers to the safety of David's flesh while he is still alive.

---

[28] *De Psalmen,* I, 45. It is notable that the words "I shall not be moved" usually express confidence in God *in the face of danger,* e.g., Ps. 10:6; 21:7; 62:2, 6.

[29] *De Psalmen,* (COT), I, 126.

[30] C. A. Briggs, *The Book of Psalms* (ICC), I, *ad loc.*

[31] E.g., C. A. Briggs, *op. cit., ad loc.;* J. De Groot, *De Psalmen,* pp. 169ff.; and more elaborately A. de Bondt, *op. cit.,* pp. 51, 177ff.

3. In verse 9 the first part of the parallelism speaks of the poet's heart and soul, the second of his flesh. In such cases "my flesh" never denotes the *dead* body, but rather man's physical side as such (e.g., Ps. 63:1; 84:2).[32]

4. It would be contrary to Old Testament usage to understand the expression "shall dwell safely" (or "secure," RSV) as referring to a body's resting in the grave. M. Noordtzij maintains that nowhere in the Old Testament is the body said to *dwell* in the grave, but rather to *lie down*.[33] A. de Bondt, however, appeals to a few instances where we read that the dead "dwell in the dust" (the grave).[34] But this argument is not conclusive with regard to the text at hand. The Old Testament may once or twice use the expression "dwell in the dust" or "dwell in silence" with regard to the dead, but nowhere is it said of the dead and buried that they dwell *in safety,* or *secure.* This expression is used only to describe those living on earth under God's protecting care (Deut. 33:12, 28; Ps. 4:8; Jer. 23:6; 32: 37).

For all these reasons the correct interpretation of verse 9b seems to be that David, after he has expressed the joy of his heart and soul (9a), i.e., the happiness of the inward man in view of the Lord's nearness to help (8), now gratefully states that he is sure also that his outward life is safe under God's protecting care.[35]

If this interpretation is correct it follows that we cannot expect verse 10 to speak of the author's resurrection from the dead. For verse 10, starting with "for," states another reason (in addition to the one given in vs. 8) why the poet is sure that his "flesh will dwell secure," i.e., that God will bless and protect his life.

Those who believe that verse 10 refers to the poet's resurrection understand the verse as stating that God will not leave David's

[32] Cf., e.g., E. W. Hengstenberg, *Commentary on the Psalms, ad loc.;* A. F. Kirkpatrick, *The Book of Psalms.*

[33] *De Achtenzestigste en de Zestiende Psalm,* p. 115.

[34] De Bondt refers to Ps. 7:5, Ps. 94:17, and Isa. 26:19.

[35] With J. J. Valeton (*De Psalmen*), N. H. Ridderbos, (*De Psalmen,* KV), and others, we prefer taking "my flesh" as denoting here the physical aspect of David's person, the outward side of his existence, rather than to regard it with, e.g., J. Ridderbos (*op. cit., ad loc.*) as a mere equivalent of "heart and soul," denoting "I." Even when we connect "also" not with "my flesh" but with the whole statement of vs. 9b, the parallelism seems to be cumulative.

soul *in* Sheol or suffer him to see *corruption*.[36]   But the verb *azab* with *lamed* means *leave to, abandon to*.[37]   With a view, therefore, to the meaning of verse 9 as well as to the wording of verse 10a, the correct interpretation of 10a seems to be that here David expresses his assurance that the Lord will protect his life amid all the dangers that are looming ahead and not abandon him[38] to Sheol, i.e., not suffer him to die and so to become death's prey.

The same thought is expressed in 10b: "or let thy godly one see the Pit" (RSV; Hebrew *shachath*).   Here instead of "my soul" the expression "thy godly one" is used, obviously to emphasize that the poet can be sure of God's protection only as one who truly fears the Lord and as such is God's own.

Some render *shachath* not by "Pit," or "grave," but "corruption," in conformity with the Greek of the Septuagint, which reads *diaphthora*.   Acts 2:27, 31 and 13:35, which quote the psalm from the LXX, use the same word.   The great majority of recent scholars, however, consider this rendering incorrect.[39]   For our purpose it makes very little difference.   Even if one translates "corruption"[40] the meaning would be that God will not suffer his faithful child to die and so to fall a prey to corruption.   The parallelism with verse 10a and the interpretation of 9b make it impos-

---

[36] Thus A. de Bondt, *op. cit.,* p. 177; J. de Groot, *op. cit.,* p. 170.

[37] Cf. BDB and KB, both *s.v.*   See also Lev. 19:10; Job 39:14.   J. Ridderbos also appeals to the rendering *eis haiden* in Acts 2:27, 31 (in conformity with the Septuagint), but this is not convincing; in the *Koine* and particularly in Luke's writings *eis* is often used in the sense of *en* (cf. ZK on Acts 2:27).

[38] We take *nephesh* here as denoting (which it frequently does) the whole person, because it stands parallel to "thine holy one" in vs. 10b.   The interesting question whether there is a special reason for using the word *nephesh* in connection with Sheol (cf. J. Ridderbos, *op. cit.,* p. 131) is not directly relevant to our subject and can therefore be ignored here.

[39] Cf. BDB, KB, both *s.v.*   H. H. Rowley (*op. cit.,* p. 174, n. 1) admits that the word *shachath* might be rendered by "corruption," but remarks that it is never used of the body in decomposition.   He deems it therefore "very improbable" that the meaning "Thou wilt not allow me to experience decomposition" would be expressed by saying "Thou wilt not allow me to witness destruction."   For that reason he favours the rendering "the Pit."   The implications of the difference between the New Testament quotation and the Hebrew text are discussed by J. Ridderbos, *op. cit.,* p. 131, n. 1.

[40] As in ASV; ERV; BV; A. de Bondt; and J. Cales, *Le Livre des Psaumes,* I, 199.

sible to think that the poet will be preserved from corruption *in* the grave.

Corresponding with the negative statements of verse 10, as just interpreted, the last verse of the psalm speaks positively of David's assurance that the Lord will grant him *life,* life in its fullness, characterized by living in blessed and unceasing fellowship with God, to whom the poet says in adoration: "In thy presence is fulness of joy; In thy right hand there are pleasures evermore."[41]

Although there appears to be no exegetical ground for understanding Psalm 16:9-11 as referring to life after death and to resurrection, yet the Septuagint translates this whole passage as speaking of hope in the grave and of resurrection from the dead, as did later Judaism.[42] In Acts 2:26ff. our passage is quoted by Peter in the Septuagint version and explained as a prophecy in which David predicts Christ's resurrection from the dead.

Passing over in silence the general problem of New Testament quotations from the Old Testament, particularly in the Septuagint version, there is reason to say that, as far as the essential meaning of Psalm 16:9-11 is concerned, Peter's conclusion, based on the Septuagint text, is not at variance with the interpretation of the Hebrew text, as given above.

The poet, as nearly all commentators emphasize, employs a strikingly general and absolute language. He does not say that he is sure the Lord will prevent him from dying a premature death and grant him a long life in the service of and fellowship with Yahweh. Though all this is doubtless implied, he goes much further by saying without any restriction that the Lord will not suffer him to die; on the contrary, life — glorious, blessed and unceasing life — is what his God has in store for him. Here his faith claims the complete defeat of death for God's own. Here he "rises above himself and above the reality of his life, which gives his statements a more or less typical-symbolic Messianic character."[43]

Viewed in this light, it is obvious that the passage under consideration has found its fulfillment in Jesus Christ, as Acts 2:26ff. and 13:35ff. declare. There may be this difference, that David spoke of invincible life which death could not even touch, whereas our Lord suffered death and so gained the victory of life; yet this difference is not a principial or basic one. Particularly in the

[41] Cf. W. O. E. Oesterley, *The Psalms,* I, *ad loc.*
[42] Cf. SB on Acts 2:25ff.
[43] A. Noordtzij, KV.

light of Jesus' statement in John 10:17ff., that when he dies he lays down his life of his own free will, having power to take it again, Jesus' resurrection manifests most completely that invincibility of life which David in Psalm 16 claims for God's faithful servant.

It is difficult to decide how much the poet realized concerning the implications of his daring statements in Psalm 16. Peter, in Acts 2:30ff., declares that David, "being therefore a prophet, and knowing that God had sworn with an oath to him that he would set one of his descendants upon his throne . . . foresaw and spoke of the resurrection of the Christ . . ." (RSV). Peter's choice of words (he was a *prophet* and *knew* that . . .) seems to imply that David, while realizing that he himself might finally die, anticipated that the Lord would grant him invincible life in the promised theocratic King, in whom his house and throne would stand forever. The language of II Samuel 7:16ff. and 23:1-5 leaves no doubt that David was greatly surprised and deeply impressed by God's promise.

Peter's statement obviously does not imply that David knew anything in detail about the fulfillment of God's promise; but just as surely it does imply that David was to *some* extent conscious of a future fulfillment of his words in his great Son.

We conclude that Psalm 16:9-11 is not a *direct* expression of David's belief in the resurrection of the flesh, but that the latter is *implied* in his absolute and unrestricted claim to invincible, glorious life for the whole man: heart, soul, *and flesh*.

There are a few more passages in the Psalms which, according to some, express belief in individual resurrection. They are the following:

Psalm 17:15b: "I shall be satisfied, when I awake, with beholding thy form"; Psalm 49:15: "But God will redeem my soul from the power of Sheol; For he will receive me"; and Psalm 73:24: "Thou wilt guide me with thy counsel, And afterwards receive me to glory."

The interpretation of these passages is, however, very uncertain, at least as far as their possible reference to resurrection is concerned. Apart from that, even if they express belief in the resurrection (which seems to be the case with Ps. 49:15), they give us no information about the nature of the resurrection-body, the subject of this study. There seems to be no reason, therefore, to give particular attention to these passages.

5. Isaiah's Prophecies

Two passages of what is called "The Apocalypse of Isaiah" (chaps. 24-27)[44] deserve special consideration. These are 25:8a and 26:19.

The first of the two passages, Isaiah 25:8a, reads: "He hath swallowed up death for ever; and the Lord God will wipe away tears from off all faces."

Instead of rendering the verb *bala'* in the perfect tense, as does the ERV,[45] it seems better to employ the future, as do many modern versions and commentators. The Hebrew perfect tense is sometimes used to denote future actions.[46] In Isaiah 25:8a the subject, according to the context, is obviously Yahweh; his future eschatological actions are the subject of the whole passage. There is therefore reason to render the beginning of verse 8 as does, e.g., the RSV: "He will swallow up death for ever. . . ."

According to some, this statement is "an isolated monostich"[47] which is out of place between the surrounding statements and therefore is to be regarded as a gloss.[48] But there seems to be little ground for this judgment. If we understand "the veil that is spread over all nations" (v. 7) as the veil of mourning and grief (II Sam. 15:30; Jer. 14:3ff.; Esther 6:12),[49] then verse 8a states *why* this veil, this symbol of suffering and death, can be destroyed; it is because death, the cause of suffering and mourning, will be completely destroyed by Yahweh! Then, as a quite natural sequel to this promise, we read in 8b that "the Lord God will wipe away tears from off all faces": when the veil has been destroyed because death has been swallowed up, the tears that still linger on the unveiled faces may now be wiped away.

Understood this way, as a prophecy within the framework of a

---

[44] We will pass over the various questions concerning authenticity, unity, and date(s) of the chapters concerned; they are of no immediate significance for our subject. The authenticity of these chapters has recently been defended by M. Beek, *Inleiding tot de Joodse Apocalyptiek van het O. en N.T. Tijdvak*, pp. 11ff., and by A. de Bondt, *op. cit.*, pp. 207ff.

[45] And several others, among whom very recently W. Kessler, *Gott geht es um das Ganze*, BAT, *ad loc.*

[46] Cf. Ges.-Kautzsch-Cowley, par. 106m.

[47] G. B. Gray, *The Book of Isaiah*, ICC, *ad loc.*

[48] F. B. Duhm, *Das Buch Jesaja*, and others.

[49] Thus G. B. Gray, *op. cit.*; J. Ridderbos (KV); A. Van der Flier (TU); and others. In view of the context (the Lord's *feast*, vss. 6ff.) this interpretation is to be preferred to that of Franz Delitzsch (KD) and J. A. Alexander, who suggest that it is the veil of spiritual blindness (cf. II Cor. 3:15).

moving description of the eschatological feast that the Lord will "make unto all people" (v. 6), verse 8a constitutes a most impressive prediction of the complete *"destruction of death,* as the great manifestation of Yahweh's power as the living One, of his glory and grace."[50]   Here, in contrast to the immediate context and also to Isaiah 65:20-22, the symbolic language is abandoned; the great deliverance from death and its consequences, as Yahweh will grant it to his people all over the world,[51] is described in clear terms[52] which at the same time are as absolute as possible.   When in Isaiah 65:22ff. the blessings of the new world are described, the inhabitants of the new Jerusalem are pictured as living very long.   In Isaiah 25:8a, however, life is safeguarded *for ever*: there is no place for death anymore.   With G. C. Berkouwer we may say: "Nowhere does the Old Testament reach out to deeper and higher perspectives than it does here."[53]

Paul is correct, therefore, when he writes that the saying of Isaiah 25:8 will come to pass when those who died in Christ are raised imperishable, and when the believers who are alive when Jesus returns are changed to glory and immortality (I Cor. 15:54).[54]   Revelation 21:4 also gives a correct paraphrase: "he shall wipe away every tear from their eyes; and death shall be no more; neither shall there be mourning, nor crying, nor pain, any more. . . ."

This prophecy of Isaiah 25:8a does not teach a physical resurrection *expressis verbis,* but the absolute language employed certainly carries this implication.   A world without death and there-

---

[50] G. C. Berkouwer, *De Wederkomst van Christus*, I, 223.

[51] That the blessings are only for the believing people of God is evidenced by 24:21ff. and 25:10ff., which speak of judgment for the enemies of God's people.   That the eschatological people of God are found among all nations, is implied in 25:6, which speaks of a feast *for all peoples* (cf. J. Ridderbos, KV).

[52] Cf. J. Ridderbos, *het Godswoord der Profeten,* II, 478.

[53] *Op. cit.,* p. 223.

[54] Paul's quotation, a true example of his stylistic freedom, is neither from the MT nor from the LXX.   His rendering *eis nikos* (in victory) instead of *for ever* (MT) is in conformity with the versions of Theodotion and Aquila, and probably has an Aramaic background.   The Aramaic connotation ("excel" or "overcome") is likely not to be entirely absent in the Hebrew (cf. E. Earle Ellis, *Paul's Use of the Old Testament,* pp. 15, 22, 140).   With F. W. Grosheide (on I Cor. 15:54) we might interpret the words *eis nikos* as meaning "so that death is overcome" and say that this is the correct meaning of Isa. 25:8a within its context.

fore without mourning and grief cannot possibly be a world with
unopened graves, in which the bodies of children of God are still
in the power of death.   Only when all deceased saints are raised
from their graves to immortal life, raised in the selfsame bodies
that death had laid hold on, only then is death "swallowed up
for ever."   That is why Paul can refer to Isaiah 25:8a at the
end of I Corinthians 15, which, as will be shown later, speaks
so clearly of the resurrection of the believers in a body of (glorified) flesh.

The second passage, Isaiah 26:19, reads: "Thy dead shall live;
my dead bodies shall arise.   Awake and sing, ye that dwell in
the dust; for thy dew is as the dew of herbs, and the earth shall
cast forth the dead."

This verse, according to some, cannot possibly speak of the
resurrection of the dead, for then it would completely contradict
verse 14.[55]   The latter verse reads: "(They are) dead, they shall
not live; (they are) deceased, they shall not rise" (ASV; similarly RSV), or as some would translate: "The dead do not live;
the ghosts do not stand up" (BV; W. Kessler, A. Van der Flier, J.
Ridderbos, et al.).

This alleged contradiction, however, is based on what seems
to be a misinterpretation of verse 14, namely that it is a quite
general, absolute statement: there is no resurrection of the dead.
But within its context verse 14 evidently does not refer to the
dead in general, but to the oppressors of Israel, the "other lords"
of verse 13.[56]   When verse 14 says that they are dead, ghosts
that will not rise again, this means obviously that as dead enemies
they cannot harm Israel any more; they cannot possibly rise from
their graves to resume their attacks on the people of God.   In
other words, the possibility of an eschatological resurrection is
not under discussion here.[57]

Various scholars recognize that Isaiah 26:19 speaks of resurrection, but they deny that a resurrection of individual dead is

[55] Thus, for example, A. Van der Flier, op. cit., p. 137.
[56] Cf. E. S. Mulder, Die Teologie van die Jesaja-Apokalypse Jes. 24-27,
p. 46; A. de Bondt, op. cit., pp. 218, 221.   J. Moffatt translates: "These
lords are dead and gone, ghosts that return no more."
[57] Cf. E. S. Mulder, op. cit.; Fra Delitzsch, op. cit., p. 448; J. Ridderbos,
KV. W. Kessler takes v. 14a out of its traditional context and places it between vv. 18 and 19, interpreting it as a desperate exclamation of Israel
that there is no hope for the dead, to which the prophet replies in v. 19
that there is hope indeed.   There is no reason for such a drastic reposition-
ing of v. 14a.

meant. They claim that since verses 15 and 19 speak of the *people* of Israel, verse 19 must refer to the restoration of Israel as a *nation,* described in terms much like those of Ezekiel 37:1-14.[58]

With K. Runia it may be admitted that the national element and the collective eschatological hope play a part in Isaiah 26, including verse 19. But Runia adds rightly that the reference here is also to an individual resurrection, in distinction from Ezekiel 37:11 and Hosea 6:2 and 13:14, which clearly speak of the nation only.[59] It may be pointed out, further, that the context undeniably contrasts the fate of the ungodly (vv. 14, 21) with that of the righteous.[60] For there can be little doubt that Yahweh is addressed in 19, as in the preceding verses, and that therefore the words "Thy dead" mean "the dead that belong to Thee, the deceased righteous."[61] The nation of Israel, therefore, is envisaged here as essentially consisting of such as truly fear the Lord and put their trust in him (cf. vv. 7-9; 16), "the congregation of the pious" (J. Ridderbos, KV; similarly F. Delitzsch, *ad loc.*). This contrast between the ungodly and the pious implies that the reference is not only to the nation, but also to individuals.

This is also seen from the next clause, "my dead bodies shall arise."[62] Some prefer the translation "my dead body" or "my corpse."[63] The Hebrew singular certainly allows for this rendering, which also makes good sense. The prophet gratefully acknowledges that he himself also will share in the future resurrection. Nevertheless, it seems better to regard the Hebrew noun *nebelah* as a collectivum, as it is also used in Isaiah 5:25 and

[58] Thus, e.g., K. Barth, CD, III/2, 619; H. H. Rowley, *op. cit.*, p. 167; H. W. F. Saggs, "Some Ancient Semitic Concepts of the Afterlife" (in *Faith and Thought,* Journal of the Victoria Institute, Winter, 1958, p. 175).

[59] *Op. cit.*, pp. 190-91.

[60] Cf. G. J. Streeder, *De Prediking van de Opstanding der Doden in het Oude Testament,* p. 14; G. F. Oehler, *Theology of the Old Testament,* ET, p. 513.

[61] J. Ridderbos, KV; E. S. Mulder, *op. cit.*, pp. 105ff.; A. Oepke, TWNT, I, 370.

[62] The indicative rendering is preferable to the optative mood, which understands v. 19 as expressing a wish. V. 20 shows clearly the certainty of the prophet that the resurrection will take place (cf. Fra Delitzsch, *op. cit.*, p. 446).

[63] For instance, BV; New Dutch Version; K. Runia, *op. cit.*, p. 191; P. A. Verhoef, *Die Vraagstuk van die Onvervulde Voorsegginge in Verband met Jesaja* 1-39, p. 324.

in other passages.[64]   For there can be little doubt in view of the context that by "Yahweh's dead" the prophet in the first instance thinks of the righteous that had already died under the "other lords" of verse 13, whereas the prophet himself is alive. Moreover, if *nebelah* is taken as a collectivum and rendered as a plural, then the first half of verse 19 contains two parallel sayings, quite in accordance with Hebrew usage.   With various authors,[65] therefore, we prefer the rendering: "my dead bodies shall arise." In speaking thus, the prophet makes himself the mouthpiece of the people,[66] and expresses "the belief that the actual body that died will be revivified" (G. B. Gray).

That this is indeed the meaning of the prophecy is evident also from what follows.   Here the dead are addressed as those that "dwell in the dust" and are exhorted to awake and sing because their "dew is as the dew of light and the earth shall revivify the departed spirits."[67]   This rendering, "the dew of light," is to be preferred to "the dew of herbs," because the dew is the symbol of life-giving power (Hos. 14:5; Mic. 5:7), whereas the realm of light must be regarded as the realm of life; the creation of life followed that of the lights of heaven (Gen. 1:14ff.)[68]

There is some difference of opinion as to the translation of the second part of verse 19[69] and the interpretation of certain details of this passage.   Its meaning, however, remains basically the same, namely that the prophetic command sounds "over the burial ground of the dead" (Fra Delitzsch), exhorting the dead to awake and sing for joy because they will come forth again from the earth. The Lord, who by means of the dew and light in nature causes the earth to bring forth plants and fruits, will raise his righteous dead from the dust of the earth in which they "dwell," quickening them by "the life-giving dew from the realm of light in

---

[64] Cf. KB and BDB, *s.v. Nebelah.*

[65] E.g., Fra Delitzsch, G. B. Gray, W. Kessler, J. Ridderbos (all *ad loc.*), and H. H. Rowley, *op. cit.,* p. 166.

[66] Many prefer the rendering *"their* dead bodies," in accordance with the Syriac and the Targum.   The difference is of no significance in connection with our subject.

[67] Thus NBG and others.

[68] Cf. O. Procksch, *Jesaja I (Kommentar zum alten Testament), ad loc.* See also Ps. 36:9, where life and light in the fellowship with the Lord are identified, and Ps. 110:3, where light, dew, and life are found in the closest combination (cf. J. Ridderbos, *Het Godswoord der Profeten* II, 478).

[69] Some translate: "For thy dew is a dew of light, and on the land of shades thou wilt let it fall" (RSV; similarly BV, *et al.*).

which God dwells."[70]   Here, indeed, is confirmed what we found to be the meaning of verse 19a: the dead will be raised in the body that died.   Whatever changes the body may undergo at the resurrection (a point not under discussion in Isa. 26), the identity of the body of flesh that was buried will be maintained.

So understood, Isaiah 26:19 is a most significant passage: it is the first clear Old Testament prophecy concerning the eschatological, physical resurrection of the individual dead.[71]   It is true that this prophecy does not speak of a general resurrection, but rather a resurrection of the righteous dead, probably especially of those faithful Israelites who had died under the "other lords" of verse 13.   Many claim, on this basis, that a general resurrection was unknown at the time; but this claim cannot be substantiated.   Isaiah 26:19 is a word of comfort for the true Israelites of that day, as they were mourning over their righteous dead.   Instead of implying that a general resurrection was unknown, the comforting words of this prophecy rather presuppose belief in such a resurrection, quite in conformity with Isaiah 25: 8a.[72]

6. EZEKIEL'S VISION

Ezekiel 37:1-10, the vision of the valley of dry bones, now deserves consideration in connection with our subject.   God brings these bones together again, clothes them with flesh and turns them into a mighty host of living men.   With a change in the metaphor the same thought is repeated in the interpretation of the vision (vv. 11-14): the dry bones lie in the graves, but the Lord opens the graves and causes the corpses to come up, revived by the almighty power of his Spirit.

These interpretative verses make the meaning of the vision obvious: the Lord will graciously restore Israel's life as a nation after it has become a "dead" nation during the exile.

Although this passage does not refer to the resurrection of the dead, it is remarkable that the vision is given in this particular form.   The question arises, Is this symbolic language not in-

[70] H. H. Rowley, *op. cit.,* p. 166, n. 4.

[71] As regards the physical element, cf. D. S. Russell, "Between the Testaments," London, 1960, p. 159.

[72] The allegedly fundamental religious difference between Isaiah's prophecy (26:19) and the individual statements of faith in an afterlife as found in Job and some of the Psalms (thus G. von Rad, TWNT, II, 860) may be passed over in silence as irrelevant to the purpose of this study.

explicable unless one assumes that the prophet and his people were familiar with the conception of a bodily resurrection of the dead as an eschatological event?

Here commentators differ widely. Many deny any relationship between the vision and belief in a resurrection of the dead.[73] Others, however, claim that the vision would be completely unintelligible for Israel if there was no common belief in a bodily (future) resurrection of the dead.[74] If the latter are right, then Israel must have envisaged that resurrection as a resurrection in a body of *flesh*.

Now it is impossible to prove, as many scholars claim, that this common belief *could not* yet have arisen in Israel. The chief reason given by these scholars is purely negative, namely that the *clear expression* of this belief is of a rather late date. On the other hand, neither does Ezekiel 37:1-14 prove that this belief *was* generally held. The reason given, namely that without belief in a future resurrection the vision would be unintelligible, seems invalid. To understand the vision, it was sufficient for Israel to believe that Yahweh is *able* to raise the dead in a body of flesh whenever it pleases him. The *power* of the Lord to do so is clearly presupposed in this passage, particularly in verse 3, where the prophet answers the Lord's question whether these dry bones *can* live. The prophet's reply: "O Lord God, thou knowest," implies that according to Ezekiel such a resurrection is *possible* with God.[75] This belief was based not only on the nature of Yahweh as the almighty Creator and King of heaven and earth, but on visible evidence of Yahweh's power in this respect: Israel knew of the three cases of physical resurrection that are mentioned in I and II Kings (see note 15).

This belief in Yahweh's *power* to raise corpses from their graves must be regarded as sufficient to make Ezekiel's vision intelligible. We hold, therefore, that in Ezekiel's day there *may* have existed a general belief in a future resurrection of the flesh, but that Ezekiel's vision does not prove it. Consequently, this passage does not make a clear contribution to our study.

---

[73] E.g., G. A. Cooke (ICC), H. G. May (IB), and A. Noordtzij (KV).

[74] So G. Ch. Aalders, *Het Herstel van Israel volgens het Oude Testament,* pp. 149ff.; A. de Bondt, *op. cit.,* pp. 172ff.; C. F. Keil (KD); to mention only these few names.

[75] This belief is so basic to the whole vision, that according to Cooke this narrative contributed towards the growth of the resurrection belief as it is expressed in Isa. 26:19 and Dan. 12.

7. DANIEL 12:2, 3

Here we find the strongest and clearest Old Testament evidence of belief in the resurrection of the individual dead: "And many of them that sleep in the dust of the earth shall awake, some to everlasting life, and some to shame and everlasting contempt. And they that are wise shall shine as the brightness of the firmament; and they that turn many to righteousness as the stars for ever and ever."

Karl Barth deems it possible that even this prophecy speaks exclusively of Israel's restoration as a nation.[76] This view is not shared, however, by the great majority of Old Testament scholars,[77] nor can it claim convincing support from the text itself. The latter speaks obviously not of the nation as a whole, but of a qualified group, viz. the "many" of verse 2. These "many," in turn, are distinguished into two groups according to the quite different conditions to which they are raised, either to everlasting life or to shame and everlasting contempt.

Some deny that verse 2 refers to a partial resurrection of the dead. They claim that "many" stands for "all" and is used to indicate that the "all" is a great number.[78] But C. F. Keil rightly remarks that *rabbim* does not mean "all" but "many." Moreover, an interpretation which reads "many shall arise, to whom belong those who sleep in the dust" is not only "very artificial" (Keil) but has also the context against it.

H. C. Leupold defends the interpretation "all" with an appeal to John 5:28, 29, where, according to him, Jesus quotes and interprets Daniel 12:2, substituting "all" for "many." But comparison between the two passages shows that the wordings are so different that it is unwarranted to speak of a quotation. There are certainly points of similarity which make it likely that Jesus had Daniel's prophecy in mind. But he was not giving an authoritative interpretation of the Hebrew text by this change of wording, as Leupold claims. Jesus rather *extended the scope* of the resurrection from the "many" of Daniel's prophecy to the "all" of the New Testament revelation.

As to the context, Daniel 12:1 speaks of an extremely severe

[76] CD, III/2, 619.
[77] See, e.g., W. Eichrodt, *op. cit.*, p. 65; E. Jacob, *op. cit.*, p. 313; S. Mowinckel, *He That Cometh*, p. 205; A. Oepke, *op. cit.*, p. 370; G. von Rad, TWNT, II, 850; and most other commentators.
[78] Thus, e.g., H. C. Leupold, *Exposition of Daniel;* and G. F. Oehler, *op. cit.*, p. 514.

tribulation that lies ahead for Israel. Out of this tribulation God's people will be delivered, namely, "every one that shall be found written in the book." In the light of other Old Testament passages that refer to a book kept by God, in which He writes the names of the "righteous," i.e., those that truly fear Him and are recognized as His own,[79] we may conclude with most commentators that verse 1 speaks of the deliverance of those Israelites who, in the midst of the approaching tribulation, remain faithful to the Lord even unto death (11:33-35).

To which specific tribulation and deliverance does verse 1 refer? The question is controversial, and cannot be discussed here in detail. Some take the whole passage as being exclusively eschatological, and identify the tribulation of 12:1 with the period of Anti-Christ.[80] Others agree that the whole passage has an eschatological aspect, but claim that it refers primarily to the oppression and deliverance of Israel in the days of Antiochus Epiphanes, whose ungodly reign is described in 11:21ff. Like other Old and New Testament prophecies, it predicts imminent historical facts but points at the same time to an eschatological future in which it finds final fulfillment.[81]

We favor the latter interpretation because it does justice to the nature of biblical prophecy which often has a contemporary as well as an eschatological aspect.[82] It makes also possible a natural interpretation of the expression "thy people" in verse 1, which obviously denotes in the first place *Daniel's* people, i.e. the Jewish nation of those days, and only secondarily the Christian Church of the end of the world.

Within this framework the statement of verse 2a, "many of them that sleep in the dust of the earth shall awake," finds its nat-

---

[79] Cf. Exod. 32:32, where Moses, praying that God may forgive the sins of Israel, continues, "and if not, blot me, I pray thee, out of thy book which thou hast written"; Ps. 69:28, where the poet asks the Lord concerning his ungodly enemies: "Let them be blotted out of the book of life, and not be written with the righteous"; and Isa. 4:3, where the holy remnant of the Messianic age is described as "every one that is written among the living in Jerusalem."

[80] Thus, e.g., S. R. Driver, *The Book of Daniel;* H. C. Leupold, *op. cit.;* C. F. Keil (KD); F. Nötscher, *Daniel;* and E. J. Young, *The Prophecy of Daniel.* J. Calvin, *ad loc.,* explains vv. 1ff. as referring to the sufferings of the Christian Church in general; the Michael of v. 1, he says, is Christ.

[81] Cf. G. Ch. Aalders, *Daniel* (COT); W. Kessler, *op. cit.;* and others.

[82] Cf. J. G. Aalders, *Gog en Magog in Ezechiel,* ch. 4; F. W. Grosheide, *Het Heilig Evangelie volgens Mattheus,* p. 356; W. Hendriksen, *More than Conquerors,* pp. 57ff.

ural explanation. The deliverance mentioned in the preceding verse concerns the faithful remnant, those who are living when the deliverance comes. This leads to the question: But how about those that have died and laid down their lives as martyrs in the faithful service of Yahweh? Will they receive no reward, whereas the faithful remnant may enjoy the blessings of the deliverance?

Verse 2a provides the answer: there will be a resurrection for many, i.e., for those Israelites that died during the years of the great tribulation. They will wake up from their sleep of death[83] in "the earth of dust,"[84] i.e., from their graves,[85] to receive from the Lord either blessing or punishment in accordance with their faithful or unfaithful conduct during the tribulation;[86] some shall awake "to everlasting life, and some to shame and everlasting contempt" (2b).

Exegetical details of verse 2b can be passed over because they are irrelevant to the subject of our study. In that respect verse 3 is more significant, since it states that the "wise" and "they that turn many to righteousness" will shine as the brightness of the firmament and as the stars. It is obvious from this verse that the main purpose of this prophecy is to comfort Israel in its concern over the righteous dead. For the "wise" and "they that turn many to righteousness" can be none other than those mentioned in 11:33, 35, where it is predicted that many of them will fall, i.e., die as martyrs. Now 12:3 says that these very people will shine as the brightness of the firmament and as the stars, which obviously implies that after they arise, their selfsame bodies[87] will

---

[83] In Job 3:13 and Jer. 51:39 death is also spoken of as a sleep.

[84] Cf. J. Calvin, *ad loc.* Similarly J. A. Montgomery (ICC), "the ground of dust"; and E. J. Young, *op. cit.,* "dusty earth." The usual translation, "the dust of the earth," is less correct.

[85] Some see in the expression "the ground of dust" a reference to Sheol in contrast to the grave (e.g., R. H. Charles, *A Critical and Exegetical Commentary on the Book of Daniel;* E. Jacob, *op. cit.,* p. 303; F. Nötscher, *op. cit.*). However, with a view to the wording used in this verse, we prefer (with Aalders, Keil, Young and others) the word "grave." Keil rightly refers to Gen. 3:19, "thou shalt return unto the ground . . . unto dust. . . ."

[86] Cf. G. Ch. Aalders, *op. cit.,* and *Het Herstel van Israel volgens het Oude Testament,* p. 223; H. W. Obbink, *Daniel* (TU), p. 143; H. H. Rowley, *op. cit., pp.* 167-68; *et al.*

[87] That the resurrection is viewed here as one of *flesh,* i.e., of the whole person, the physical body included, is evident from the fact that in v. 2 the resurrection is called an "awakening" of such as "sleep in the ground of dust." In this connection Dan. 7:27 is also significant because it announces that the Messianic Kingdom will be established on *earth.* This implies that

be full of *visible glory*. Here, for the first time, mention is made of a change that will take place in the bodies of the saints.

In summary, Daniel 12:2, 3 does not refer directly to a *general* resurrection of both good and evil, but only to that of the people of Israel. The pagan nations are not mentioned. We may not conclude from this omission that Daniel would *deny* such a general resurrection. Obviously he was not writing a doctrinal treatise on the resurrection in general, but primarily a word of comfort in a very concrete situation of Israel's history, when many had to die a martyr's death. For that reason it is not surprising that only *Israel's* dead are mentioned. This is also in accordance with the Old Testament as a whole; Israel forms the center of the history of salvation and of God's revelation in the books of the Old Covenant. It was left to the New Testament revelation to illuminate the role of the pagan nations in God's plan of salvation, and thus to explain the nature of their resurrection.[88]

8. HOSEA 13:14

In this most interesting passage the Lord speaks to his people about ransoming them from the power of the grave, redeeming them from death.

According to many older and some recent commentators this is a promise of salvation. A. de Bondt, who defends this interpretation, says that God promises Israel's restoration as a nation, especially spiritually: he will not completely destroy his people by the severe judgments announced in this chapter, but will restore them in his grace.[89] E. Earle Ellis, who holds the same view, says that Paul quoted our passage in I Corinthians 15:55 because he recognized it as the description of God's deliverance of his people out of utter destruction, in conformity with the view of the early Church.[90] H. Frey also interprets our passage as a promise of salvation, but takes it as referring to the future resurrection of the dead, "the destruction of death itself, as the finale at the end of history."[91]

---

the risen saints will live there, though the glorification of their bodies (12:3) suggests a far-reaching change in life's conditions on earth (cf. E. Jacob, *op. cit.,* p. 313). The nature of this glorification will be discussed further in connection with relevant N.T. passages.

[88] Cf. G. Ch. Aalders, *op. cit.,* p. 309.

[89] A. de Bondt, *op. cit.,* pp. 87-91, which also gives a comprehensive survey of the various opinions on this passage.

[90] *Paul's Use of the Old Testament,* pp. 50, 96, 125n., 138n., 144-45.

[91] H. Frey, *Das Buch des Werbens Gottes um seine Kirche* (BAT), p. 278.

Most modern commentators, however, assert that our passage cannot be a promise of salvation, because the preceding as well as the following context doubtless refers to judgments which the Lord will bring upon Israel. They translate the verse as a question, followed by a negative answer. The question is: "Shall I ransom them from the power of Sheol? Shall I redeem them from death? O Death, where are your plagues? O Sheol, where is your destruction?" (RSV) The answer follows in the words: "Compassion is hid from mine eyes" (RSV), i.e., I shall have no mercy.[92]

We agree with the latter group of commentators. The context speaks so explicitly of judgment that verse 14 is most naturally explained as a statement of the same nature.

Even on the other interpretation our passage is only a promise of national restoration for Israel. The idea of individual resurrection is completely out of line with the general contents of this chapter. For this reason we find no suggestion concerning the nature of the resurrection-body in Hosea 13:14.[93]

In conclusion, we may say that the Old Testament teaches with increasing explicitness the resurrection of man in his physical body, which for the believer will be a glorified body. The final victory of this belief, moreover, as shown in Daniel's prophecy, is not necessarily the result of foreign influences, particularly from Persia, as some maintain.[94] We have tried to show that there is sufficient ground in the Old Testament literature to claim that the resurrection belief is of Israelite origin,[95] finding its deepest roots in God's revelation to his people.

---

[92] This interpretation, to mention only a very few recent examples, is favored by J. Mauchline (IB); J. Ridderbos (KV); and W. H. Gispen, *Hosea* (COT). Gispen evaluates particularly the argumentation of de Bondt.

[93] As to the connection between Hos. 13:14 and I Cor. 15:55, we agree with J. Ridderbos that the inspiration of Scripture allows for the possibility that Paul used these words with a meaning different from what the prophet first had in mind. We would add that in I Cor. 15:55 the actual quotation is from Isa. 25:8. What follows need not necessarily be regarded as an authoritative interpretation of Hosea 13:14 in the Hebrew context. With L. Morris (TNT on I Cor. 15:55) we are of the opinion that Paul here "in language reminiscent of Hosea 13:14 sings of the triumph that will be wrought."

[94] E.g., M. A. Beek, *Das Danielbuch,* pp. 75-76; H. Birkeland, "The Belief in the Resurrection of the Dead in the Old Testament," in *Studia Theologica,* III (1950-51), pp. 75ff.; H. W. Obbink, *op. cit., ad. loc.;* and A. Oepke, TWNT, I, 370.

[95] Cf. A. de Bondt, *op. cit.,* pp. 148-64; E. Jacob, *op. cit.,* pp. 314ff.; H. H. Rowley, *op. cit.,* pp. 167-68, *et al.*

So, too, it is characteristically Israelitish to hold that the resurrected body will be a body of *flesh*.   The Greek conception of
matter as being intrinsically evil was completely foreign to the Hebrew mind.[96]   This applies to the Hebrew conception of *man,* as
we have found, as well as to his eternal future in the eschatological
malkut of Yahweh, which Kingdom is always depicted as com-
prising heaven and *earth*.[97]   "The Jew is only to be comforted by
a new earth in which dwells righteousness. . . . Here it is that the
heart of Israel beats, very religiously; Israel could never forget
Genesis 1."[98]   Little wonder, then, that the resurrection-body was
regarded as a body of *flesh,* of glorified flesh as far as the true
Israelites are concerned (Dan. 12:3).

It cannot be denied that in the later apocalyptic and rabbinical
literature this eschatological hope took on remarkable "materialistic" features[99] which, as we shall see later, are unbiblical, as also
are certain conceptions of the church fathers.   But it should be
realized that such a development was possible only on the basis
of an existing strong Old Testament belief in the resurrection of
the whole man-of-flesh-and-blood.[100]

[96] Cf. SB, III, 330.

[97] Cf. K. G. Kuhn, TWNT, I, 568.

[98] P. A. Van Stempvoort, "De Opstanding des Vleses in I Kor. 15" (in
Vox Theologica, p. 176).

[99] A. Oepke, TWNT, II, 336.

[100] Cf. SB, *op. cit.,* II, 618ff.   For the various conceptions of the resurrection and the resurrection-body in Judaism we may refer to SB, IV (Vol.
II), pp. 1166-98, and D. S. Russell, *op. cit.,* pp. 157ff.

CHAPTER THREE

FLESH AND BODY IN THE NEW TESTAMENT

1. THE NON-PAULINE WRITINGS

a. *The Synoptics and Acts*

The words *sarx* and *soma* do not occur often in the Synoptics and Acts. In most places where they do occur they obviously have no ethical implication and therefore may be ignored. The following passages, however, require special attention.

(i) In Matthew 5:29, 30, 18:8, 9, and Mark 9:42, our Lord warns his disciples not to let their eye, hand, or foot cause them to sin (ASV). If that should happen, however, he demands that they pluck out or cut off the offending member and cast it away, so that they may be saved.

Leaving aside those matters which bear upon the synoptic question and the composition of the Gospels, we are faced with the question whether the members of the body as depicted here are in themselves an actual cause of sin.

W. H. Bolkenstein answers affirmatively, and accepts the full consequence of his interpretation by stating that it may be necessary to mutilate the body in order to escape the temptation arising from some part of it.[1]

Most commentators, however, hold rightly that Jesus was using metaphorical language, or as S. E. Johnson puts it, an "Oriental hyperbole" (IB). The following reasons may be adduced for *not* taking the body as the cause of sin in these passages: (1) it is practically impossible to sin with the right eye only (Matt. 5) apart from the left; (2) throwing away one eye, hand, or foot would not prevent a person from sinning with the other;[2] and (3) if Jesus was literally advocating dismemberment because *parts* of the body (or flesh) are sources of sin, then when the *whole* body is involved in sinning he should logically have advocated suicide. But this latter is absurd.

---

[1] M. H. Bolkenstein, *Het Verborgen Rijk* (PNT).
[2] Cf. G. A. Buttrick (IB), F. W. Grosheide (KNT), H. N. Ridderbos, (KV), and others.

To discover the real meaning of these verses we should consult the context of Matthew 5:29, 30. As indicated by verse 28, the immediate subject (though not necessarily the only one) is the sin of *adultery*. Jesus points out that adultery can begin and even be committed with the eye. But for such adultery Jesus obviously holds the *person* responsible, not just, e.g., the eye. Therefore in the passage under consideration the members of the body are not the actual cause of sin (which cause, according to Jesus, is the "heart," Matt. 15:18,19; Mark 7:21), but rather they are potential *"instruments of lust"* (W. C. Allen, ICC) or "the *medium* [*viz.,* the eye] through which temptation comes" (R. V. G. Tasker, TNT). Accordingly, Jesus does not demand the mutilation of the body but the avoidance of "sight and contact which stimulate passion" (W. C. Allen, ICC).

(ii) In Matthew 16:17 Jesus says to Peter that "flesh and blood" have not revealed to him the knowledge of Jesus as "the Christ, the Son of the living God." There is a contrast here between "flesh and blood" and God. Commentators agree, however, that the expression "flesh and blood" does not denote parts of man but man as a whole, regarded as a mere creature, not able to understand the things of God without divine revelation.[3]

(iii) In Matthew 19:5,6 and Mark 10:8 Jesus, denouncing divorce, refers to Genesis 2:24, where it is stated that in marriage man and woman shall "become one flesh." Since the statement of Genesis 2:24 has been given ample attention in the first chapter of this study, it may suffice here to say that "becoming one flesh" obviously denotes the physical union, the sexual intercourse, by which the unique union of the two partners in marriage is expressed.[4] Jesus declares this to be the ordinance of the Creator, which means that according to our Lord there is not only nothing wrong with the flesh as such or with sexual life, but rather that in marriage they can and must be used in the obedient service of God.

(iv) In Matthew 26:41 and Mark 14:38 the Master warns the disciples: "Watch and pray, that ye enter not into temptation: the spirit indeed is willing, but the flesh is weak."

---

[3] H. N. Ridderbos (KV). The expression "flesh and blood," often used in Jewish literature "to mean humanity as contrasted with divinity" (S. E. Johnson, IB), appears first in the *Book of Jubilees* (cf. TWNT, VII, 118).

[4] Cf. H. N. Ridderbos (KV), R. V. G. Tasker (TNT), Th. Zahn (ZK), *et al.*

The contrast between spirit and flesh in this statement has received different interpretations. Some think of the divine Spirit over against man in his creatureliness.[5] The context, however, seems to point in the direction of a contrast *within* man, viz. between the spirit of the disciples and their flesh, and so most commentators interpret it.

How then are we to understand this opposition between spirit and flesh in the disciples? R. C. H. Lenski (Comm.), F. W. Grosheide (KNT), and others find here the Pauline ethical contrast between the inner man, regenerated by the Holy Spirit, and the old, sinful nature. But since the flesh is only called *weak,* which adjective does not necessarily have an ethical connotation, this interpretation seems to be pressing the word "flesh" too much.[6]

When we read Jesus' statement in its context, it seems best to interpret the word "flesh" here in a truly Old Testament sense, as denoting man in the frailty of his earthly nature.[7] The disciples find it difficult to watch with Jesus, for they are frail creatures of flesh; at the end of a day full of tension they are physically tired and need the rest of sleep. Their spirits (i.e., their *believing hearts*) can overcome this weakness of the flesh only by watching and praying that God will strengthen them.[8]

If this interpretation is correct it is obvious that the flesh, including the substance of the body, does not receive *blame* for the disciples' sin. Moral responsibility in connection with this temptation is laid upon the *spirits,* the hearts of the disciples.

The tempter (Satan; cf. Luke 22:31) may of course use the weakness of the flesh to bring the believer to sin, as is equally implied in Jesus' words. But then the flesh with its weakness is only the ethically neutral instrument through which Satan tries to influence the human heart. As H. W. Robinson, speaking of Mark 14:38, writes: "The flesh is not the spirit's enemy, but the spirit's weakness, the gate of the city through which the peril may easily come."[9]

---

[5] So, e.g., J. Schniewind, *Das Evangelium des Markus.*

[6] E. Schweizer also goes too far when, in this connection, he speaks of "sinful flesh" (TWNT, VI, 394).

[7] Cf. V. Taylor, *The Gospel According to St. Mark;* F. C. Grant (IB); and others.

[8] Cf. F. J. Pop, *op. cit.,* pp. 151, 345.

[9] *The Christian Doctrine of Man,* p. 81.

(v) In Luke's writings the passages Luke 24:39 and Acts 2:26,30,31 are of paramount significance with regard to our subject. Not only do they show that the flesh is not unworthy of resurrection, but they give convincing proof that in our risen Savior our flesh has already been raised in principle. These passages, however, will receive ample consideration in the next chapter, which deals with the resurrection of Christ.

Concluding our brief survey of the Synoptics and Acts, we may say that flesh and body occur here in a characteristically Old Testament way. There is "no trace of the dualism of body and soul, matter and spirit, which we associate with Greek thought."[10]

b. *The Johannine Writings*[11]

In the gospel according to John the word *sarx* occurs infrequently, but in most of the few cases there are certain significant implications.

(i) In John 1:13 we read that believers were born "not . . . of the will of the flesh . . . but of God." It is not easy to decide what precisely is meant here by the word "flesh." Various interpretations are given, such as "sexual impulse,"[12] "sinful man who does not possess salvation,"[13] and "natural life in its continuity,"[14] of which we prefer the first. In any case, it is obvious that the contrast between the "flesh" and God, as expressed in this verse, does not denote an ethical contrast between the substance of the human body and God.

This is also proved by the next verse, John 1:14, where the evangelist states that the Word became flesh. Here the exegete must face many problems, which we need not discuss. But there is general agreement that the "flesh," as John speaks of it in this connection, is not something wholly other than the substance of the human body. The Logos became man in the

---

[10] H. W. Robinson, *op. cit.,* p. 81. Similarly E. Schweizer, TWNT, VII, 123.

[11] Here the Gospel and the three General Epistles which tradition ascribes to the apostle John, are regarded as genuine Johannine writings. For the General Epistles see S. Greydanus, *Bijzondere Canoniek van de Boeken van het Nieuwe Testament,* II, 320ff., 362ff.; and D. Guthrie, *Hebrews to Revelation,* pp. 186ff., 251ff. The book of Revelation contains no relevant passages and it therefore will not be discussed here.

[12] Thus, e.g., J. H. Bernard (ICC), F. W. Grosheide (KNT), W. Hendriksen (NTC), and W. F. Howard (IB).

[13] E. L. Smelik (PNT).

[14] E. Schweizer, TWNT, VII, 139.

full sense of the word: man of flesh and blood.[15] He who was with God and who himself was God (1:1) adopted our flesh in such a way that he became fully one with it in order to overcome sin and death. This seems to exclude the possibility that Christ would ever abandon his body of flesh, for this would mean that he ceased to be fully man, the truly and abiding *incarnate* Word. Of particular importance in this connection is I John 4:2, which verse will be discussed later.

(ii) John 3:6 reads: "That which is born of the flesh is flesh; and that which is born of the Spirit is spirit." Here our Lord, in his discourse with Nicodemus, is speaking of "two orders of generation, flesh and spirit."[16]

According to E. Schweizer the word "flesh" does not here imply the sinfulness of man, because 15:22-24 states explicitly that the cosmos contained no sin until Jesus came.[17] This, however, makes John contradict the whole Bible with its teaching that since the Fall every man is sinful and needs salvation (cf., e.g., Rom. 1:18ff.). It would also entail that no one can be saved as a sinner unless he first rejects Jesus in unbelief, thus becoming a sinner — which is a conception utterly foreign to the New Testament. The sin referred to in 15:22ff. can only be the special sin of rejecting the grace offered in Christ, as nearly all commentators understand it.

As to the meaning of the word "flesh" in Jesus' statement to Nicodemus, we agree with E. L. Smelik (PNT) that "it does not denote the substance but the actual condition of human existence."[18] Various commentators are rightly of the opinion that the sinfulness of the flesh (understood as human nature after the Fall), although it is not emphasized here, must not be excluded in view of the context.[19] It seems best therefore to understand the "flesh" in this connection as denoting natural man in his sinful opposition to God, which makes him bring forth an offspring as sinful as he himself is.

Thus interpreted, our passage in no way depreciates the flesh as the substance of the human body.

---

[15] Cf. Hebr. 2:14.

[16] Sir Edwyn Hoskyns, *The Fourth Gospel.*

[17] TWNT, VII, 139.

[18] Similarly C. K. Barrett, *The Gospel According to St. John.* Lenski remarks rightly, "Thus *sarx* includes the human soul, the human psyche, and the human *pneuma*. . . ."

[19] Cf. J. H. Bernard (ICC), F. W. Grosheide (KNT), W. Hendriksen (NTC), G. H. C. MacGregor (MNTC), and A. J. Gossip (IB).

(iii) John 6:51ff. contains Jesus' teaching that his flesh is the bread of heaven, which every one who desires to have eternal life must eat.

The scope of this study permits a few remarks concerning the Roman Catholic and Lutheran interpretations, which take the word "flesh" here in its literal sense. With the great majority of non-Lutheran Protestant scholars we regard our Lord's description of the communion with himself (eating his flesh and drinking his blood) as metaphorical. This is evident from the fact that in the context "to believe in him" is equivalent to "eating his flesh" and effects the same result, viz. eternal life (John 6:40,47ff.).[20] F. W. Grosheide (KNT) refers also to verse 57, where Jesus, speaking of eating him, uses the present tense (*ho trogon me*), i.e., eating him there and then in the Synagogue of Capernaum. We agree with Grosheide that this saying of Jesus is incompatible with a literal interpretation of the words "flesh" and "blood" in John 6.

The "flesh" of Jesus, as spoken of in our passage, may be described as "the whole of his person and work in the historic reality of his life upon earth."[21] We should realize the significance of this fact: Jesus chooses the word *sarx* to denote himself in his person and work, not only once but often and emphatically.[22] This entails that we are not to think of Jesus' person and work apart from his being and having "flesh" in the sense of 1:14, i.e., apart from his being a man of flesh and blood, the *incarnate* Word of God. When Jesus, in verse 51b, states that he will give his "flesh" for the life of the world, the reference is doubtless to his bloody sacrifice on the Cross, where he would suffer and die *in his body of flesh*.[23] Can it be different when Jesus in the same context more than once speaks of eating his flesh as the only way to eternal life? This expression is admittedly figurative, as we have seen. It means having communion

[20] John Calvin denies the identification and makes a distinction between the two. According to him "eating Christ" follows after believing, as an "effect and work of faith." The wider context, however, does not support such a distinction (cf. F. W. Grosheide, KNT).

[21] F. J. Pop, *op. cit.*, p. 355.

[22] Whatever the relationship may be between John 6:51b-58 and "the words of institution" spoken in the upper room, we regard it incompatible with the inspiration of Scripture to consider this passage a later addition (R. Bultmann), if this implies that Jesus himself did not actually say what the Gospel narrative records here.

[23] Cf. Grosheide, Hendriksen, MacGregor, A. Schlatter (Erl.), *et al.*

with Christ by faith.[24]   But we wonder if this communion with the risen and glorified Christ, as it is now possible and necessary unto salvation, could be called "eating his *flesh*" if Christ in his glorified state is no longer the *incarnate* Word whose flesh once clothed him on earth, died on the cross, rose from the grave, and is now glorified in heaven.

We are inclined to answer this question in the negative.   Our passage not only shows convincingly that there is nothing wrong with the flesh as such, but also suggests that Christ still has a body of flesh and that, consequently, there is an eternal future for the flesh of all believers.

(iv) The words of Jesus in John 6:63, "It is the spirit that giveth life; the flesh profiteth nothing," must be interpreted in the light of our foregoing discussion.   The context, where we hear Jesus' disciples discuss Jesus' teaching about "eating his flesh," shows that in verse 63 the word "flesh" refers in the first instance to Jesus' flesh (cf. Grosheide, Hendriksen, MacGregor, *et al.*)[25]   It is important, however (as Dean Alford, Bernard, and others remark), that Jesus does not say "my flesh" but "the flesh."   This means, in the light of the context,[26] that according to our Lord not only his own flesh but flesh in general has no power *as such* to give eternal life.   If the disciples, as apparently was the case, understood Jesus to say that they should literally eat his flesh, then they needed to be told that Jesus never meant that.   Human flesh, even the flesh Jesus had, cannot quicken unto eternal life.   That is the privilege of the Spirit, here denoting the Spirit of God, dwelling in Jesus.[27]

It is obvious that no depreciation of the flesh is involved here; only its limitations are emphasized.

(v) I John 2:16 speaks of "the lust of the flesh," which is "not of the Father, but . . . of the world."   It is evident that "flesh" with its *epithumia* (lust) has an ethically unfavorable sense here. With most interpreters we take "the lust of the flesh" to mean "all the cravings of unregenerate man" (A. N. Wilder, IB), the evil significance of the phrase lying in "lust," not in "the flesh" (P. W.

---

[24] Grosheide (KNT, pp. 465-66) points out that it means a communion with the *whole* Christ.

[25] It seems incorrect, therefore, to understand the contrast "flesh-spirit" in our passage in the Pauline sense of the old Adam versus the Holy Spirit, as do H. Sasse (*op. cit.*, p. 355), and others.

[26] V. 60 refers back to vv. 52-58.

[27] Cf. also E. Hoskyns, *op. cit., ad loc.*

Hoon, IB). It is possible that the reference is in the first instance to unsanctified sexual lust,[28] but Lenski refers rightly to all New Testament "lists of vices"; every desire contrary to God's revealed will is condemned here, not only those arising from bodily appetites. The fact that Jesus Christ "came in the flesh" (4:2) implies that the bodily appetites "are in themselves wholesome" (P. W. Hoon, IB).[29]

(vi) I John 4:2, like II John:7 (to be discussed subsequently), speaks of confessing Jesus Christ as coming in the flesh. In both passages the confession of Jesus Christ as "come in the flesh" is presented as the norm for determining whether a certain teaching is of God or not of God.

The meaning of I John 4:2 depends partly on the identity of those false teachers whom John denounces in his writings. With S. Greydanus (KNT, p. 368), W. Hendriksen (NTC, *Commentary on John's Gospel*, p. 33) and D. Guthrie (*op. cit.*, p. 193), we favor the opinion that John intended to refute the errors of his contemporary Cerinthus.[30] The latter taught that Jesus was merely human and that the heavenly Spirit-Christ hovered over Jesus from his baptism until his suffering began. Then Christ left him again, for a Spirit-Christ cannot suffer.[31]

Against this background the meaning of I John 4:3 becomes evident: every teaching which does not confess Jesus *as the Christ,* as the divine *Word-become-flesh,* is a teaching "not of God" (Greydanus, Lenski, *et al.*). This negative statement of 4:3, in turn, illuminates the positive statement of 4:2: "Every spirit that confesseth that Jesus Christ is come in the flesh is of God." Here also the identity of Jesus and Christ is emphasized over against the teachings of Cerinthus, who separated them. The historical Jesus, John declares, was not merely human. He was the divine Christ, come in the flesh.

In connection with the purpose of our study two things are significant in this passage.

1. John does not say that Christ came *into* the flesh (which would refer to the historical fact of the incarnation), but that he has come into the world *en sarki* (in the flesh; lit. in flesh), i.e.,

---

[28] Cf. E. Schweizer, TWNT, VII, 141; J. Willemze (TU); *et al.*
[29] See also R. Bultmann, ThNT, I pp. 104-05.
[30] Cf. Irenaeus, *Against Heresies,* III, 2,1;11,1.
[31] Irenaeus, *op. cit.,* I, 26, 1; III, 16, 5-6, 8; Hippolytus, *The Refutation of All Heresies,* Ch. VII.

as one (the divine Word) clothed with flesh; one who is as truly human, man of flesh and blood, as he is divine.[32]

2. The perfect participle is used (*eleluthota*). This means, according to John, not only that Jesus Christ once came in the fullness of time as one clothed with flesh, but that thus he is *still present*. What happened at the incarnation has not been undone. He is a Christ who "is come, who came and who abides in the flesh."[33]

If this interpretation is correct, our passage shows that any theory which claims that Christ abandoned his flesh at or after the ascension is unscriptural.[34]

(vii) In the second passage, II John:7, the anti-Christian deceivers are portrayed as men who "confess not that Jesus Christ cometh in the flesh." The expression "in (the) flesh" is the same as in I John 4:2, but it is remarkable that the present participle has replaced the perfect participle. This is generally understood as a timeless present, having virtually the same meaning as the perfect of I John 4:2. S. Greydanus, however, puts in a strong plea for understanding the expression "coming in the flesh" as denoting Christ's second coming. It cannot be denied that John may have had this in mind when he wrote our passage, but we cannot be sure. In either case the consequence for our study is the same: Christ is still in the flesh.

In conclusion we may say that John's conception of the flesh does by no means exclude the possibility of the believer's resurrection in a body of flesh; on the contrary, it positively suggests that this will happen. For if the glorified Christ is still in the flesh, we may expect that the believers, who according to I John 3:2 "shall be like him," will also be raised in a body of flesh.

c. *The Epistle to the Hebrews*

(i) Hebrews 5:7 contains this statement about our Lord: "Who in the days of his flesh, having offered up prayers and supplications. . . ." The question arising here is, Does the phrase "in the days of his flesh" present a contrast with his pre-incarnation state or with his glorified post-ascension state? If the latter

---

[32] The absence of the article emphasizes the quality: Christ adopted human FLESH.

[33] A. Ross (NIC). Similarly S. Greydanus and R. C. H. Lenski. P. W. Hoon (IB) interprets: "The incarnation is in one sense an event; in another sense it is also a process eternally going on. . . ."

[34] These theories will be discussed in a later section of this book.

were meant, this text would seem to deny by implication that Christ still has a body of flesh. The context, however, makes it clear that "the days of his flesh" stands in contrast to Christ's glorious pre-existence as the Son appointed by God to be "a priest for ever" (5:1-8; cf. 1:5 and 2:14). "The days of his flesh" denotes the eternal Son's incarnate life on earth, and the word "flesh" is doubtless used to emphasize the great self-humiliation of the Son of God in adopting human nature with all its weakness, suffering, and need.[35]

There is therefore no ground to infer from this passage, as some do,[36] that after his life on earth Jesus discarded the flesh. When Jesus ascended he passed from humiliation to glory, as our epistle repeatedly states (2:7, 9, 10; 3:3), but this does not mean that he abandoned his body.

(ii) Hebrews 10:20 speaks of Jesus as the high priest who "through the veil, that is to say, his flesh" dedicated for us a new and living way into the heavenly sanctuary.

Concerning this difficult verse we need raise only the following question: Was Jesus' flesh an obstacle to his entering the heavenly sanctuary, so that he needed to abandon his flesh-body in death and thus gain deliverance from the deadly power of matter?[37]

Our answer, with the great majority of recent commentaries, can only be in the negative. The background of this epistle is not Hellenistic and Neo-Platonic thought[38] but the Old Testament.[39] Furthermore, as F. W. Grosheide rightly remarks, the interpretation which considers Jesus' flesh an obstacle for *himself* fails for the simple reason that the text reads ". . . the way which he dedicated *for us*" (Greek *hemin*).

The flesh of Jesus is, indeed, referred to as an obstacle (the veil, curtain)[40] between us and the heavenly sanctuary. But "the context warrants our seeing here only a reference to the necessity

[35] Cf. F. W. Grosheide (KNT, CNT), Th. Hewitt (TNT), H. M. van Nes (TU), H. van Oyen (PNT), *et. al.*

[36] E.g., E. Schweizer, TWNT, VII, 142-3; and M. R. Vincent, *Word Studies in the New Testament*, IV, 500.

[37] Thus the *Religions-geschichtliche* interpretation, which finds gnostic-mystic elements in Hebrews. This theory has recently been favored, e.g., by E. Käsemann, *Das wanderende Gottesvolk*, pp. 140ff.

[38] Cf. Feine-Behm, *Einleitung in das Neue Testament*, p. 223.

[39] Cf., e.g., D. Guthrie, *op. cit.*, pp. 44-50; and H. van Oyen, *op. cit., ad loc.*

[40] With many others we see here a reference to the curtain in the temple, through which the high-priest on the day of atonement entered the inner sanctuary.

of the death of Christ, his physical death, that his redemptive blood (v. 19) might be available as the effective sacrifice."[41]

No depreciation of the flesh can be derived from this passage.

(iii) A few comments are in order regarding the use of the word *soma* (body) in Hebrews. Chapter 10:5 speaks of the *soma* that God had prepared for his Son, whereas 10:10 declares that we are sanctified through the offering of the *soma* of Jesus Christ.

The reference in the first verse is doubtless to the incarnation, as the context shows. The difficult question why the LXX, which is quoted in this passage, renders the Hebrew expression "digged my ears for me" by the words "prepared a body for me," is irrelevant to our subject. Significant, however, is the fact that the author of Hebrews, following the LXX in this passage (and also in v. 10) uses *soma* to denote Christ's human nature and earthly life, while in other parallel passages he speaks of "flesh," as we have seen, or "flesh and blood" (2:14). This means that to the author the two words *sarx* and *soma* are synonyms, without any essential difference in meaning. (See also 13:11, where *somata* denotes the carcasses of sacrificial animals.)

There is no ground, therefore, for alleging Hellenistic influences behind the use of the words *sarx* and *soma* in Hebrews, as has been suggested by E. Käsemann.[42]

d. *The Rest of the General Epistles*

The Epistle of James contains no passage of special significance for our subject.

In I Peter a few statements do, however, require careful consideration.

(i) I Peter 3:18 states that Christ was "put to death in the flesh, but made alive in the spirit." This clause belongs to a Scripture passage which is a most outstanding *crux interpretum*. The exegesis of the clause depends partly on that of the whole passage, 3:18-22.

Since space does not permit a lengthy discussion of all the exegetical problems involved, the following remarks may suffice.[43]

---

[41] A. C. Purdy (IB). Similarly, for example, F. W. Grosheide (CNT; KNT); Th. Hewitt (TNT); R. V. G. Tasker, "The Gospel in the Epistle to the Hebrews," p. 30; G. Vos, "The Teaching of the Epistle to the Hebrews," p. 110.

[42] *Leib und Leib Christi*, p. 95.

[43] A valuable reference to recent special discussions of this passage may be found in D. Guthrie, *New Testament Introduction*, II, 109, n. 2.

1. In the clause under consideration *sarki* and *pneumati* stand in contrast to each other, and since they are both without the article or a preceding preposition they must be considered datives of the same nature. Hence the translation "in the flesh" and "by the Spirit," as the KJV has it, must be rejected.

2. Some regard the datives as instrumental.[44] This gives a very good sense to the phrase "made alive by the Spirit," but leads to a forced interpretation of the phrase "put to death by (the) flesh." Calvin takes this as referring to the weakness of Jesus' flesh, which caused his death, whereas Lenski argues that because Jesus had flesh it was *possible* for him to be put to death. But, as I.A. Mombert remarks, the participle *thanatotheis,* denoting violent death, does not well suit this interpretation.[45]

3. Most modern translations render the clause as follows: "being put to death in the flesh, but made alive in the spirit."[46] The datives are taken here as datives of sphere, or of reference: "as regards the flesh . . . as regards the spirit."

This seems to be the correct translation, but it presents us with a difficult problem of interpretation. What is meant here by Christ's flesh and spirit?

Some scholars take "flesh" and "spirit" as denoting respectively the "material" side of his human nature and personality, and the spiritual side. The clause is then interpreted to mean: Christ died as far as his flesh, his physical life was concerned, but was made alive (immediately after he died) as regards his human spirit. In that spirit he went to the evil spirits in Hades, between his death and resurrection.[47]

But this interpretation cannot be reconciled with the fact that the expression "Christ died . . . but was made alive" always refers in the New Testament to Jesus' death and resurrection (or: resurrection-life), as in Romans 14:9, II Corinthians 13:4, and I Timothy 3:16. Moreover, in Colossians 2:13 it is said of the believers that they have been "made alive" with (the *risen*) Christ, i.e., they have been raised with him. Here, for "made alive," the Greek uses a form of the same verb *zoopoieo,* which occurs in the clause under consideration.[48]

[44] For example, Calvin and Lenski.
[45] In J. P. Lange's *Commentary of the Holy Scriptures.*
[46] For example, ERV; RSV: J. Moffatt; NEB; R. F. Weymouth; see also E. Schweizer, TWNT, VI, 446.
[47] So, very recently, A. M. Stibbs (TNT).
[48] R. Bultmann, TWNT, II, 877; see also Ch. Bigg (ICC); E. G. Selwyn, *The First Epistle of Peter.*

Therefore, with most commentators we interpret this clause as speaking of Christ's death and *resurrection,* which is also in conformity with verse 21, where Jesus' resurrection is mentioned not as a new fact but as one already referred to.[49]

4. Of the greatest importance in connection with our subject is this question: does the contrast between Christ's flesh and spirit in I Peter 3:18 mean that his resurrection was not physical but purely spiritual? This seems to be A. M. Hunter's interpretation (IB). This scholar interprets the verb "made alive" as denoting the resurrection. The spirit of Christ, he says, is the higher aspect of Christ's being, the "Divine vital principle" in virtue of which Christ was raised. In this spirit, writes Hunter, "as distinguished from the flesh," Christ went to Hades to preach to certain spirits imprisoned there.

Selwyn's interpretation is basically similar. He quotes as "an excellent note" Dean Alford's statement: "He, the God-man Christ Jesus, body and soul, ceased to live in the flesh, began to live in the spirit; ceased to live a fleshly, mortal life, began to live a spiritual resurrection-life."[50] If this statement means (which is not perfectly obvious) that Christ rose from the grave in a body which was no longer a body of flesh, we would raise serious objections to this interpretation as well as to that given by Hunter. Though these interpretations can be defended on grammatical grounds, they are, as far as we can see, unacceptable in view of the *analogia Sacrae Scripturae.* For they attribute to Peter[51] a teaching which is clearly contradicted not only by the teachings of the Gospels, as we shall see later, but also by Peter's own testimony in his speeches, recorded in Acts, which imply the empty tomb and the preservation of Jesus' flesh.[52] Unless

---

[49] As regards the alleged preaching by Christ (in the Spirit or as a Spirit) in Hades, we would agree with H. Bavinck (*Gereformeerde Dogmatiek,* III, 461ff.; IV, 695ff.), S. Greydanus, *ad. loc.,* and others that the words "in which he went" (v. 19) refer to Christ's ascension. With these scholars we regard the preaching to the evil spirits as having taken place at and through the ascension itself: by the fact that Christ, after his resurrection, made his triumphant entry into heaven, he proclaimed his victory to the evil spirits in Hades.

[50] Dean H. Alford, *The Greek Testament,* IV, 364-65.

[51] With S. Greydanus, *Bijzondere Canoniek van de Boeken van het Nieuwe Testament,* pp. 284-92, we regard Peter as the author of 1 Peter. (See also D. Guthrie, op. cit., pp. 97ff.).

[52] In particular, Acts 2:26-32, which will also be discussed later. Selwyn does recognize a contrast between Acts 2:27,31 and I Peter 3:18 (*op. cit.,* p. 34).

one admits the possibility of doctrinal contradictions in Scripture, which we consider incompatible with its inspiration, I Peter 3:18 cannot possibly say what the scholars mentioned above read in it.

5. We favor the following interpretation: the expressions "put to death in (as regards) flesh" and "made alive in (as regards) spirit" both refer to the whole man Jesus, body-of-flesh and soul alike.[53] "Flesh" and "spirit," anarthrous in the Greek text, emphasize quality and denote here the respective conditions of Jesus' existence before and after the resurrection. "Flesh" denotes the condition of his humiliation, with all the emphasis on his being subject to the weaknesses and divine punishments appropriate to our fallen state; "spirit" denotes the unlimited power, the imperishable life and glory, which Jesus through the Spirit (the Holy Spirit, cf. Rom. 1:4) received in body (flesh) and soul at the resurrection, and possesses for ever.

This, then, is what the clause seems to declare: Jesus was (violently) put to death as one who in body and soul was "flesh," i.e., in a state of humiliation because of our sins; but in the resurrection he was made alive as one who in body (flesh) and soul was and is "Spirit," i.e., full of the Holy Spirit's power, life, and glory.[54]

This interpretation fits naturally into the context and is in conformity with the teaching of I Corinthians 15:45,46 concerning Christ as the lifegiving Spirit, who as the last Adam is spiritual.[55]

If this interpretation is correct, the clause under consideration does not deny that the risen Christ has a body of flesh.

(ii) I Peter 4:6 is, again, a very difficult passage. Here the Apostle declares: "For unto this end was the gospel preached even to the dead, that they might be judged indeed according to men in the flesh, but live according to God in the spirit."

Various recent commentators see this passage as parallel to 3:19-22, where it is said that Christ preached the gospel to the wicked spirits in Hades.[56] Against this interpretation there is,

---

[53] Cf. Hoffmann, *Schriftbeweis,* 2, 337, as quoted in P. J. Lange's commentary, *ad loc.*

[54] Cf. e.g., S. Greydanus (KNT) and G. Wohlenberg (ZK).

[55] Later we hope to show that this passage does not deny that the risen and glorified Christ has a body of flesh.

[56] E.g., Ch. Bigg (ICC), A. M. Hunter (IB), H. M. van Nes (TU), and H. Windisch, *Die katholischen Briefe.* J. Moffatt, although preferring a different interpretation, deems this one also possible.

first of all, the fact that the expressions employed in both passages differ greatly: 3:19 has "the spirits," while 4:6 speaks of "dead" without the article; 3:19 speaks of a proclamation to the spirits (*ekeruxen*), 4:6 of preaching the Gospel (*eueggelisthe*). Secondly, the "dead" to whom 4:6 refers are dead now, but this does not imply that they were dead at the moment that the gospel was preached to them. On the contrary, the second half of the verse shows clearly that their death as men in the flesh followed *after* the preaching. When the Gospel came to them they were alive. Third, "No Jew and no Gentile of the first century ever thought of the evil spirits as 'dead.' "[57]

I Peter 4:6 must be interpreted in close connection with the preceding context. Here (vv. 1-5) Peter draws a conclusion from what he wrote about Christ's passion and death in chapter 3 and particularly in 3:18. He says that the passion and death of Christ mean victory over sin, and therefore his readers, as believers in Christ and partakers of his suffering and death, must abstain from sin. They must be quite different from the gentiles, conscious of the fact that Christ (cf. Acts 10:42) will judge the living and the dead.

It is this line of thought that is continued in verse 6. In what way? The answer is by no means easy to give. Many different interpretations are presented by commentators. We would prefer an interpretation along the following lines. In verse 5 Peter has mentioned the coming judgment of the living and the dead. In verse 6 he adds a few words concerning some of the dead, namely the Christians that had died, perhaps as martyrs for Christ's sake. The readers (as Moffatt and Selwyn suggest) may have been troubled with the anxiety felt by some Macedonian Christians (I Thess. 4:13) and may have wondered what benefit their deceased brethren had received from their faith in Christ, their suffering for his sake, their abstaining from sin. Here, in verse 6, is the answer: the preaching of the gospel to those Christians that are now dead was not in vain. Though[58] "according to men" (i.e., as it is man's lot since the Fall) they had to die, bearing the common judgment of death in their "flesh" (i.e., their earthly, bodily existence), the preaching of the gospel, which they believed, yielded the glorious fruit at which it aimed, namely that they might live as regards the spirit

---

[57] Selwyn, *op. cit.*, p. 337.
[58] With Greydanus (KNT) we regard this part of the sentence as concessive.

(i.e., a truly spiritual life), "according to God" (i.e., in conformity with his holy being and will), and have this life unceasingly, eternally.[59]   The readers may be comforted: their deceased brethren still possess that Spirit-dominated and Spirit-empowered life. And when Christ comes to judge the living and the dead they will be manifested as such and receive that life in its fullness, in body and soul.

If this interpretation is correct, we again have the same contrast between flesh and spirit in connection with dying and living, as we found in 3:18. Here in 4:6, as in 3:18, "flesh" and "spirit" have the dative case and are without the article, so that the emphasis is on the quality: though the deceased brethren died as regards their weak, earthly frame which is burdened with the effect of God's judgment (death), they were granted immortal life full of the Spirit's power and glory.

Consequently there is no indication here that the saints will exist forever as spirits only. The contrast is not between flesh and spirit as "substances," but between perishable, weak, and imperfect life ("flesh") and imperishable, powerful, perfect life ("spirit"), a life that in either case concerns the whole man, body and soul.

(iii) The word *soma* occurs once in I Peter, namely in 2:24, where it is stated of Christ that "he bare our sins in his body upon the tree." This statement shows how flesh and body were equivalent to Peter, for in 3:18 and 4:1 he speaks of Christ's suffering and dying in the *flesh.*

In II Peter two passages require attention.[60]

(iv) There is first II Peter 2:10, where we read of great sinners "that walk after the flesh in the lust of defilement, and despise dominion." In this verse the characteristic expression, different from the Pauline "to walk *kata sarki,* i.e., according to the flesh," is: "to walk *opiso sarkos.*"

In view of the context the word "flesh" must be taken here in its most literal sense and as generally as possible: these men (who in v. 12 are called "mere animals") are "trailing along

[59] With Greydanus and Stibbs we regard this to be implied in the use of the present continuous tense of the verb "live" (Gr. *zosi*), especially since this present continuous tense stands in contrast to the aorist *krithosi,* which refers to their being judged (death) at a certain point of time.

[60] With E. M. B. Green (*II Peter Reconsidered*) we regard II Peter as written by the apostle of that name. See also Greydanus and Guthrie, both *op. cit.*

behind flesh" (Lenski), irrespective of sex or kinship (Grey-danus). Wherever and whenever they see flesh, be it male or female, their lust is incited and they follow it as their leader in complete dedication.[61] Here Peter "seems to have in view the darker forms of impurity which were common throughout the Roman Empire" (Rom. 1:24-28).[62]

E. Schweizer (TWNT, VII, 144) declares that according to II Peter sexual desire for flesh is sinful in itself. But this finds no support in the context, which clearly speaks of misusing and abusing sexual life (vv. 6,14,18). Schweizer's appeal to the words *en epithumiai miasmou* ("in the lust of defilement") is invalid. In this connection *epithumia* can only denote *sinful* desire.[63]

According to this passage the flesh as such is not evil; the sin is to be found in those who abuse and misuse the flesh by giving in to unbridled lusts and passions.[64]

(v) II Peter 2:18 declares of the same ungodly men that they entice the newly converted "in the lusts of the flesh, by lascivious-ness." The fact that the lusts of the flesh are declared to be *aselgeiais* ("by excesses," denoting particularly sexual excesses)[65] shows that the phrase "in the lusts of the flesh" probably refers to the type of activity in which the seducers enticed others by their excesses, namely, the evil lusts of the flesh (Greydanus). In this connection "flesh" is best regarded as denoting sinful human nature.[66]

Though commentators differ in details of exegesis and inter-pretation, it is obvious from the context that flesh-substance and sexuality are not considered sinful in themselves. Peter is not arguing in favor of asceticism, but against the sexual immorality of sectaries, who were much like the Nicolaitans of Revelation 2:3.[67]

The word *soma* is not used in II Peter.

Turning now to the last of the General Epistles, that of Jude, we may ignore the problem of the relationship between II Peter 2 and the letter of Jude.

---

[61] H. Seesemann, TWNT, *s.v. opiso.*
[62] E. H. Plumptre (CBSC).
[63] See F. Büchsel, TWNT, *s.v. epithumia.*
[64] Cf. most commentators. See also Green, *op. cit.,* pp. 25-26.
[65] Cf. O. Bauernfeind, TWNT, *s.v. aselgeia.*
[66] "Passions of the flesh include all phases of human nature, which are put to wrong uses. . ." (A. E. Barnett, IB).
[67] E. B. Green, *op. cit.,* p. 26.

(vi) Of importance for our subject is Jude 8, where false teachers are charged with "defiling the flesh" as did the people of Sodom and Gomorrah. The reference is certainly to immorality, and probably to unnatural sexual practices.[68]

The characterization of this gross immorality is remarkable. It is called a defilement of "flesh," which word occurs here without the article, so that "flesh" has a qualitative sense and denotes human flesh in the literal sense of the word. It is stated here that this flesh is *defiled* by the immoral false teachers; hence we may infer that the flesh in itself is good and pure. It is defiled when it is used contrary to its intended use. Sinning *in* and *with* the flesh one is at the same time sinning *against* the flesh.

(vii) The word *soma* is used in Jude 9 to denote Moses' dead body, from which use it is obvious that in Jude's letter *soma* is synonymous with *sarx*.

We conclude our survey of the General Epistles by stating that nowhere is the flesh, as the substance of man's body, disqualified ethically, nor is *soma* viewed as being essentially different from the flesh.

2. THE PAULINE EPISTLES[69]

In connection with the problem under consideration, the main questions requiring our attention in studying Paul's conceptions of *sarx* and *soma* are the following:

a. Does the Apostle teach that the flesh as substance of the human body, and this body itself as far as it is a body-of-flesh, are intrinsically evil? Is their nature inevitably involved in sin, and are they therefore not capable or worthy of participating in the resurrection?

b. Does the Apostle make an essential distinction between *sarx* and *soma,* implying that not the former but only the latter can be expected to be raised?

These two questions will provide an outline for the discussion that follows.

---

[68] The problem of what is meant by "strange flesh" in v. 7 cannot further be discussed. With E. H. Plumptre (CBSC) and many other commentators, we regard it as referring to homosexuality.

[69] Here all the letters which bear Paul's name as the author are recognized as genuine. Cf. S. Greydanus, *op. cit.,* II, 1-249, and D. Guthrie, *New Testament Introduction,* I, *passim.* For an admirable survey of recent trends concerning the authorship of the Pastorals, see E. E. Ellis, *op. cit.,* pp. 49-57.

a. *Whether Body and Flesh Are Both Intrinsically Evil*

There is a growing tendency among New Testament scholars to emphasize the Hebrew background of Paul's teachings in general and of his anthropology in particular. Though all recognize that Paul's conception of *sarx* is more advanced than that of the Old Testament, this advance is now seen to be a very natural development on the basis of all the Old Testament connotations of *basar*.[70]

In Paul's writings *sarx* is used a few times, as in the Old Testament, to denote "the bare, literal, external flesh of the human body" (J. T. Darragh, *op. cit.*, p. 287). This usage can be found in those passages which contrast the true, spiritual circumcision with one that is merely in the flesh (Rom. 2:28-29; Eph. 2:11; Col. 2:13).

Again, Paul follows Old Testament usage when he employs the word *sarx* to denote the human body, or rather "the bodily existence of man in its totality" (E. Schweizer, TWNT, VII, 124). Thus, for example, II Corinthians 12:7, where Paul refers to the "thorn in the flesh," which the great majority of commentators regard as a physical disability. To this category belongs also Galatians 4:13, where Paul speaks of "an infirmity of the flesh," and Colossians 1:24, where the Apostle declares: "I . . . fill up . . . the afflictions of Christ in my flesh."[71]

In conformity with the Old Testament usage, again, is the expression "no flesh" in Romans 3:20 and I Corinthians 1:29, which is simply the negative of the Hebrew *kol basar,* and means nobody, not a single member of the human race.

Once more, Paul's letters sometimes employ the Hebrew connotation of "flesh" as meaning man in his weakness, dependence, and perishableness (as fallen man), particularly in contrast to God and his Spirit. So the word is used, for example, in II

---

[70] David W. Stacey, e.g., in contrast to W. Bousset and many others of the older liberal school, who claimed that in Paul's anthropology the governing factor was Hellenistic, arrives at the conclusion that Paul's whole anthropology, even where he emphasizes the ethical meaning of "flesh," has "a Jewish background . . . [in] the Old Testament rather than Rabbinic writings" (*op. cit.*, pp. 172, 223ff.), Similarly E. Schweizer, TWNT, VII, 425,433. See also the brief survey given by E. E. Ellis, *Paul and his Recent Interpreters,* pp. 29-32.

[71] J. A. T. Robinson (*The Body,* p. 19) claims that here "flesh" is simply a periphrasis for "I" or "my person." But in the light of II Cor. 11:24-27 it seems evident that Paul is referring in particular to the many sufferings he had to endure for Jesus' sake in his *body of flesh.*

Corinthians 4:11, where Paul speaks of "our mortal flesh"; in Galatians 1:16: "I conferred not with flesh and blood," i.e., with what is merely "human, the creaturely, in itself, in its frailty" (H. N. Ridderbos, NLC); and in Ephesians 6:12, where the same expression is found with the same connotation: "For our wrestling is not against flesh and blood."

Sarx denotes further, as in the Old Testament, human descent, as for example Romans 1:3: ". . . his Son, who was born of the seed of David according to the flesh" (cf. also Rom. 9:3, 5).

Sometimes Paul uses *sarx* to denote human descent in contrast to a humanity regenerated by the Spirit of God. So in I Corinthians 10:18, where the Apostle distinguishes "Israel after the flesh" from "the true Israel, the Christian Church" (L. Morris, TNT), and also in Galatians 4:23,29, which passages speak of Ishmael as "born after the flesh," i.e., "according to the order or law of the flesh, that is, according to the natural procreative process" (H. N. Ridderbos, NLC).[72]

With the Old Testament background so evident in Paul's view of man, our first impression is that Paul, like the Old Testament, finds nothing evil in human flesh as such.

This impression is substantiated when we consider the many statements in Paul's letters which imply that the flesh, understood as the "substance" of the human body or as the human body itself, is God's good creation and a suitable instrument to glorify God.

Romans 1:3 and 9:5, already referred to, speak of Christ as adopting human flesh and doing his redeeming work in it. And so does I Timothy 3:16, "He who was manifested in the flesh," i.e., whose previous existence was unveiled in a human life like ours, a life in the weakness of the *sarx* (W. Lock, ICC, *et al.*).

In Colossians 1:22 we find the pleonastic, Hebraistic expression "the body of his flesh"[73] used of Christ: "And you . . . hath he reconciled in the body of his flesh through death." This expression is evidently employed here to emphasize the fact that it was by suffering death in a body, consisting of real, human

---

[72] E. Schweizer (TWNT, VII, 126) rightly remarks: "*sarx* is in such cases not understood as sinful and at enmity with God, but only as limited and preliminary."

[73] The Hebrew equivalent of this expression is found in the Qumran Commentary on Habakkuk 2:7. There the context shows that the physical body is meant.

flesh, that Christ performed all that was required for our salvation. J. A. C. van Leeuwen (KNT) rightly regards this verse as an indirect refutation of the Colossian heretics who taught that asceticism is the way to be freed from the powers of darkness — an asceticism against which 2:23 clearly speaks in contrast with the saving power of Christ's death (2:20).[74] According to van Leeuwen Colossians 1:22 says not only that Christ adopted a body of real flesh, but that his death in such a body makes it unnecessary for believers to punish their flesh-body by hard ascetic measures; our sins *have* been punished in the *flesh.*

If this interpretation is correct, Paul is here protecting the flesh of the believers, as he also does in 2:20. This means that he did not consider the flesh evil in itself.

Occasionally Paul uses the word *soma* as an equivalent to *sarx* to denote the real human body of the historical Jesus, in which he suffered, died, and rose again. Thus Romans 7:4: ". . . my brethren, ye also were made dead to the law through the body of Christ," i.e., "by the doing to death of His sacred Body for you, on His atoning Cross . . ." (H. C. C. Moule, *The Epistle to the Romans*). In addition, I Corinthians 10:16, "The bread. . . a communion of the body of Christ," and I Corinthians 11:24, "This is my body, which is for you," are passages in which the word "body" denotes Christ's body which he sacrificed on the cross.[75]

The fact that the Son of God adopted our humanity, the flesh-substance included, to do the work of reconciliation in and through that humanity, shows clearly that the flesh as such and in itself cannot be evil.[76]

Some scholars have adduced Paul's statement in Romans 8:3, that God sent his Son "in the likeness of sinful flesh," as evidence of the sinfulness of Christ's flesh, at least in the sense that it was capable of sinning, or was inclined to sin.[77]

[74] Similarly F. F. Bruce (NIC), *et al.* Bruce, however, like others, puts more emphasis on the reality of the incarnation.

[75] Cf. H. D. Wendland, *Das Neue Testament Deutsch, ad loc.*; F. W. Grosheide (NLC); and many other non-Lutheran Protestant commentators. The doctrinal controversy concerning these and similar passages cannot be discussed here.

[76] See also Luke 1:35; Acts 4:27, 30.

[77] Thus, e.g., Pfleiderer and Holsten, referred to by W. Sanday and A. C. Headlam (ICC); C. K. Barrett, *A Commentary on the Epistle to the Romans,* who speaks of "a proclivity to sin" in Christ, which he "constantly overcame" (p. 156); E. Käsemann, *op. cit.,* p. 116; and (with a slight difference) A. Nygren, *Commentary on Romans,* p. 315.

Again it is impossible to discuss all exegetical problems connected with this passage. The following remarks may suffice.

1. If Paul meant to say that Jesus' flesh was in any way sinful he would contradict himself, for in 5:14 the Apostle depicts Christ as the new Adam, in whom through God's creative act a new beginning was made for mankind. This implies that it was an absolutely sinless beginning in the flesh (Zahn, ZK). In II Corinthians 5:2, moreover, Paul declares emphatically that Christ knew no sin.

2. The interpretation discussed is to be rejected also because it contradicts God's own testimony about Jesus, given through the angel Gabriel to Mary. In Luke 1:35 Gabriel calls the child to be conceived in Mary and born of her "the holy thing" (or: "that holy Offspring," BV).[78] From this it is evident that Jesus did not have to obtain holiness by constant struggling against the unholy inclinations of his flesh, but that he was holy in every respect from the very beginning of his earthly existence in Mary's womb.

3. Most commentators emphasize rightly that the expression "in the likeness of" has already been used by Paul in 1:23, 5:14, and 6:5 (cf. also Phil. 2:7). In none of these passages does the expression denote a mere appearance or imitation. In all of them it refers to an actual "being like." Hence Paul's statement does not convey the docetic thought that Christ had human flesh only seemingly, which interpretation has also been given.[79]

4. The interpretations of C. K. Barrett (Comm.) and J. Knox (IB) that the flesh of Christ was real human flesh but different from ours in that it was unfallen flesh and not (as ours is) sinful flesh cannot be accepted because it is based on the assumption that our human flesh as such is sinful, which is contrary to the clear teachings of Scripture. It is also in essence a docetic

---

[78] With S. Greydanus (KNT), NBG, BV, et al., we prefer this rendering to the more frequently favored: "He will be called holy, the Son of God" (ERV, RSV, et al.) Both renderings, however, have the consequence shown above. N. Geldenhuys (Commentary on the Gospel of Luke) is right when he says that the words do not mean that Jesus would become the Son of God. He was the Son of God and would reveal himself and be recognized as such. If this is correct, it applies also to the word "holy," which then must be understood as suggested above.

[79] Thus, e.g., H. A. Bakels in Circa Sacra, 1935, pp. 5ff., as quoted by G. C. Berkouwer, De Persoon van Christus, pp. 168ff. Berkouwer remarks: "It was Paul who wrote the words, so repugnant to Marcion, that Christ was born of a woman."

theory because it makes Jesus' flesh different from that of his mother Mary.[80]

5. The main question is how the expression "sinful flesh" (lit. "flesh of sin") must be understood. In the light of all that we have found in Scripture up to now regarding our human flesh, it cannot possibly mean that the flesh as such is sinful or inherently inclined to sin. This will be shown further when we deal with Paul's conception of "flesh" in its ethically loaded sense.

The expression can be satisfactorily understood and explained in two ways:

(a) The flesh of sin is "the material of our bodies, in which sin has set up its throne and which in this sense belongs to sin" (J. A. Beet). If we understand this as meaning that the flesh as such is not sinful, but only the instrument and vehicle of sin — which is a scriptural thought, as we have found — then Paul's statement can be explained as follows: God sent his Son in a body of the same flesh as we have, which flesh may be called "flesh of sin" (flesh belonging to sin) because in and through this flesh we reveal and experience the sinfulness of our hearts.

In this case the Apostle purposely uses the expression "in the likeness of" to prevent the impression that Christ's flesh is the instrument and vehicle through which *he* sinned. Though Christ had precisely the same flesh as we have, he did not sin in and with that flesh.

(b) The flesh of sin is the "human existence which is qualified by sin" (H. N. Ridderbos, CNT), or "our identical nature, under all those conditions of earthly life which for us are sin's vehicles and occasions" (H. C. G. Moule).[81] Here "flesh" is taken in a wider sense than in the first interpretation, but the conception is the same: God sent his Son in precisely the same humanity as we possess; in that humanity we constantly sin, but Christ did not.

For the same reason as mentioned above under (a), Paul speaks of Jesus' being "in the likeness of sinful humanity."

Whichever interpretation one prefers, in neither of them is the flesh of Christ understood as being sinful in itself.

There is still further evidence that according to Paul the flesh, in the sense of "the material element in human nature," is

---

[80] Sanday and Headlam (ICC) may also favor this interpretation, for they declare that "the flesh of Christ is 'like' ours inasmuch as it is flesh; 'like,' because it is not sinful."

[81] Similarly C. H. Dodd (*The Epistle of Paul to the Romans*), S. Greydanus (KNT), J. Murray (NLC), *et al.*

"morally indifferent" (C. H. Dodd, *op. cit.,* p. 136). In several statements the Apostle refers to the part that flesh and body play in the Christian life, as instruments suitable to be used for the glorification of God. II Corinthians 4:10,11 reads: ". . . always bearing about in the body the dying of Jesus, that the life also of Jesus may be manifested in our body. . . . For we who live are always delivered unto death for Jesus' sake, that the life also of Jesus may be manifested in our mortal flesh."

With F. V. Filson (IB) and most commentators we regard verse 11 as a repetition of the thought of verse 10, for the purpose of emphasis.

We notice, first, that in these verses *soma* and *sarx* have essentially the same meaning. The body is the body-of-flesh, the flesh is the "substance" of the body. In verse 11 Paul speaks of *flesh* instead of *body* (v. 10), probably in order to emphasize the weakness and vulnerability of the body (cf. F. W. Grosheide, KNT).

There is no ground in these verses to substantiate W. D. Stacey's claim (*op. cit.,* p. 183) that in this passage Paul "confused" *soma* and *sarx,* using *sarx* "for a function that really belongs to *soma.*" It is true that Paul's use of *sarx* and *soma* in this connection does not fit into the *sarx-soma* scheme which Stacey regards as Pauline. But this shows only that this scheme is not in accordance with Paul's conception of *sarx* and *soma.*

Second, the context which speaks of persecutions proves that it is incorrect to speak of "body" and "flesh" in these verses as being "simply a periphrasis for 'I,' or 'my person.' "[82] A. Schlatter is right when he writes: "In his body Paul has Jesus' death with him, because the attack of the world is directed against his body: it is his body which has to endure persecutions and sufferings. . ." (Erl.). Most commentators agree with this view.

In the third place, various commentators understand the manifestation of Jesus' life in Paul's body, his mortal flesh, as denoting the power of Jesus' resurrection-life as it revealed itself in letting the Apostle miraculously escape death time and again, and in using Paul's sufferings for the extension of his kingdom.[83] Others, however, understand it as referring also to Paul's future

[82] So J. A. T. Robinson, *The Body,* p. 19.
[83] E.g., Filson (IB), Grosheide (KNT), Lenski (Comm.), Pop (PNT), and Tasker (TNT).

resurrection, when the Cross will be followed by the Crown.[84] If the latter are right, we have in our passage a direct Pauline statement of the resurrection in a body of *flesh*. Then the manifestation of Christ's resurrection-life in the human, mortal flesh of Paul implies also that, finally, his *mortal* flesh, by putting on immortality and incorruption (I Corinthians 15:53-55), will become *immortal, incorruptible* flesh.

It is not easy to make a choice, but even if one prefers the first interpretation it is obvious that for Paul the body of the believer, his body of mortal flesh, is the "sphere in which" and "the means by which"[85] the risen Christ manifests his resurrection-power in order to build his Church. It is hard to understand how the phrase "the resurrection of the flesh" would have "horrified"[86] the man who wrote II Corinthians 4:10-11.

In II Corinthians 7:1 Paul exhorts the believers to cleanse themselves "from all defilement of flesh and spirit. . . ." The combination "flesh and spirit," denoting the whole man, shows that here "flesh" signifies the body, and "spirit" the soul.[87]

W. Barclay (*The Mind of St. Paul*, p. 199) adduces this passage as an evidence of "the filthiness of the flesh." This seems incorrect. With J. Reid (IB), H. D. Wendland (NTD), and most commentators we hold that the combination "flesh-spirit" with regard to the *molusmos* (defilement) of both, implies that *sarkos* and *pneumatos* are objective genitives: flesh and spirit do not defile but can *be* defiled, the flesh "by such sins as unchastity and overindulgence in food and drink," the spirit by sins such as "covetousness, pride, the unforgiving temper" (J. Reid, IB). Paul exhorts the believers to cleanse their flesh and spirit from such defilement, i.e., to abstain from such sins. It is quite obvious that Paul regards the flesh as God's good creature (cf. I Tim. 4:4) which has to be protected against defilement.

---

[84] So, e.g., J. Calvin, Ch. Hodge (Comm.), A. Schlatter (Erl.), and H. D. Wendland (NTD).

[85] With Grosheide, *et al.*, we regard the preposition *en* as having this double meaning.

[86] Thus C. H. Dodd, *The Meaning of Paul for Today*, p. 58.

[87] "Body" and "Soul" are used here in the popular sense, denoting the two aspects of man's existence. That Paul regards man as a dichotomy in the Greek sense, or, as some have thought, as a trichotomy (cf. I Thess. 5:23) will be hard to defend. Paul did not teach a systematic anthropology (as his fluid terminology shows), but the revelation of God in Christ. From this Apostle we can "learn little about the constitution of man, but very much about man in relation to God" (Stacey, *op. cit.*, p. 241; cf. Robinson, *The Body*, p. 27).

Ephesians 5:29, "for no man ever hated his own flesh; but nourisheth and cherisheth it even as Christ also the church," is a most striking evidence of Paul's favorable evaluation of the human body-of-flesh. Loving it and caring for it can even be a symbol of Christ's love and care for his Church.

In Ephesians 5:31 Paul quotes from Genesis 2:24: a man shall "leave his father and mother, and shall cleave to his wife; and the two shall become one flesh." This marital unity is referred to as symbolizing the mysterious unity between Christ and his Church. Though "becoming one flesh" does not exclusively signify sexual intercourse, the latter is certainly included and probably prominent (cf. T. O. Wedel, (IB); F. W. Grosheide, (CNT); et. al.). This proves beyond doubt that to Paul, as in the Old Testament, sexual life is not evil but part of God's good creation. The answer to the question, Can it be that Paul associated original sin and sex?,[88] would have to be in the negative. Not only Ephesians 5:29ff. proves this, but also passages such as I Corinthians 7:3, where husband and wife are exhorted "to render their marital obligation to each other" (Lenski, ad loc.) precisely to *prevent* sin (v. 1); I Timothy 4:4, where the Apostle rejects those who forbid marriage; and Colossians 2:23 and other passages in which Paul condemns asceticism and "unsparing treatment of the *body*," the latter understood "in its ordinary sense" (F. F. Bruce, NIC).

As to Ephesians 5:29ff., E. K. Simpson (NIC) objects to "the omission in modern recensions of the text of the additional clause 'of his flesh and of his bones.'" These words, he argues, echo the words of Adam in Genesis 2:23 and correspond with the immediately following quotation from Genesis 2:24 in verse 23. If Simpson is right, then in Ephesians 5:30 the glorified Christ is stated to have flesh and bones, as is done in Luke 24:39, a verse to be discussed later.

It would not be difficult to add more passages in which Paul's evaluation of the flesh-in-itself is evidently favorable, but the statements discussed may suffice.

---

[88] Thus John Bowman in *The Reformed Theological Review*, Melbourne, Oct. 1960, p. 69. Professor Bowman's appeal to I Cor. 7:1, "It is good for a man not to touch a woman," cannot be regarded as valid. Paul was not the man to contradict his God, who according to Gen. 2:18 said: "It is *not good* that the man should be alone." The Apostle wrote the statement of v. 1 "for the Corinthians and for their specific circumstances at the time" (Lenski, ad loc.).

We have already shown amply that "flesh" and "body" (in its ordinary sense) are equivalent conceptions in Paul's writings and that both are regarded as God's good creatures; this follows from those passages cited above in which *soma* and *sarx* are used interchangeably. We will now add a further selection of passages that bear upon the same point.

Romans 1:24 states that God gave the heathen up "unto uncleanness, that their bodies should be dishonored among themselves." The reference, as the context shows, is apparently to "sensual, sexual perversities; . . . the body is regarded here as the organ in which man reveals himself . . . but special emphasis is placed on the dishonoring of the body as such" (H. N. Ridderbos, CNT).

In Romans 12:1 Paul exhorts the Christians to present their "bodies a living sacrifice, holy, acceptable to God." We would agree with Moule when he remarks: "Not now your spirit, your intelligence . . . but *your bodies* . . . . It is only through the body practically, that we can serve our generation by the will of God" (Comm.).

In I Corinthians 6:13-18 Paul sounds a powerful admonition against fornication, appealing to the fact that our "bodies are members of Christ" (v. 15), temples of the Holy Spirit (v. 19), while the Apostle also declares that a man who commits fornication "sins against his own body" (v. 18). Many varying interpretations of this pericope can be ignored here as irrelevant to the subject under discussion. We note with interest, however, the "uncompromisingly physical . . . language"[89] of the context, which leaves no doubt that the Christian in his *physical soma,* his body-of-flesh, is declared to be a member of Christ, a temple which is so holy that committing fornication means to *sin* against it.[90]

In I Thessalonians 5:23 Paul writes: "And the God of peace himself sanctify you wholly; and may your spirit and soul and

---

[89] J. A. T. Robinson, *The Body,* p. 52.

[90] According to W. Barclay (ExT, June, 1961, p. 26), this Pauline conception of the *soma* is exactly "the main line of Stoic thought," as the Stoics regarded the body as "inhabited by its divinity. . . ." Paul, however, knows nothing of a divine anthropological *pneuma* dwelling in the body of every man. The Spirit of whom I Cor. 6:19 speaks is God the Holy Spirit, and only the body of one who is *in Christ* is a temple of the Spirit (Acts 1:5; 2:33; Rom. 8:9, 14; I Cor. 2:12, 13; Jude: 19). This is, indeed, a far cry from the Stoic line of thought.

body be preserved entire, without blame at the coming of our Lord Jesus Christ."

We agree with G. Milligan that "the triple subject must not be pressed, as if it contained a psychological definition of human nature."[91] Though commentators differ on this and other points of exegesis, they all rightly emphasize that Paul's prayer for the sanctification and preservation of the Christians concerns them as *entire men,* in every aspect of human existence, the body as the corporeal frame included.

Most commentators regard the "preservation" mentioned in verse 23b as the result of the sanctification for which the Apostle prays in the first half of this verse. According to them the "preservation" will occur in the Day of Judgment: instead of being condemned like the ungodly, the sanctified ones will be declared blameless and so will be preserved from eternal death.[92]

Others argue that the preservation takes place in this life. The phrase *en tei parousiai* is then translated "with a view to," or "in connection with" (Lenski), or "unto" (KJV), or "until" (J. W. Bailey, IB).

The difference is not very great. Whichever interpretation one prefers, the implication for our subject remains the same: it is Paul's prayer that the *entire man,* nothing excluded, may be blameless in the Day of Judgment. From this it is evident, in the first place, that flesh and body cannot possibly be intrinsically evil in Paul's estimation. What is essentially unholy cannot be kept holy. Second, Paul's statement entails that *this* body of flesh, in which the sanctification takes place, will be raised at the coming of Christ and glorified. It makes no sense to speak of the sanctified body being preserved at the Judgment, if *this* body, in which the sanctification occurs, vanishes at death never to return. The essential identity of this body of flesh and the resurrection-body cannot be denied in the light of this passage.

That it is *this* body which will be raised, is also taught in two passages in Romans.

The first is Romans 8:11: ". . . he that raised up Christ

---

[91] G. Milligan, *St. Paul's Epistles to the Thessalonians.* Similarly J. A. C. van Leeuwen (KNT), W. Neil (MNTC), A. Plummer, *A Commentary on St. Paul's First Epistle to the Thessalonians, et al.* A most interesting survey of the various theories on trichotomy in connection with this passage may be found in W. Hendriksen, *I-II Thessalonians* (NTC), pp. 146-50.

[92] So, e.g., J. Hutchison, J. A. C. van Leeuwen, L. Morris (NTC), A. Plummer, and G. Wohlenberg (ZK).

Jesus from the dead shall give life also to your mortal bodies through his Spirit that dwelleth in you."

Leaving aside exegetical details, we need not doubt that the phrase "your mortal bodies" denotes this present body, i.e., our whole outward existence, including the flesh as the body's "material." Concerning this body Paul gives us the assurance that it will be raised through the power of the same Spirit ("unmistakably the divine Spirit")[93] through whom Jesus was raised, since this Spirit is dwelling in the body of the believer too. Now Jesus was raised in the *same* body-of-flesh as that in which he died, as will be shown later. Hence the believer may be certain of his resurrection in the *same* body of flesh as that in which he lived and (if he is not alive when Jesus returns) died.

The second passage, Romans 8:23, ". . . waiting for . . . the redemption of our body," requires similar interpretation. We agree with J. Knox (IB) that the meaning of 8:11 and 8:23 is the same. It is true that the genitive *tou somatos* can be taken either as one of separation (deliverance *from* the body) or as an objective genitive (the body itself will be redeemed).

If one prefers the former, "body" must be understood in its ethically loaded sense, which, as we shall see later, is also Pauline. Then it denotes our humanity as it is corrupted by sin and subject to the consequences of sin.[94]

With Zahn and the great majority of commentators, however, we prefer the interpretation which regards the body as the subject of the expected redemption. The context speaks of the future deliverance of the whole creation from the "bondage of corruption (v. 21), which certainly denotes "physical evil" (Moule), and hence the redemption of our bodies is most naturally understood as a deliverance "from the 'ills that flesh is heir to'" (Sanday and Headlam).[95]

J. A. T. Robinson suggests that Paul's use of the word "body" in the singular, over against the plural in 8:11, shows that the Apostle is referring to "the one Resurrection-body," *viz.,* the Church.[96] C. K. Barrett, however, rightly rejects this inter-

---

[93] J. Knox (IB).

[94] So, e.g., A. Nygren (*op. cit., ad loc.*), who refers to 7:24: "Who shall deliver me out of the body of this death?"

[95] Similarly J. A. Beet, G. R. Cragg (IB), R. C. H. Lenski, J. Murray (NLC), S. Greydanus (KNT), *et al.*

[96] *The Body,* p. 79n. (cf. pp. 81-82).

pretation with the convincing remark, ". . . the Church is never the body of *us* but the body of *Christ*."

It may be admitted that the "body" which will be redeemed is not only our physical body of flesh but "our present, human mode of existence" (H. N. Ridderbos, CNT). But we would underline the words "not only." Our physical body is certainly included and will "be liberated from the slavery of corruption (v. 21), on account of the price paid by Christ."[97]

We can agree, further, with G. R. Cragg (IB) that the body referred to by Paul in this passage will not be raised in its present form, which would be "a most un-Pauline doctrine" and excluded by the very words of this passage. On the other hand, Cragg rightly emphasizes that according to Paul the resurrection-body will not be "wholly unrelated to the bodies we now use." There will be "continuity."

As far as we can see, this continuity implies that the resurrection-body will be a body of flesh. For how can our present body, which certainly is a body of flesh, be delivered from "the slavery of corruption" if it has no future at all as a body of flesh?

b. *Whether Paul Makes an Essential Distinction between Flesh and Body.*

According to J. A. T. Robinson, the Apostle makes an essential distinction between *flesh* and *body,* implying that not the former but only the latter can be raised. After referring to numerous passages in Paul's letters in which *sarx* and *soma* are completely identical (*The Body,* pp. 27-30), he declares that the two are not identical in all respects, the difference being that whereas *sarx* signifies "man in his 'otherness' from God, in his frailty and mortality . . . . *soma,* on the other hand, while it can be identified with *sarx* in all man's sin and corruption, is also the carrier of his resurrection" (p. 26). Or, as he formulates the point on page 31: ". . . however much the two may come, through the Fall, to describe the same thing, in essence *sarx* and *soma* designate different aspects of the human relationship to God. *While sarx stands for man, in the solidarity of creation, in his distance from God, soma stands for man, in the solidarity of creation, as made for God"* (italics Robinson's). According

---

[97] Cf. Lenski. For "redemption" (Greek *apolutrosis*) reference may be made to A. Deissmann's interpretation in *Licht vom Osten,* pp. 275-78.

to Robinson this does not mean that *sarx* and *soma* are to be regarded as different *parts* of man, or that the one should be material and mortal, and the other not. The only thing that matters is that *soma* designates the whole man as utterly subject to Spirit, whereas *flesh* denotes the whole man as not. That is why man as *soma* can be raised, not man as *sarx*. The question whether the resurrection-*soma* will be material or not, is out of the picture here. It has nothing to do with the *soma* understood as "man, wholly subject to the Spirit." He may be subject to the Spirit without having a material body.[98]

One is eager to learn the passages in Paul's writings that prove Robinson's contention. Apart from Colossians 2:11, which according to Robinson allows for the possibility of a *soma* which is not *tes sarkos,* the only proof adduced is from I Corinthians 6:13ff.: "Meats for the belly, and the belly for meats: but God shall bring to nought both it and them. But the body is not for fornication, but for the Lord." The significance of the *koilia* ("the stomach," RSV) is the same as that of the *sarx,* according to Robinson, "something inherently perishable and transient. But the body (which stands throughout this passage for the "personality") is not created for a purely corruptible function and destiny . . . it is for the Lord." Therefore, only "man as *soma*" can inherit the Kingdom of God.[99]

Against this theory the following objections can be raised.

1. It is not in accordance with sound hermeneutics to build a theory on one Scripture passage when there are numerous passages which teach differently. Robinson himself has given abundant proof that *sarx* and *soma* as a rule are identical in Paul's letters. Now only a single passage, which seems to teach the opposite, is deemed sufficient to prove that *sarx* and *soma* are not at all identical but constitute an absolute contrast, signifying mutually exclusive conceptions. A sound method of exegesis should lead us to ask whether that one passage could be reconciled with the rest.

2. The Pauline anthropology does not contrast *flesh* with *body,* but rather *flesh* with *spirit*, and as we shall see, this contrast is not ontological but religious, which Robinson himself admits

---

98 *The Body,* p. 31n.

99 *Ibid.,* p. 31. Cf. W. G. H. Simon (TBC), who claims that *"belly* here stands for the same thing as St. Paul's word *flesh."* L. Morris (TNT) in his interpretation of this passage also introduces the contrast "flesh-body," with an appeal to Robinson.

(p. 31n.).   Now, suddenly, this prominent Pauline contrast "flesh-spirit" is replaced by the contrast "flesh-body," expressing practically the same thought as that of "flesh-spirit."   It is not reasonable to suggest that Paul, who always describes the two basic relationships of man to God in terms of *flesh* and *spirit,* should on a single occasion use a different pair of terms for the same idea.

3. The passage to which Robinson appeals, *viz.,* I Corinthians 6:12ff., does not distinguish flesh from body in such a way that the former denotes the whole man in his otherness from God, etc., while the latter denotes man as "made for God."   The context makes it clear that *koilia* does not denote the whole man, or even the whole body regarded as flesh, but one very special *part* or *function* of the body.

Paul is warning the Corinthians against fornication.   Apparently some Corinthians ("Gnostic libertines," IB) defended this sin with an appeal to the slogan: "Meats for the belly and the belly for meats."   That is to say, food has been created to satisfy the stomach (the digestive organs) and the stomach was given to us for taking food.   Eating and drinking, therefore, are quite natural activities.   The same holds true (thus they must have argued) for the whole body with all its organs and activities, the sexual included.   Of course, adultery is forbidden in God's law, but fornication is something quite different.   It means sexual intercourse with a harlot, an activity which is quite as natural for the human body as are eating and drinking.

Paul refutes this argumentation, in which *part* of the body, *viz.,* the stomach and its function, is identified with *the body as a whole,* i.e., with man in his bodily existence.   The Apostle makes it clear that there is a great distinction, not between man as *flesh* and man as *body,* but between one specific organ or function of the body and the body as a whole.   The distinction is not merely formal.   The belly, Paul argues, has significance for this earthly life only.   It will be destroyed, abandoned; the resurrection-body will not need digestive organs or food.   The Corinthians, therefore, are wrong if they infer from what is only a transient part or function of the body, to the body as a whole and to what the body as a whole may or may not do.[100]

Then, according to Paul, the distinction between the belly and the body has another characteristic: the belly, indeed, was

[100] Cf. C. T. Craig (IB), F. W. Grosheide (CNT; KNT), A. Schlatter (Erl.), H. D. Wendland (NTD), *et al.*

made for food; taking food is its aim within the framework of the body. But the body itself, though it has sexual organs, is not qualified by sex, nor does it find its aim in it, nor is it destined for sexuality. The body is man's outward existence, man himself in his outward existence.[101] As such it has a specific destination: the body of the Christian is for the Lord, i.e. for Christ, destined to be used in his service and to his glory. The Lord, on the other hand, is for the body: he protects it and will raise it in glory, but this body will be without "stomach," i.e., without the need of food.

The connection between the body of the believer and Christ is such a close one that the body can be called a member of Christ: one and the same life-giving Spirit dwells in Christ and in the Christian's bodily existence. To commit fornication, therefore, is a horrible sin; it means making a member of Christ a member of a harlot, a godless woman. For according to God's ordinance in Genesis 2:26 ("the twain shall become one flesh"), sexual intercourse always effects a complete union of the two persons involved and thus is quite different from eating or drinking something. Becoming one *flesh* with a harlot means becoming one *body* with her, i.e., being united with her in every respect, in her shameful sinning as well. What a contrast with being united with the Lord through the Spirit, which is the destination of the Christian's body![102]

4. The whole argumentation in I Corinthians 12:13-20, moreover, proves the untenability of Robinson's contention that it is irrelevant whether the body (as v. 13 speaks of it) is material or immaterial and whether the resurrection-body will be material or immaterial. In general Paul, speaking of man's body, never thinks in modern terms of an immaterial "personality" and the

---

101 J. Short (IB), W. G. H. Simon (TBC), *et al,* claim with Robinson that Paul uses "body" in this passage as equivalent to the term "self" or "personality." But the context shows clearly that although "body" stands for more than "flesh-matter" and denotes the whole man, nevertheless the "material aspect" is included and even prominent. How much Paul had this material aspect in mind may appear from the fact that Craig (IB) criticizes Paul as proving too much when in v. 16 he appeals to Genesis 2:24, "The two shall become one flesh," the relevance of which verse (according to Craig) "depends on the identification of *body* (*soma*) and *flesh* (*sarx*)." Indeed, when speaking of the body in this connection Paul also has the *sarx* in mind.

102 Cf. F. W. Grosheide.

like,[103] and he most certainly does not do so in the passage under consideration. The fact that he interchanges the expressions "becoming one *flesh*" (v. 17) and "becoming one *body*" proves again that to him "flesh" and *soma* are essentially the same. Particularly in this connection, where the issue is fornication and becoming one body with a harlot, the material side of the body has everything to do with it. It is this *body* of *flesh* in which the fornicator becomes one with the harlot. For a Christian this is a horrible sin just because this *body* of *flesh* is for the Lord, and will be raised for an eternal glorious future.[104]

5. We conclude that I Corinthians 6:13ff. has nothing to do with an essential difference between *sarx* and *soma,* but rather that Paul remains consistently in the Hebrew tradition on this point. In his letters the Greek word *soma* has essentially the same connotation as the Hebrew word *basar.* Both denote man's outward existence, the flesh-substance included. This outward existence is not evil as such, but can be used either in the service of God or in the service of Satan and sin. Which of the two it will be depends on the condition of a man's heart, which is the religious center of his being.[105]

There remains one difficulty which needs to be discussed. Although it cannot be denied that Paul speaks of flesh and body in such a way that they cannot be intrinsically evil, there are certain passages which create a completely different impression. They are those passages in which *flesh* and *sin* are practically identified. In Romans 7:14, for instance, the Apostle complains that he is *sarkinos,* i.e., carnal, fleshly, which he identifies with being "sold under sin." According to verse 18, "in me, that is, in my flesh, dwelleth no good thing," and in verse 25 Paul declares that with the flesh he "serves the law of sin." In Romans 13:14 we are warned not to make "provision for the flesh, to fulfil the lusts thereof": the flesh apparently has evil lusts. In Galatians 5:16, 17 "the lust of the flesh" is mentioned again, and it is declared to be diametrically opposed to the Spirit. The evil works which the flesh produces are listed in verses 19-21, and it is obvious

---

[103] Cf., e.g., C. H. Dodd's "form" in *The Meaning of Paul for Today,* p. 58, and A. M. Hunter's "organic principle of identity" in *Interpreting Paul's Gospel,* p. 54.

[104] Cf. J. Calvin, F. W. Grosheide, Ch. Hodge, R. C. H. Lenski, A. Schlatter, *et al.*

[105] The word *kardia* ("heart") occurs with this meaning no less than forty-eight times in the Pauline epistles.

that there is no evil which the flesh cannot produce. In Ephesians 2:3, too, the flesh is characterized by evil lusts and desires.

There are, moreover, passages in which the expressions "in the flesh" and "after the flesh," especially when used with a verb, are equivalent to living or acting in a sinful way. Thus, e.g., Romans 8:8: "they that are in the flesh cannot please God;" and Romans 8:4, where the believers are depicted as those "who walk not after the flesh, but after the Spirit."

Indeed, judging from these and similar statements, flesh and sin seem to be inseparably connected, and it is quite in conformity with this fact that Galatians 5:24 declares: "they that are of Christ Jesus have crucified the flesh with the passions and the lusts thereof."

As to the *body,* here too we meet with statements that seem to contradict our earlier conclusions. Romans 6:6 declares that union with Christ results in "the body of sin" being done away. In Romans 6:12 we are admonished not to obey the lusts of our mortal body. In Romans 7, which so often speaks of the sinfulness of the flesh, we find in verse 23 that the word "flesh" is replaced by "members" (of the body), whereas in verse 24 the deliverance from the flesh is called a deliverance "out of the body of this death." In 8:13 "not living after the flesh" is identified with mortifying, by the Spirit, "the deeds of the body." According to Colossians 2:11 the Christian has been circumcised in Christ "with a circumcision not made with hands, in the putting off of the body of the flesh," whereas in 3:5 the believers are told: "Put to death therefore your members which are upon the earth. . . ."

It is evident that in all these passages "flesh" and "body" have a morally loaded meaning, and the question arises how these conceptions can be harmonized with Paul's main line of thought.[106] Must we now, finally, suspect Paul of following two mutually exclusive lines of thought, the one Hebrew, the other Hellenistic?[107]

If this were the case it would imply that the Apostle was hopelessly confused on a matter of fundamental importance, contra-

[106] W. D. Davies, after tabulating the incidence of the term "flesh," comes to the conclusion that "the term *flesh* with a moral connotation occurs far less frequently in the Pauline Epistles than discussions of Pauline theology would lead one to expect." As to *soma*: it occurs *very* seldom with a moral connotation. (*The Scrolls and the New Testament,* ed. K. Stendahl, p. 163).

[107] A survey and description of such opinions, as held by many of the older liberal theologians and some of more recent times, may be found in W. D. Stacey's work, already referred to, pp. 41-43.

dicting himself in a most serious way. But this hypothesis is incompatible with the care and consistency of Paul's argumentation in general. *A fortiori,* to suppose that Paul contradicts himself in the same letter is most unlikely.

It would seem to follow, then, that where Paul uses "flesh" and "body" with an ethically unfavorable connotation, he cannot be referring to the flesh-substance or the body-of-flesh as such. We find this confirmed when we turn to the passages concerned. There is first the significant fact, pointed out by W. D. Davies,[108] that almost all the instances where Paul uses "flesh" with a moral connotation occur either in Romans 7 and 8, where Paul is concerned with his personal experience of sin, or in the polemic portion of Colossians, or in the pareanetic section of Galatians. On the other hand, in Romans 1, 2 and 5, where the Apostle is dealing with the origin of sin in general, the term "flesh" is not used in a morally loaded sense. This indicates that Paul did not view the flesh as intrinsically evil. If he did, he could not have neglected to give it a prominent place in his teachings on the origin of sin.[109]

To this *argumentum ex silentio* can be added the following evidence. In Romans 13:14, Galatians 5:16ff., and Ephesians 2:3 the lusts and desires of the flesh are mentioned with a moral connotation. Are they meant as the lusts and desires of the *flesh-substance* or of the *body-of-flesh* as such? They are not, as clearly appears from Galatians 5:19ff., where the evil works of the flesh are listed. By far most of these "flesh-works" certainly do not have their origin in the physical flesh or body; idolatry, enmities, jealousies, wraths, factions, divisions, heresies, and envyings are very markedly sins of the soul, the heart. "Flesh," therefore, in these and similar passages, must denote that sinful human nature which finds its center in the human *heart*.[110]

As far as the Christian is concerned, the flesh in its moral sense is identical with Paul's conception of the "old man," which according to Ephesians 4:22 the believers must put away. In this pas-

---

[108] *Op. cit.,* p. 163.

[109] It is remarkable, as Davies shows (*op. cit.,* p. 164), that the same usage of "flesh" is found in the Scrolls: the moral connotation is only in the Psalms, where we hear of the personal experience of sin. "Where the Scrolls present a system of belief the term is notably absent." This implies that Paul's usage of the word "flesh in *all* its aspects has a Jewish background.

[110] There is a striking similarity between the list of sins of the flesh in Gal. 5:19ff., and that of the sins which our Lord declared to proceed from the human *heart* (Mark 7:21ff. and parallel passages).

sage Paul declares of the old man that it "waxeth corrupt after the lusts of deceit," and that it means "your former manner of life" (v. 22).

On the basis of these statements we may conclude that "flesh" and "body," where they have a moral connotation in Paul's writings, and the "old man," stand for one and the same thing: sinful human nature, with its sinful manner of life.[111]

This conclusion is confirmed by other passages. In Galatians 3:3, for instance, Paul asks the Galatians: "having begun in the Spirit, are ye now perfected in the flesh?" Here the connotation of "flesh" is determined by the context, where the contrast is between living by faith in the crucified Savior (v. 1) and living in self-righteousness by doing the works of the law (v. 2). "Flesh" in verse 3, therefore, cannot possibly denote the flesh-substance or the body-of-flesh, but rather it stands for human nature and its achievements as the object of religious confidence and boasting.[112]

In Colossians 2:11 Paul reminds the readers that they have been circumcised with a circumcision "not made with hands, in the putting off of the body of the flesh. . . ." Here not only "flesh" but also "body" has a moral connotation, but the "body of the flesh" cannot possibly be the physical body or its flesh-substance. The Colossians certainly did not put that off. The context proves that the body of the flesh must be human nature in its sinful state. The unusual expression "the body of the flesh" is employed to emphasize the fact that the spiritual circumcision, to which the "putting off of the body of the flesh" refers, is a thorough one. The Jewish circumcision consisted in putting off only a small part of the body-of-flesh. Spiritual circumcision means, however, that the *whole* "body of the flesh," i.e., the sinful human nature in *all* its aspects, must be abandoned.[113]

In Colossians 3:5 the believers are urged to put to death their "members which are upon the earth." Neglecting various exegetical problems connected with this verse and that which follows, we concentrate on the question whether the "members" in question are actual members of the physical body. The answer, of course, must be negative. In the first place, in the Epistle to the Colossians Paul is "battling against gnostic trends in the

---

[111] Cf. W. Barclay, *The Mind of St. Paul*, pp. 199ff.
[112] H. N. Ridderbos (NLC).
[113] J. A. C. Van Leeuwen (KNT). Similarly F. F. Bruce (NIC), H. N. Ridderbos (CNT), J. E. Uitman (PNT), *et al.*

Church,"[114] propagated by innovators who were trying to impose an unchristian *askesis* upon the addressees.[115] In 2:23 he condemns their "severity to the body." Second, Paul himself explains what he means by the "members" that have to be put to death, by adding a double catalogue of vices (vv. 5, 8, 9).[116] Some of these vices are particularly connected with the physical body, but others concern primarily the condition of the heart as, e.g., evil desire, anger, wrath. The "members" of Colossians 3:5 therefore denote again the evil human nature, the sinful manner of life, the "old man" (v. 9).

Though all the preceding passages prove that Paul does not regard the flesh-substance and the physical body as evil in themselves, it cannot be denied that he connects them very closely with sin. The very fact that "flesh," "body," and "members" are used to denote sinful human nature points in that direction. And with good reason: man on earth is always man-in-the-flesh, in the literal sense of the word. It is by means of his flesh, his biological body, that man expresses himself, whether in his sinfulness or in his holiness. Even merely "spiritual" sins such as hatred and pride express themselves in the way a man looks, bears himself, and acts. Even unbelief, the most "spiritual" sin, expresses itself this way. The physical body, therefore, as man's instrument of expression, certainly has a part in his sinning, just as it plays a part in his living by faith.

There is even more. As a tool misused by man after the Fall to express the sinfulness of his heart, the flesh, the physical body with its members, has in the course of history acquired certain tendencies, inclinations, and habits which cause it to be a mighty organ of sin. The tool, shaped by the sinful soul, has become the soul's master — not because there is anything intrinsically wrong with the flesh-substance or the physical body, but because man has corrupted them and *made* them his soul's master.[117] The responsibility rests with man in the center of his personality, his heart, not with his flesh or physical body as such. This is obviously Paul's teaching in Romans 6:13, "neither present your

---

[114] J. Horst, TWNT, *s.v. melos*, p. 571.

[115] F. F. Bruce (NIC).

[116] With Bruce, Van Leeuwen (KNT), and others we see no reason for making a heavy stop after "your members which are upon the earth," introducing an anacoluthon, as J. B. Lightfoot suggests.

[117] W. Schlatter, *op. cit.*, p. 39. See also J. van Andel, *Paulus' Brief aan de Colossensen*, p. 52, and H. N. Ridderbos, *Aan de Romeinen* (CNT), p. 136.

members unto sin as instruments of unrighteousness; but present yourselves unto God, as alive from the dead, and your members as instruments of righteousness unto God." Here it is implied that the "lusts of the mortal body" which should "not be obeyed" (v. 12) have no independent existence: "your mortal body" and "your members" are interchangeably used with "yourselves." Man is responsible for the fact that in his body lusts demand to be "obeyed"; he is responsible for using his members either as instruments of sin or as instruments of dedication to God.

In this light we are to understand the ethically loaded sense of "flesh" and "body" found in Romans 7. In this chapter Paul is speaking in a very personal way. It is true that what he has to say concerns all Christians, as appears from verses 1-6. But beginning with verse 7 the plural "we" is replaced by the singular "I": Paul feels himself to be completely involved in the battle with sin which all Christians must wage.[118]

In verse 18 the Apostle says, "For I know that in me, that is, in my flesh, dwelleth no good thing." According to W. Bauer, Paul deviates here from the Old Testament tradition and stresses the "necessary relationship between flesh as a substance, and sin," in line with the Greek conception of the flesh.[119] In the light of all that we have found, nothing can be farther from the truth. The Greek dualism was ontological: the body was regarded as evil because it was matter, and it was inhabited by the *nous*

---

[118] H. N. Ridderbos has recently put in a vigorous plea for the interpretation which regards Rom. 7:14ff. as referring to Paul's inward struggle before his conversion (*Aan de Romeinen* (CNT), *ad loc.*). Professor Berkouwer, in a few articles in *Gereformeerd Weekblad,* 14th Year, Nos. 37ff., records his disagreement. We agree with the latter and with those commentators who hold that Paul's statement records the inner struggle of a regenerated man. Only thus can the expression "I delight in the law of God after the inward man" (v. 22) and similar expressions in Rom. 7:14ff. be satisfactorily interpreted.

[119] A-G, *s.v. sarx* par. 7. Much the same opinion is given by W. Barclay in ExT, June 1961, p. 261, where the "sideline" of Stoic thought as found "mainly in Seneca and Epictetus" is described as a conception "in which the body is hated and despised, a line which echoes the Orphic catchword *soma sema,* the body is a tomb. The flesh is evil, much as Paul saw it . . . this line is part cf the Gnostic dualism. . . ." Fortunately, Professor Barclay can be refuted with his own words in *the Mind of St. Paul,* where he emphatically denies that the Greek conception of the essential evil of all material and bodily things was Paul's conception: "Paul was very far from holding such a view of the body" (p. 201). This is also Schweizer's conclusion concerning Paul's anthropology (TWNT, VII, p. 133, par. 8).

(mind), which was conceived as divine.[120]   This conception was absolutely foreign to the Hebrew mind, which saw man in his totality in opposition to God.   It is foreign to Paul's mind, too. It has already been shown, and a closer study of Romans 7:14ff. will show it again.

When Paul complains in Romans 7:18 that in him, that is in his flesh, no good dwells, he distinguishes between "I" and "flesh" (C. K. Barrett).   Sanday and Headlam take "I" as denoting "the higher self" or "conscience," but the distinction between a higher and a lower part in man is more in conformity with Greek thought than with biblical teaching.   It seems better, with S. Greydanus (KNT), H. N. Ridderbos (CNT), J. Murray (NLC), and others, to think of the "I" as the person, the ego, the center of personality. In verse 22 this is called "the inward man," in verse 25 "the mind."

Here, in the center of his humanity, Paul as a man, regenerated by the Holy Spirit, has a desire to do God's will (vv. 21, 22).

Then, over against this desire stands his "flesh" in which "no good dwells," but rather sin (v. 20b).   This sin works in his "flesh," in his "members," as a "law," i.e., as a "constraining principle" (Sanday and Headlam), constantly seeking to make Paul its prisoner of war,[121] causing him to obey the law of sin instead of the will of God, which his mind desires to do and, indeed, does do (vv. 22, 25b).

What does Paul in this connection mean by his "flesh" and his "members"?   J. A. Beet interprets it as denoting "the outer and material side of his nature," whereas J. Knox identifies the "flesh" completely with the flesh-substance (IB on Rom. 7:15).

It cannot be denied that the latter is included.   But it can only be part of what Paul means by "flesh."   For flesh is distinguished from the "I," the inward man, the mind, the center of the personality.   "Flesh," therefore, must mean more than just the flesh-substance of the body.   With Ridderbos we take it as denoting "man in his concrete, bodily mode of existence," or (as Greydanus interprets) "all that is not his Ego: his bodily and psychic powers." With C. H. Dodd we might call it "human nature" if we add: as distinguished from the ego.

Does Paul say that his "flesh," so understood, is essentially evil?   He does not, as most commentators recognize.[122]   The

---

[120] Cf. Bertrand Russell, *History of Western Philosophy,* p. 286.

[121] H. C. G. Moule, who remarks that the present tense does not necessarily indicate the full success of the strategy, but its aim.

[122] E.g., C. K. Barrett, C. H. Dodd, J. Knox, and Sanday and Headlam.

Apostle declares that sin *dwells in* his "flesh," and that the law of sin is *in* his "members." In other words his humanity, apart from his ego, is occupied by sin, under its dominion, and for that reason it is "a constraining and paralyzing power" (Zahn), preventing his ego from doing those God-honoring actions which can be performed only through the medium of the "flesh."

From all this it is evident that in Romans 7 the "flesh," which includes the body-of-flesh, occurs as "the instrument and sphere of operation of the law of sin" (Murray, p. 269), in precisely the same way as we find it everywhere in Scripture. It is in and through his physical body that Paul constantly experiences the corrupting power of his sinful nature, his old man, still working in him.

It is also evident that Paul does not mean to say that he is an innocent victim of his "flesh" and of the sin dwelling in it. Though he distinguishes "I" from "flesh," he does not separate them. He declares (v. 18), "In *me* there dwells no good." He calls the flesh "*my* flesh." In verse 25, he confesses: "*I myself* . . . serve . . . with the flesh the law of sin." The battle of which Paul speaks in Romans 7:14ff. is the fighting of the renewed Paul against what (in his whole existence) is left of the old Paul.

With this background we may understand correctly his desperate longing for deliverance: "Wretched man that I am! who shall deliver me out of the body of this death?" (v. 24).

It is striking that precisely here in this chapter, where we find the loaded meaning of "flesh" in stronger terms than anywhere else, Paul uses the word "body" as an equivalent. It shows again that any essential difference between flesh and body is absolutely foreign to the mind of the Apostle.

It shows also that it is wrong to identify the flesh in its loaded sense with the flesh-substance of the body, for which according to J. Knox (on Rom. 7:15, IB) there can be no redemption. If that were true, there could be no redemption for the body either, in view of the identification of flesh with "body of death" in Romans 7:24.

Since "flesh" and "body of death" are obviously identical, the latter must denote, like "flesh," humanity as distinguished from the ego, humanity (the flesh-body included) still in the power of sin. Paul calls it "the body of *death*," meaning that, because sin is reigning in it, it is "doomed to death" (BV, J. Knox, *et al.*) or "under the dominion of death, which is already working in it" (H. N. Ridderbos, *et al.*).

From *this* body Paul wants to be delivered. This cannot mean that Paul desires to be a spirit without any body at all. His positive teachings on the resurrection of the body exclude any such idea. What he wants to be delivered from is a humanity (the flesh-body included) which is under the power of sin and death, which in I Corinthians 15:53 is called "this corruptible" and "this mortal." He wants to receive an incorruptible and immortal body, a body in which not sin but God's Spirit reigns supreme, a humanity wholly sanctified and glorified.

If Paul desires this for the *body*, he must desire this also for the *flesh* (as substance), for in Romans 7 flesh and body are identified. When will this deliverance from the body take place? Some suggest: at death.[123] But since Paul's chief emphasis is clearly on the resurrection hope (cf. 8:11, 23), it seems better to say with A. Nygren that "Paul is reaching forward in hope toward the time when the perishable puts on the imperishable, and the mortal puts on immortality (I Cor 15:54)."

Our examination of Paul's epistles results in the conclusion that there is no trace of Hellenistic dualism in his anthropology.[124] His conceptions of flesh and body are fully in line with the Old Testament conception of man as *basar*. Where he goes somewhat beyond the Old Testament usage of *basar*, he nevertheless does not contradict it. Where he uses Greek terms and expressions, he fills them with a Hebrew content. It was not necessary for him to derive these terms and expressions from Hellenistic sources: they were commonplace in the Jewish literature of the Scrolls, though the anthropology and theology of the sect differed widely from Paul's.[125]

According to the Apostle there is nothing ethically wrong with the flesh-substance or with the body-of-flesh in themselves. After the Fall, however, there is very much wrong with *man, as far as his relationship to God is concerned.* Man has even seen fit to bring his body-of-flesh, God's good creature, under the bondage of sin. But by the grace of God the body may participate in the redemption through Christ. For the believer it becomes a temple of the Holy Spirit, and its members become weapons of righteousness instead of weapons of unrighteousness, despite the remaining struggle against the old nature. And complete deliverance is

[123] E.g., J. A. C. van Leeuwen and D. Jacobs (KV).
[124] Cf. also J. G. Machen, *The Origin of Paul's Religion*, pp. 275ff.
[125] W. D. Davies, *op. cit.*, pp. 171,182.

awaiting those that are Christ's: in the day of resurrection the whole man will rise in glory, his body included.

Indeed, in the *essence* of the flesh-substance or the body-of-flesh there is nothing which makes it impossible for the body to be raised as a body of glorified *flesh*.   In Paul's teachings, as we have studied them thus far, the latter is even implied.

The same conclusion applies *mutatis mutandis* to the other New Testament teachings on flesh and body.   There is no essential difference between Paul's theological anthropology and that of the New Testament in general.   Both are completely in line with the Old Testament and in neither of the two do we find the slightest trace of contempt for, or disqualification of, the flesh-substance or the body-of-flesh.

Especially the strong statements of Professor Cullmann, mentioned at the beginning of Chapter 1, find no ground whatsoever in the writings either of Paul or of the New Testament in general, and the conclusions drawn from these and similar statements must be considered invalid.

CHAPTER FOUR

THE RESURRECTION-BODY OF JESUS CHRIST

The resurrection of Jesus Christ is not only the basis on which the resurrection-hope of the believers rests,[1] but it is also the pattern of their resurrection. When Christ returns from heaven, he "shall fashion anew the body of our humiliation, that it may be conformed to the body of his glory" (Phil. 3:21). "And as we have borne the image of the earthy, we shall also bear the image of the heavenly" (1 Cor. 15:49). "We know that, if he shall be manifested, we shall be like him" (1 John 3:2).

Since according to these and other passages Christ's resurrection-body is "type and model of our own,"[2] the question concerning the kind of body in which Jesus Christ was raised from the dead is of the utmost importance for our subject.

1. DEFINITION OF THE TERM

In the light of recent theological discussions, it is necessary first to define more closely the term "the resurrection-body of Christ." The fact that Paul repeatedly calls the Church the body of Christ[3] has led various theologians to identify the Church with the body in which Christ rose from the grave or with the body that he possesses in heaven after the ascension. J. A. T. Robinson, for instance, claims that "it is almost impossible to exaggerate the materialism and crudity of the Church as literally now the Resurrection *body* of Christ,"[4] and that "there is no real line between the body of His Resurrection and the flesh bodies of those who are risen with Him, for they are members of it."[5] Robinson even goes so far as to say that the risen body in which Christ appeared to Paul on the road to Damascus was that of "his post-ascension form," i.e., "the resurrection body of Christ not as an individual,

---

[1] John 11:25; I Cor. 15:21; Phil. 3:10, 11; I Thess. 4:14ff.; I Pet. 1:3ff.
[2] W. Milligan, *The Resurrection of the Dead*, p. 154.
[3] I Cor. 12:13ff.; Eph. 1:23; 2:16; 3:6; 4:4ff.; Col. 1:18, 24; 2:19; 3:15.
[4] *The Body*, p. 51.
[5] *Ibid.*, p. 53.

107

but as the Christian Community."[6]   Alan Richardson refers to
John 2:21, where, according to him, Christ himself "speaks of
raising the Church, the temple of his resurrection-body."[7]

According to Cullmann the Church on earth is Christ's resurrection-body, "the only *soma pneumatikon* in existence at the
moment," though "none of them individually possesses a resurrection-body, since all are still clothed with a body of flesh."[8]   He
declares, with an appeal to 1 Corinthians 6:15,16 that Paul con-
ceives membership in the Church, the risen body of Christ, to be
"a physical relationship."[9]   A. H. Curtis regards the resurrection
of Christ as "the season in the life of Jesus after death at which
He obtains life within His disciples. . . .   He was raised . . . in
His Body the Church."[10]   E. Schweizer thinks it possible "that
Paul conceived of the body of Christ in a material manner, as a
kind of fluid issuing from the Exalted One and embracing all
those who belong to him."[11]   Some go so far as to say that the
Church as the Body of Christ "is Christ himself . . . as He is
present among and meets us upon earth after his resurrection."
The Church, in its turn, "is, in its essence, nothing other than this
presence of Christ."[12]   Others call the Church "the extension of
the Incarnation,"[13] and Käsemann says that Jesus' death and resurrection resulted "in the manifestation of the pre-existent Church,"
a Church in which "Christ Himself as well as the individual are
deprived of their historic individuality."[14]

It is impossible within the limits of this study to deal extensively
with the various aspects of this problem.   Others have done so
ably,[15] and in the following remarks we will rely on their works.

---

[6] *Ibid.*, p. 58.
[7] *An Introduction to the Theology of the New Testament*, p. 255.   See
also Bonhoeffer, *The Cost of Discipleship*, p. 221.
[8] "Proleptic Deliverance of the Body," in *The Early Church*, p. 168.
[9] *Ibid.*, p. 172.
[10] *The Vision and Mission of Jesus*, pp. xxxi, 111, 295ff.
[11] *Lordship and Discipleship*, p. 111.
[12] Thus A. Nygren, *Christ and His Church*, p. 96, as quoted by F. I.
Andersen in *The Westminster Theological Journal*, May 1960, p. 132.
[13] E.g., Robinson, *The Body*, p. 57.
[14] *Op. cit.*, p. 184.
[15] E.g., L. B. Smedes, *The Incarnation: Trends in Modern Anglican
Thought*, and W. D. Jonker, *Mystieke Liggaam en Kerk in die Nuwe
Rooms-katolieke Teologie*.   Both are doctoral dissertations written at the
Free University in Amsterdam.

1. As is the case with Paul's usage of the word *sarx,* the term "body of Christ" is used with different connotations.   It can denote Christ's personal, literal body, in which he died, rose from the dead, went to heaven, and will come again;[16] the Church;[17] and the bread in the Lord's Supper.[18]   Though the three are related, they are not identical.

2. Those who appeal to certain passages in which Paul seems to identify these different connotations, without taking into account passages which clearly show that they are not identical, are not following sound hermeneutical methods.

Cullmann and Robinson, e.g., refer extensively to 1 Corinthians 6:15ff., which passage with its "uncompromisingly physical type of language" (Robinson) demonstrates, according to them, that the members of the Church are materially and physically members of Christ.   It is noteworthy, however, that this very passage proves the opposite.   Speaking of fornication Paul quotes Genesis 2:24, "The twain, saith he, shall become one flesh" (v. 16).   Then the Apostle goes on to speak of the unity of the believer with the Lord.   Does he use uncompromisingly physical language in *this* connection, speaking of the believer as becoming one *body* with the Lord, as one might expect with a view to the conclusions of Cullmann and Robinson?   By no means.   Rather the Apostle says: "But he that is joined unto the Lord is one spirit [with him]" (v. 17).   Precisely here, where the nature of the comparison invites misunderstanding, the Apostle emphasizes that we become one *spirit* with the Lord.   This means that the union is spiritual, not physical.   The body of the believer *participates* in the union with the Lord because the body is one aspect of his whole being. Nevertheless the union is *effected* not in the outward, physical existence but in the inner man, in the spirit of the believer.[19]

3. The fact of the Ascension makes it obvious that the personal resurrection-body of Christ is to be distinguished from the Church as his body.   The heavenly messengers said to the disciples: "this Jesus, who was received up from you into heaven, shall so come in like manner as ye beheld him going into heaven" (Acts

---

[16] John 20:12ff.; Acts 2:22ff.

[17] See references in n. 3, above.

[18] Luke 22:19; I Cor. 11:24.

[19] See, e.g., Grosheide (KNT), Lenski, and L. Morris (TNT). Wendland claims that there is no difficulty here if we realize that Christ's body is a *divine* reality according to Paul.   But this would imply that Christ has ceased to be very *man,* which is contrary to the continually-reiterated teaching of the New Testament.

1:11). It was in his personal, risen body that the disciples had just seen Jesus and talked with him. In that body they had seen him go to heaven, and now they are assured that "in like manner" he will come again.

It was only on the basis of this fact, of which the Apostles had been ear- and eyewitnesses, that Peter could declare on the day of Pentecost that the same Jesus whom the Jews had crucified was raised up by God and placed at his right hand in heaven to be both Lord and Christ (Acts 2:33-36).

It is clear that none of these passages speak of the *Church* as raised from the grave, residing in heaven and returning at the end of the ages, but rather of Christ in his personal, literal resurrection-body. Similarly, Paul could not possibly have meant to identify the Church with Christ's personal, literal resurrection-body, since the *kerygma* that he preached was the same as that of Peter (cf. Acts 13:29ff.).

Thus it is particularly the ascension, the lordship, and the second coming of our Lord, as taught in these passages of Acts, which "rule out any idea of a mystical fusion between Christ and the Church. . . . Christ stands over against the Church."[20]

4. If the Church is regarded as the resurrection-body of Christ in a literal sense, identical with himself or at least with part of himself, then the absolute pre-eminence of Christ (Rom. 1:4; Col. 1:18; 2:10) is implicitly denied. Such a conception of the Church as the body of Christ "would have horrified the apostle."[21]

The same holds true for conceptions which speak of the Church as "the extension of the Incarnation," "the presence of Christ," etc. It is not possible to blend Christ and the Church into one ontological unit without robbing Christ of his unique prerogatives as God and Savior.

5. Leaving aside any further interpretation of Paul's conception of the Church as the body of Christ, the conclusion may be drawn from the foregoing that Christ's resurrection-body, as the personal body in which he rose from the grave, ascended into heaven, and

---

[20] Cf. Bonhoeffer, *op. cit.*, p. 218. In *Sanctorum Communio*, pp. iiiff., Bonhoeffer posits that the Church is "Christ Himself present" (quotation from H. Sasse's article, "The Second Vatican Council," in *The Reformed Theological Review*, Melbourne, 1961, p. 70). Bonhoeffer's statements are contradictory: if Christ "stands over against the Church," the latter cannot possibly be identical with the former. See also L. Newbigin, *The Household of God*, pp. 82ff., 113, 128.

[21] G. S. Hendry, *The Holy Spirit in Christian Theology*, p. 67.

is coming again, is essentially distinct from the Church. In this chapter we deal not with the latter but with the former.[22]

2. RELIABILITY OF THE SOURCES

For the knowledge of Christ's resurrection-body we are dependent in the first place on the Gospel records of Jesus' resurrection and his post-resurrection appearances. Some passages of Acts and 1 Corinthians 15:3ff. may be added to this primary source. Nowhere else in the New Testament do we find such clear and unequivocal statements with regard to the nature of Christ's resurrection-body.

There is a tendency in recent works on eschatology to make light of the Gospel narratives, as far as our issue is concerned, by quoting certain statements of Paul against some statements in the Gospels. The scholars concerned appeal to Paul's declaration that flesh and blood cannot inherit the kingdom of God (1 Cor. 15:50), and that the resurrection-body of the believer will be a spiritual body (1 Cor. 15:45). This means, according to them, that the resurrection-body of the believer will consist of spirit, or of a spirit-like material, but by no means of flesh. And since the resurrection-bodies of the believers and of Christ are of the same nature, Christ's resurrection-body cannot possibly have been one of flesh either, whatever the Gospels may report.[23]

Against this method of interpretation some serious objections must be raised. In the first place, Scripture teaches us that Christ's resurrection-body is the model of that of the believer (Phil. 3:21), not the reverse. Second, if Paul's statements actually do contradict those of the Gospels (they do not, as will be shown later), the latter should be given preference because they record what ear- and eyewitnesses saw and heard, which cannot be said of Paul's statements concerning the future resurrection-body. Third, it is begging the question to say that according to Paul the resurrection-body of the believer will not consist of flesh. Many

---

[22] To what strange contradictions and inconsistencies the identification of the two leads appears from the fact that Cullmann, who so strongly rejects the idea of a *spiritual* body of *flesh,* calls the Church the only existing *spiritual* body, although the members of that body "are still clothed with a body of *flesh*" ("*Proleptic* Deliverance of the Body," p. 168).

[23] E.g., E. Brunner, *Das Ewige als Zukunft und Gegenwart,* p. 164; O. Betz, NTS, July 1957, p. 325; H. E. Fosdick, *op. cit.,* p. 285; Vincent Taylor, *The Life and Ministry of Jesus,* pp. 222-25; Kirsopp Lake, *op. cit.,* p. 35; and H. J. Heering, *op. cit.,* p. 114.

theologians, not all of them conservative, deny that in 1 Corinthians 15:45,50 Paul is dealing with the *substance* of the resurrection-body.[24] It is unjustifiable to depreciate statements of the Gospels which *undoubtedly* deal with the substance of Jesus' resurrection-body in the name of other statements by Paul which perhaps do not. Good hermeneutics requires that we explain less lucid passages by those that are clear, not the reverse.

Another preliminary question, even more far-reaching in its implications, concerns the historical trustworthiness of the Gospels themselves, particularly with regard to the resurrection of Christ and the post-resurrection appearances. Many scholars claim that these events did not take place as the Gospels describe them. Even Paul's teachings, they say, contradict those of the Gospels. Not only is Paul's conception of the resurrection-body different from that of the Evangelists,[25] but Paul in 1 Corinthians 15:3ff. still knows nothing of the empty grave[26] — a fact much stressed in the gospels. Moreover, the list of appearances in 1 Corinthians 15:5ff. differs from what the Gospels tell us.

The Gospels themselves are also said to be full of discrepancies and contradictions, which create doubt as to the reliability of the resurrection narratives at least in their details. Luke, e.g., locates the appearances in Jerusalem, Matthew says that Jesus appeared to the gathered disciples only in Galilee, whereas John locates the appearances in Jerusalem *and* Galilee. Luke 24:39 describes the body of Jesus as flesh and bones, but according to John 20:19 Jesus entered the room where the disciples were gathered through closed doors. In John 20:17 the risen Lord forbids Mary to touch him, but in 21:27 Thomas is invited to do the very thing that Mary was not allowed to do, etc. How could such "confused accounts of the resurrection-appearances"[27] provide any reliable knowledge of the Easter and post-Easter events?[28]

Finally, there are the objections raised by the Form-critics who, by studying the literary forms of the narratives, try to discover which elements are historically trustworthy and which are to be regarded as legends, myths, stories, etc. produced (for

[24] Special attention will be given to these passages in Chapter 6.
[25] See n. 23, above.
[26] R. Bultmann, ThNT, I, 45. Many others hold the same opinion.
[27] W. Strawson, *Jesus and the Future Life*, p. 223. It must be added that in general Strawson regards the historical value of the Gospels very highly (*op. cit.*, pp. 2ff.).
[28] For objections of this kind see, e.g., Kirsopp Lake, *op. cit., passim.*

apologetic and other purposes) by the evangelist or by the Christian community in which he worked.   The Gospels are looked upon as the *kerygma* of the early Church, and the question is, How much historical fact does this *kerygma* contain?

If one believes, like Bultmann, that "the course of nature can [not] be interrupted or, so to speak, perforated by supernatural powers,"[29] he can easily use the tool of form-criticism to "expose" myths in the Gospel accounts of Christ's resurrection and later appearances.   Bultmann declares: "The accounts of the empty grave . . . are legends,"[30] and according to him the resurrection stories are based, not on fact but on the Easter faith of the Church, which in this way tried "to surmount the scandal of the cross."[31]   But nothing of essential value is lost by this reinterpretation, if we may believe Bultmann.   Our faith does not rest upon historical facts but upon the *kerygma* of the Church, a *kerygma* in which God speaks to man in an existential way, making real to him his personal relation with God.[32]   The myths contained in this *kerygma* need not be eliminated but must be interpreted so that their deeper meaning may be discovered.[33]

For all the reasons mentioned, many theologians deny altogether that Jesus Christ really rose from the dead, leaving the tomb in the same body in which he had been buried.

G. Bornkamm, e.g., evaluates the resurrection narratives much in the manner of Bultmann, and although he believes in certain "appearances," they are of such a kind that "the resurrection faith has nothing to do with the empty tomb."[34]   Emil Brunner criticizes Bultmann's interpretation of the "Easter faith" and maintains that Christ *is* the Risen One, whose resurrection is the ground of our hope for the future.   But he does not recognise Holy Scripture as the ground of that hope, since the world-view of the Bible cannot be ours any more.[35]   Accordingly, he says, a resurrection which consists of a dead man being raised to physical life is crudely mythical.[36]   Paul Tillich speaks contemptuously of the physical resurrection theory, calling it absurd and blasphe-

[29] R. Bultmann, *Jesus Christ and Mythology,* p. 15.

[30] ThNT, I, 45.

[31] *Ibid.,* p. 45.

[32] *Jesus Christ and Mythology,* p. 59.

[33] *Ibid.,* p. 18.   Here Bultmann recognizes that the word "demythologizing" is unsatisfactory.

[34] G. Bornkamm, *Jesus of Nazareth,* pp. 183-85.

[35] *Das Ewige als Zukunft und Gegenwart,* p. 122.

[36] *Ibid.,* p. 26.

mous because it gives rise to "the absurd question . . . as to what happened to the molecules which comprise the corpse of Jesus of Nazareth."[37] Karl Barth's position, again, is not clear. He speaks of the resurrection as an unquestionable reality, but when it comes to the question whether it is a historical fact independent of subjective faith Barth is evasive. According to him we have to distinguish between history and *Geschichte*.[38] To history belong such events as take place within the framework of historical time and can be subjects of historical investigation. To *Geschichte* belong those events which occur outside of time and cannot be historically investigated. Many questions have arisen in connection with this contrast between history and *Geschichte*. Barth's own disciples are asking him to elaborate the terms; so far, however, he has declined.[39]

Nevertheless, say the critics, the Easter *faith* of the early Christian community is an undeniable fact. Many theories have been offered to explain the rise of this faith, some of which are:

1. The vision-theory, which suggests that the appearances were either subjective experiences of the disciples[40] or that they were objective, being visions in which Jesus revealed to the disciples his new existence, his non-material body, full of divine light and glory.[41]

2. The spiritualistic theory, which depicts the appearances as manifestations of the immortal soul of the man Jesus.[42]

3. The theory which suggests that there have been appearances in an immaterial way of a new Being, Christ, the Spirit, who made the disciples experience his spiritual presence and power as the "continuation" of Jesus of Nazareth.[43]

---

[37] *Systematic Theology,* p. 156.

[38] CD, III2, 446ff.

[39] See Carl F. H. Henry's Article, "Between Barth and Bultmann," in *Christianity Today,* 1 July, 1961.

[40] So, e.g., R. Bultmann in *Kerygma and Myth,* pp. 38ff., and H. J. Heering, *op. cit.,* pp. 152, 166ff.

[41] Walter Künneth, *Theologie der Auferstehung,* pp. 67-68. See also W. Barclay, who rejects the vision-theory but regards the appearances to the disciples and to Paul as "in kind" not different from what Francis of Assisi and A. J. Gossip are said to have experienced and others may still experience today (*Crucified and Crowned,* pp. 162,164,170). Similar opinions are held by C.E. Raven, *op. cit.,* p. 46.

[42] E.g., Kirsopp Lake, *op. cit.,* pp. 245, 272ff.

[43] So, e.g., Tillich, *op. cit.,* pp. 156-57; Hugh Anderson, in his article "The Historical Jesus" in *Scottish Journal of Theology,* June 1960, p. 129.

All these and similar theories are, of course, only their authors' subjective ideas. They are the outcome of the rejection of the historical trustworthiness of the Gospels and show the uncertainty in which such a rejection must necessarily result. The Gospels are our only source for obtaining knowledge about Jesus Christ and if their witness is not unreservedly believed we shall never have any certainty as to the person, life, death, resurrection, and exaltation of our Lord.

There is a growing conviction, even among Bultmann's followers, that certainty about what actually happened in this respect is of vital importance for the Christian faith. Many reject, and rightly so, Bultmann's theory that faith has nothing to do with historical facts but consists only in an existential encounter with God as he speaks through the "demythologized" *kerygma* of the Church. Putting "faith and history into two totally separate compartments of the mind"[44] means a flat denial of the whole biblical concept of faith, as having to do with "the mighty works of God" (Acts 2:11). These mighty works of God are his works of salvation in Christ, which took place in history, in time and space. They are historical facts, recorded throughout the Bible.[45] However much their nature, implications, and consequences may differ from other events which are not "mighty works of God in the history of Salvation," *as historical facts* they are not different at all. Their meaning, indeed, can only be understood by faith, but their factuality is completely independent of faith.[46] They have not been created by faith, as Bultmann asserts, but they themselves, preached as historical facts of salvation, create faith (Acts 2:37ff., Rom. 10:17).

Realizing the inseparable relationship between history and faith, various authors have started a fresh quest for the historical Jesus. Among these, to mention a few, are J. M. Robinson, who declares that "the kerygma is centrally concerned with a Jesus 'in the flesh' . . . a historical person";[47] R. H. Fuller, who rightly remarks:

[44] Lesslie Newbigin, *A Faith for This One World?*, p. 63.
[45] For an elaboration of these statements the author may refer to O. Cullmann, *Christ and Time*; F. V. Filson, *The New Testament Against Its Environment*; P. Althaus, *The So-called Kerygma and the Historical Jesus*; H. N. Ridderbos, *Bultmann, passim*; and N. B. Stonehouse, *Paul Before the Areopagus*, Chapters 5 and 6.
[46] See also Cullmann, *The Early Church*, p. 11, and D. M. Baillie, *God Was in Christ*, pp. 222ff.
[47] *A New Quest of the Historical Jesus*, p. 88.

"Inadequate or false reconstruction of Jesus of Nazareth cuts at the heart of Christianity";[48] and E. Stauffer, who writes that the ideal of the new quest is a history of Jesus which gives "the clear, strictly objective statements of those facts which can still be actually discerned."[49]

It is highly regrettable, however, that several scholars who are taking part in this investigation start from the conviction that the Gospels are unreliable as historical sources. They may *contain* many historical facts, but only in company with many legends, elements of religious fiction, and dogmatic insights. It is therefore the task of the historian to separate these facts of history "from the colouring of dogma"[50] and the like. To this end "the accepted principles of literary and historical criticism" have to be applied,[51] form-criticism of course being the main tool. It will also be necessary "sometimes to make conjectures and even to essay the use of a scientific imagination controlled by facts."[52]

The problem, however, is to find an objective criterion that will enable the scholar to decide which are historical facts and which are not. But no such criterion is available; the result, therefore, can only be a boundless subjectivism and a deplorable uncertainty as to what actually happened. The great variety of opinions expressed in these studies speaks volumes. It is, moreover, readily admitted. For example, R. H. Fuller calls his task "hazardous and delicate" and likens it to grasping a nettle.[53] Vincent Taylor states: "At a hundred points, therefore, the writer's results will be open to question, and in the end he may satisfy no one. . . ."[54] George Ogg admits "there is as yet no consensus of opinion as to what in the Gospels is history and what interpretation"; but then we are comfortingly told that with regard to the results of form-criticism "extreme scepticism is without foundation"[55] — a statement in which the word "extreme" is significant. W. Barclay criticizes numerous theories of radical critics, but

---

[48] *The Mission and Achievement of Jesus,* p. 13.
[49] *Jesus and His Story,* p. 8.
[50] E. Stauffer, *op. cit.,* p. 7.
[51] V. Taylor, *The Life and Ministry of Jesus,* p. vi.
[52] *Ibid.*
[53] In *The Book of the Acts of God,* as quoted by the editor of ExT, June 1961, p. 257.
[54] *Op. cit.,* p. vi.
[55] NTS, Jan. 1961, p. 173.

when he comes to the question as to what actually happened on Easter Day and after, he makes the vague statement: "That something happened is certain beyond all doubt."[56]   His careful evaluation of the pros and cons concerning Jesus' resurrection results in the vague conclusion: "In view of the existence of the Church it is more difficult not to believe in the Resurrection than it is to believe in it."[57]   As to the ascension the same scholar writes: "We do not know what actually happened at the time of the Ascension."[58]

It is deplorable that such uncertainty should attend the great saving acts of God; surely nothing is more needful today than confidence in matters of faith.   Yet the uncertainty must be accepted *if* it follows by unexceptionable procedures from a sound starting point.   It is precisely the starting point, however, that we must question.   The critics start from the conviction that the *kerygma* is a mixture of historical facts and fictituous elements; the only task is to separate the two.   But this starting-point is purely dogmatic; it remains to be proved beyond doubt that the Gospels actually contain historically untrustworthy elements. Numerous scholars regard the evidences presented by the critics as being absolutely unconvincing.   Moreover, strong arguments can be advanced in favor of the trustworthiness of the New Testament documents and of the Gospels in particular.[59]

As to form-criticism, various recent scholars have protested against the way that some critics have used this method as a

---

[56] *Crucified and Crowned,* p. 160.

[57] *Ibid.,* p. 161.

[58] *Ibid.,* p. 175.

[59] For the historical trustworthiness of the New Testament in general see *The New Testament Documents — Are They Reliable?* by F. F. Bruce. The trustworthiness of Luke's Gospel, which is crucial to the present study, has recently been ably defended by N. B. Stonehouse, *The Witness of Luke to Christ.* The allegedly irreconcilable differences among the gospel narratives as to the place of Jesus' post-resurrection appearances have been thoroughly investigated in a thesis, publicly defended at the Free University, Amsterdam, called *De Verschijningen onzes Heeren te Jeruzalem en in Galilea,* by H. H. Holtrop. Dr. Holtrop concludes: "As to the place of Christ's appearances the various accounts of the New Testament offer no intrinsic contradiction" (p. 247).   Similar conclusions are reached by C. F. D. Moule in his article "Jerusalem and Galilee Appearances," NTS, Oct. 1957, and by A. M. Ramsay in *The Resurrection of Christ,* pp. 68ff. For the trustworthiness of the resurrection narratives in general see, e.g., F. F. Bruce, *The Dawn of Christianity,* pp. 62ff., and F. Morison, *"Who Moved the Stone?"*

weapon to attack the integrity of the Gospels.[60]   According to
T. W. Manson form-criticism should restrict itself to "the study of
the various units of narrative and teaching, which go to make up
the Gospels, in respect to their forms and that alone."[61]   We
may add that this branch of theology is completely unable to decide whether the Gospel narratives are reliable or not.   C. H.
Dodd has written a masterly essay on form-criticism, applying
the latter to the accounts of the appearances of the risen Christ.[62]
Though one of Dodd's conclusions is that the literary forms under
consideration offer no ground to justify the term "myth" for the
resurrection narratives of the Gospels as a whole,[63] he rightly
abstains from drawing any conclusion concerning the historical
reliability of the narratives.   For the historical reliability of the
Gospels cannot be decided by any scientific means of criticism.   Even trying to decide on it by such means, as many
are doing at present, cannot be justified, since it implies the rejection of the *kerygma* of the Apostles and of Christ himself, a
kerygma which by its very nature is reliable in every respect.   One
need not call into question the honest intentions of scholars who
wish to find out what actually happened in the history of salvation by approaching the New Testament accounts of that history
in a scientific way, with an unbiased mind, and prepared to accept
whatever results their historical research may produce.   Nevertheless, two very serious objections must be raised against this
method.

In the first place, it is self-deception to assume that unbiased
historical research in the history of salvation is possible at all.
Such research is always prejudiced: it assumes *a priori* the possibility that the Gospel narratives are *not* historically reliable
in every respect, and that the nature of the Gospels does *not*
exclude the mixing up of the history of salvation with myths,
legends, and other fictitious elements.   Kirsopp Lake, e.g., after
rejecting the historicity of the empty tomb, admits that "the
story of the empty tomb must be fought out on doctrinal, not on
historical or critical grounds."[64]   In the second place, the facts

[60] E.g., T. W. Manson in "The Background of the New Testament
and its Eschatology," ed., W. D. Davies and D. Daube, Ch. 11; W. Strawson, *op. cit.,* pp. 2ff.; and N. B. Stonehouse, *Paul Before the Areopagus,*
chapters 5, 6.
[61] *Op. cit.,* p. 212.
[62] In *Studies in the Gospels,* ed. D. E. Nineham, pp. 9ff.
[63] *Ibid.,* p. 34.
[64] *Op. cit.,* p. 253.

in the history of salvation, with which the Gospels deal, are such that they cannot be verified by any scientific method whatever.

To confine ourselves to the resurrection of Christ, Wilbur Smith thinks it possible to distinguish the *fact* of the resurrection from its *meaning*. The former, he says, is a historical matter which can be decided upon by historical evidence, whereas the meaning of the resurrection is a theological matter.[65] This distinction, however, seems invalid. The fact of the resurrection is not just that a certain man, called Jesus of Nazareth, came to life again after he had died on a cross and had been buried. Jesus' resurrection as a historical *fact* is of a unique kind with very specific constituent elements. As a historical *fact* Jesus' resurrection is the resurrection of God-in-the-flesh (John 1:14); of him who as the lamb of God died to take away the sins of the world (John 1:29). It is his declaration as the Son of God (Rom. 1:4); his obtaining a life which is imperishable and victorious (Rom. 6:9); the fulfillment of the Old Testament Scriptures and of his own words (Luke 24:25ff; 44ff.); the beginning of the new and last age in the history of salvation (Acts 2:17,32); the virtual deliverance from death of all who are in Christ (Eph. 2:5,6); the seal of their justification (Rom. 4:25); the actual beginning of the resurrection of all believers, because Christ rose as "the first fruits of them that are asleep" (John 14:19; 1 Cor. 15:20). All this is not just a theological interpretation of Christ's resurrection, but an essential part of this resurrection as a fact in the history of salvation.[66] That is why scientific, unbiased, historical research can never discover or verify this fact as it truly is. It can be known only by faith, because it is a fact revealed by God in the New Testament, in which Christ himself provided an authoritative, authentic, fully reliable account of the history of salvation. Historical research is certainly justified, since "the whole point of the gospel is that in Christ the power and grace of God entered into human history to bring about the world's redemption."[67] But the historian, like everyone else, is not permitted to do his research without faith in the revelation of God's great saving acts contained in the gospel. If he lacks this faith he will not be able to discover the facts as they really are. The confusion as to what actually happened on and after Easter

[65] *Therefore Stand,* p. 386.
[66] ". . . interpretation implies the facts, just as these include interpretation." O. Cullmann, "The Early Church," p. 67.
[67] F. F. Bruce, *The New Testament Documents . . .,* p. 67.

Day, as it prevails in many recent theological works, gives ample proof of this.

This is not the place for a lengthy digression on the authority of the New Testament. Let it suffice here to say that this authority rests in him who is its center and contents, Jesus Christ. He chose the twelve, "whom also he named apostles" (Luke 6:13), and who "from the beginning were eyewitnesses and ministers of the word" (Luke 1:2). These men he commissioned to bear witness concerning his person, his words and works "because," said he, "ye have been with me from the beginning" (John 15:27). Since it was necessary for future believers to have *certainty* concerning the great acts of God in Jesus Christ and no merely human witness can be infallible, Jesus promised his apostles the Holy Spirit, assuring them: "he shall teach you all things, and bring to your remembrance all that I said unto you" (John 15:26). As the Risen One he himself gave them indubitable proofs of his resurrection, instructed them during forty days in "the things concerning the Kingdom of God" (Acts 1:3), and commissioned them to be his witnesses "both in Jerusalem, and in all Judea and Samaria, and unto the uttermost part of the earth" (Acts 1:8, Matt. 28:19).

This task could not be performed by an exclusively oral transmission of the gospel tradition. It certainly started that way, but to be witnesses "unto the uttermost part of the earth" and to all nations, the apostles and their helpers had to resort to passing on the gospel tradition in written form.[68] This also was done under the inspiration of the Holy Spirit, promised to them for this very purpose (John 15:26).

To the original apostles Paul was added as the last eye- and earwitness of Jesus Christ as the Risen One (1 Cor. 15:8), commissioned by Christ himself to "bear my name before the Gentiles and Kings, and the children of Israel," as a man "full of the Holy Spirit" (Acts 9:15ff.). From the other apostles themselves Paul "received" the apostolic tradition concerning Jesus' life, words, and works up to the ascension (1 Cor. 11:23, 15:1; Gal. 1:18), and he was accepted by them as an authentic and faithful co-worker, set apart for the ministry among the Gentiles (Gal. 2:9ff.).

In passing on the apostolic tradition Paul was aware of being the mouthpiece of the Lord himself (1 Cor. 7:10), and in giving

[68] Cf. H. Riesenfeld, *The Gospel Tradition and its Beginning*, pp. 16ff.

his own apostolic teaching he speaks as one who "hath obtained mercy of the Lord to be trustworthy" (1 Cor. 7:25).

Out of all this the New Testament grew, under the promised special inspiration of the Spirit, in whom Jesus Christ himself was with the apostles (Matt. 28:20) and spoke in and through them (Luke 10:16; John 16:14,15). In the New Testament, therefore, the exalted Lord himself is present and speaking to us, and such not only in the Gospels but also and in the same way in Paul's writings.[69]   The New Testament documents "are not simply historical records (although they are that) but . . . the Holy Spirit confronts the believing reader directly with Christ."[70]

As to the assumption of some form-critics, that the written Gospels, as they were published, showed a deviation from the original apostolic tradition, we can say that this theory breaks down on the simple fact that at the time the Gospels were published many ear- and eyewitnesses must still have been alive. E. F. Harrison rightly remarks that such a deviation would have brought on serious controversy within the Church.   "Of such controversy we have no record or hint."[71]

In this study, therefore, the gospel records of Christ's resurrection and appearances are recognized as divinely inspired sources in which the Lord himself is speaking and which, for that very reason, are fully reliable.[72]

3. Paul's Witness

As we now turn to the New Testament data concerning Christ's resurrection, our single concern is whether our Lord was raised with a *body of flesh.*

[69] Cf. D. Bonhoeffer, *The Cost of Discipleship,* p. 205.

[70] O. Cullmann, *The Early Church,* p. 81.

[71] In *Contemporary Evangelical Thought,* p. 53.   Riesenfeld (*op. cit.,* pp. 18-23) describes the extreme care, in accordance with Rabbinical custom, that was taken in transmitting the Gospel tradition, first by reciting it in stereotyped form and rather early by literary fixation.   The careful choosing of men to whom this responsible task could be entrusted was based on the conviction that the Gospel tradition found its *Sitz im Leben* in Jesus' own words and deeds, and therefore was *Holy Word of God,* equal with the Old Testament.

[72] For more extensive argumentation we refer to a few (out of the many) recent publications, viz. A. Lecerf, *An Introduction to Reformed Dogmatics,* Chs. 9 and 10; J. I. Packer, *Fundamentalism and the Word of God, passim;* H. N. Ridderbos, *When the Time Had Fully Come,* Ch. 5; *Heils-geschiedenis en Heilige Schrift, passim;* and K. Runia, *Karl Barth's Doctrine of Holy Scripture,* Ch. 3.

It is generally agreed that in 1 Corinthians 15:1ff. we have the first written record of Christ's resurrection and of some of the appearances. Paul is reminding the Corinthians of the gospel he had preached to them as a missionary, the central theme of which was Christ's death and resurrection (vv. 3, 4). Paul himself had "received" this gospel (v. 3) and "delivered" the same to his readers. We agree with H. N. Ridderbos that the verbs *paralam-bano* and *paradidomi* in this passage speak of the gospel-*paradosis* (tradition) as different from a purely human tradition, "a more or less fixed creed of the Christian community."[73] The fact that Paul lists the apostolic eyewitnesses to guarantee the truth of the gospel received and transmitted, implies that the tradition concerned "represents an authoritative, personal institution, that is the institution of the apostles . . . the teaching to which the community has to submit in obedience."[74]

Of importance for our subject is the question whether Paul's preaching included the sign of the empty tomb. Some have denied this,[75] but verses 3 and 4 show that they are mistaken. For in these verses we hear not only of Christ as the one who died and was raised, but between these statements we read the words "and that he was buried." This special reference to the fact that Jesus' dead body was laid in the grave implies that Paul, speaking of Christ's resurrection, understood that resurrection as a coming out of the grave in which he had been buried.

The empty tomb, indeed, was part of the original tradition,[76] and in Paul's indirect reference to it we have a first indication that the risen Lord, as Paul preached him, possessed a body identical with that in which he had been buried, a body of flesh.

We find this confirmed by the fact that Paul speaks of Christ's resurrection as having taken place "according to the Scriptures."[77]

---

[73] *When the Time Had Fully Come*, p. 85. Cf. also Riesenfeld, *op. cit.*, p. 17, and O. Cullmann, *The Early Church*, pp. 67ff.

[74] H. N. Ridderbos, *op. cit.*, p. 86. Ridderbos refers also to 1 Cor. 11: 23, where the Apostle identifies the apostolic tradition with the word of the living Lord (cf. O. Cullmann, *loc. cit.*).

[75] To the references mentioned above in n. 26 may be added E. L. Allen, *The Lost Kerygma*, in NTS, July 1957, p. 351.

[76] So C. T. Craig (IB) and most recent commentators. Cf. also A. Richardson, *An Introduction to the Theology of the New Testament*, p. 196; E. Stauffer, *op. cit.*, p. 118; W. Künneth, *Theologie der Auferstehung*, pp. 71ff.; and E. Dentler, *Die Auferstehung Jesu Christi*, pp. 51ff.

[77] With L. Morris (TNT) and others we take the phrase "according to the Scriptures" with "rose again" and not with "the third day."

We need not search the Old Testament ourselves to find passages which Paul may have had in mind when he wrote these words. Luke, for many years the Apostle's companion, gives us a brief account of Paul's missionary preaching in Acts 13:17ff. Here we are told that Paul preached Jesus as raised up from the dead, "now no more to return to corruption" (v. 34), an expression which in itself suggests that Paul conceived of Jesus' resurrection-body as identical with that in which he had been buried. Still more striking, however, is Paul's appeal to the Scriptures of the Old Testament. The resurrection of Jesus was promised, Paul argues, when God said, "I will give you the holy and sure *blessings* of David" (v. 34). In verse 35 we are told what blessings God had in mind, according to Paul. They were the blessings of a resurrection to eternal life, as David spoke of it in Psalm 16:10: "Thou wilt not give thy Holy One to see corruption." This promise, Paul said, was not fulfilled in David himself, for he died, was buried, and saw corruption. It was fulfilled in Christ, David's son and heir; "he whom God raised up saw no corruption" (v. 37).[78]

Two things should be noticed. First, Paul refers to the same psalm that Peter quoted on the day of Pentecost (Acts 2:24ff.) and with the same implications. This proves how faithfully Paul "delivered" the original apostolic tradition.[79] His preaching was in complete agreement with that of the first apostles, as 1 Corinthians 15:11 also states. Second, the verse from Psalm 16 quoted by Paul speaks clearly of a resurrection of the *flesh*. Peter, in Acts 2:25ff., gives the full quotation, including the words "Moreover my flesh also shall dwell in hope: Because thou wilt not leave my soul unto Hades . . . ."

When T. P. Ferris, in his exposition of Acts 13:30ff. (IB), declares that it is "not likely that the modern preacher would set forth the resurrection in these terms," and then tries to explain Jesus' resurrection in spiritualizing terms "relevant to a contemporary congregation," his remarks contain the silent recognition that Acts 13:30ff. does indeed speak of Jesus' resurrection

[78] For the interpretation of Ps. 16:10 in its Hebrew context we may refer to Chapter 2 of this study. Though the LXX version of the verse, quoted by Paul (and Peter, Acts 2:27) differs from the Hebrew text, the use the apostles make of the quotation is certainly in accordance with the far-reaching implications of Psalm 16, as we have tried to show.

[79] Cf. C. H. Dodd, *The Apostolic Preaching and its Development*, p. 22. For the literary relationship between Luke and Paul, see pp. 18-22 of Dodd's book.

as a resurrection of the same body of flesh in which he had died.

Against this background we may conclude that Paul, speaking in I Corinthians 15:3 of Christ as raised up "according to the Scriptures," must have had in mind a physical and literal resurrection of Jesus in his body of *flesh*.

In I Corinthians 15:5ff. Paul lists several appearances of the risen Lord, some of them not mentioned in the Gospels, whereas the latter describe various appearances not found in Paul's list.

E. L. Allen tries to solve the problem of the differing accounts by suggesting that Paul handed on to his churches the original apostolic tradition, which "was content to relate those incidents that were of special force, appearances to leaders of the community or to a number of witnesses," whereas the Evangelists committed to writing such items as "served the needs of a Church that had to defend against criticism what had come to her from the past."[80] The Evangelists selected and interpreted such stories as served apologetic purposes.

This entirely plausible suggestion, which takes into account the *Sitz im Leben* of the respective biblical accounts, illustrates the positive value of form-criticism.[81]   But when Allen says that in some cases the Gospel narratives may be a fresh creation of the Church,[82] then form-criticism is once more overplaying its hand. Without any reasonable ground it is suggested that the Church may have *created* "stories" for the purpose of convincing her opponents of the reality of Christ's resurrection!   This is a serious accusation against the Evangelists and the Christian-community of their day.   For it implies that they are regarded as capable of *deceiving* their opponents by presenting mere fancies as historically reliable facts (Luke 1:3; John 21:24).   The ultimate authorship of the Holy Spirit, as has been pointed out above, rules out any such possibility.   One may readily admit that in the Gospels certain facts might have been selected for apologetic purposes.   But why assume that to this end "stories" were created? As Frank Morison has remarked, the stories could be used with the same effect if they were true.[83]   We would rather say: with better effect.   For if in a public defense part of the evidence submitted is not according to fact, the whole defense usually fails.

On the basis of Paul's statements in I Corinthians 15:3,4, as

---

[80] *Op. cit.,* pp. 351, 353.
[81] Cf. also Dodd's study of the appearances, referred to above in n. 62.
[82] *Op. cit.,* pp. 352-53.
[83] *Op. cit.,* p. 236.

seen in the light of Acts 13:17ff., there can be no doubt that the appearances listed in verses 5ff. were regarded by the Apostle as appearances of the Lord in his resurrection-body of flesh, precisely as the Gospels depict them.   It is not true that the fourfold repetition of *ophthe* confirms the vision-theory or makes it difficult to believe in bodily appearances.[84]   H. Holtrop refers to Acts 7:26, where Stephen says that the following day Moses appeared (*ophthe*) unto them as they were fighting, which indeed shows what Luke meant by *ophthe*.   Luke 24:34 also gives evidence that *ophthe* speaks of a real, bodily appearance, for in that verse the disciples say that "the Lord is risen indeed, and hath appeared to Simon."   The *ophthe Simoni* is adduced as proof that Christ really and bodily rose from the dead, which shows again the realistic significance of *ophthe*.[85]

When in I Corinthians 15:8 Paul speaks of Christ's appearance to him on the Damascus road, it is obvious that he is describing a real, bodily appearance.   Many have denied this, suggesting that Paul's experience on that occasion was like many other spiritual experiences throughout history, but certainly not an experience of Jesus in the body.[86]   This suggestion, however, must be rejected on the following grounds:

1. Our investigation has shown that in I Corinthians 15:4 Paul refers to a bodily resurrection of Jesus, and that in verses 5-7 he recites various bodily appearances of the risen Lord as evidence of this resurrection.   Then in verse 8 Paul mentions the appearance on the road to Damascus as the *last* one, using the same word (*ophthe*) that he employed for the other appearances (W. G. H. Simon, TBC).   He adduces this appearance as being completely on a par with the other ones, and equally proof of Jesus' bodily resurrection.   Hence the Apostle must have regarded Jesus' appearance to himself as being of precisely the same kind.

2. Acts 9:7 says that those who traveled with Paul "stood speechless, hearing the voice but beholding no man" (*medena*). It seems logical to suppose that a person who could be *heard* could also be *seen*.   If Paul had seen a private vision, those that accompanied him would not have heard a voice.

---

[84] W. Barclay, *Crucified and Crowned*, p. 153.
[85] Cf. H. Holtrop, *op. cit.*, p. 125.
[86] E.g., C. E. Raven, *op. cit.*, p. 46, and W. Barclay, *Crucified and Crowned*, pp. 161ff.

3. In Acts 9:10 we read that the Lord appeared to Ananias *in a vision* (Greek: *en horamati*). During this vision Ananias is informed that Paul saw *in a vision* (the same Greek expression) how Ananias would come and lay his hands on Paul (v. 12). In verse 17, however, where Ananias, speaking to Paul, refers to what happened on the Damascus road, we do not find the word "vision" (neither do we find it in vv. 1-8) but the well known *ophthe*. This is very significant. It suggests that Luke is safeguarding his readers against the idea that Paul's experience on the Damascus road was visionary only.[87]

4. Paul received many special revelations from the resurrected Christ after his experience on the Damascus road, but it is always made clear, either by Paul himself (II Cor. 12:1; Gal. 2:2) or by Luke (Acts 18:9), that these cases have to do with visions. Both Paul and Luke appear to be making a sharp distinction between what happened on the road to Damascus and later revelations of the risen Lord.

5. In I Corinthians 9:1 Paul asks: "Am I not an apostle? have I not seen Jesus our Lord?" Here, no doubt, he refers to the appearance of Jesus on the road to Damascus. Paul adduces it as *the* piece of evidence that he is a true apostle, not in the least inferior to the other eye witnesses. If the appearance of Acts 9:1-8 had been a vision of the same kind as Paul's later visions, he could never have written I Corinthians 9:1. Moreover, it is difficult to see how those who regard that first appearance as a vision can escape the conclusion that everyone (e.g., Francis of Assisi, etc.) who is said to have experienced a similar vision is to be accepted as an apostle, an authoritative eyewitness of the risen Lord, equal with "the twelve." If for Paul such a vision gave sufficient warrant to call himself an apostle and to speak with apostolic authority, why not for others? It is clear, however, that this would mean the denial of the unique character of the apostleship.

Our conclusion from the foregoing is that I Corinthians 15:1-8 speaks of a bodily resurrection of Jesus, and that all the appearances mentioned as evidence of it were bodily as well.[88] There

---

[87] Cf. F. W. Grosheide (KNT). The fact that in Acts 26:19 Paul speaks of the heavenly "vision" does not make the argument invalid. The word used there (*optasia*) can also mean "appearance" (cf. Liddell and Scott, *Greek-English Lexicon*). In that sense it is used in Luke 24:23 of the angels appearing to the women, which certainly was not a vision.

is no reason to contrast Paul's "spiritual" account of Christ's appearances with the more "materialistic" accounts found in the Gospels.[89]

4. THE GOSPEL AND ACTS

Turning now to the Gospels,[90] we read in Matthew 28:5-7 about the message of the angel at the empty grave. He tells the women that the *crucified Jesus* is risen. He invites them to satisfy themselves that the places where the Lord lay are empty. He charges them to tell the disciples that the Master goes before them into Galilee, where they will see him.

We should notice that in verse 5 (as in Mark 16:6) the perfect participle *estauromenos* is used, for which reason W. C. Allen rightly renders the phrase: "Jesus the crucified" (ICC).[91] With Grosheide and others we hold that this text characterizes the risen Lord not only as one who was crucified a few days ago, but in whom the results of the crucifixion are still present (cf. I Cor. 1:23; 2:2). This implies that Jesus arose in essentially the same body of flesh as that in which he was crucified.

Apart from grammatical detail, the words recorded by Matthew as spoken by the angel have this import: *God himself* made it known from heaven that the same Jesus who was buried (his buried body of flesh) was raised from the grave.

This is confirmed by verse 9, where we read that Jesus met the women and spoke to them, after which they took hold of his feet and worshipped him.

C. H. Dodd suggests that the women were in doubt, and touched Jesus to make sure that their Master had really risen.[92] For this suggestion, however, there is no support in the context. Moreover,

---

[88] S. Greydanus, *Is Hand. 9 en 15 in Tegenspraak met Gal. 1 en 2?*, investigates the alleged contradiction between Acts 9 and 15 and Galatians 1 and 2. On page 89 he concludes that those who regard the appearance to Paul as a vision can do so only on the subjective ground of their own dogmatics. (Cf. also J. G. Machen, *op. cit.*, pp. 55ff.).

[89] The fact that only Paul saw the risen Lord and not those traveling with him (Acts 9:7) belongs to the mysterious elements that characterize all of Christ's appearances in the great forty days. They will be discussed in the following pages.

[90] The traditional order of the Gospels is followed here because the synoptic question has no direct bearing on the subject under consideration.

[91] Most versions (e.g., KJV, BV, ERV, RSV, NEB) render: "who was crucified," which does not sufficiently bring out the meaning of the perfect participle.

[92] *Studies in the Gospels*, p. 12.

the Gospels always mention the presence of doubt (Matt. 28:17; Luke 24:41).

We may rather assume that the women believed the message of the angels, for without such faith the great joy of which Matthew 28:8 speaks cannot be explained. When Jesus himself met them they knelt at his feet to worsĥip him and in their enthusiasm, gratitude, and love they touched his feet.[93] Needless to say, the fact that Jesus had tangible feet must have greatly strengthened their faith that he was precisely the same Jesus whom they had buried.

When Matthew, who certainly received first-hand information from these eyewitnesses, narrates their taking hold of Jesus' feet, he gives the Church of all ages the implicit assurance that Jesus rose from the dead in a body of flesh. This assurance shipwrecks the vision-theory in its various forms, unless one is willing to degrade the Evangelist (or an alleged later editor of the Gospel) into an unreliable fantast or the women into false witnesses.

For the same reason we cannot accept the theory that Matthew embellished the tradition and embroidered his Markan source.[94] Even if the Markan Hypothesis is the key to the synoptic problem (which still is a controversial matter),[95] it does by no means imply that additional elements in Matthew's and Luke's accounts of the resurrection must be considered embroideries of the Markan source. Suggestions of this kind are not based on any verifiable fact.

The witness of Mark regarding our subject is the same as Matthew's: the women find the grave empty and a heavenly messenger tells them that Jesus is risen. In Mark, too, Jesus is called the crucified one who is risen, and the women are invited to satisfy

93 H. Greeven, TWNT, VI, 764, shows that in the New Testament the verb *proskuneo* is always used in the sense of paying homage to one who is considered divine. The women recognized Jesus' divine sonship, as it was powerfully evidenced by his resurrection from the dead (cf. Rom. 1:4). Their worship is virtually the same as that of Thomas (John 20:28).

94 A. M. Ramsey, *The Resurrection of Christ*, pp. 60ff., *et al.*

95 Serious objections against the Markan Hypothesis may be found, e.g., in S. Greydanus, *Bijzondere Canoniek*, pp. 156-209, and H. Mulder, "Het Synoptische Vraagstuk" (in *Exegetica*), Delft, 1952. Since H. Riesenfeld's *The Gospel Tradition and its Beginnings*, the whole problem of Gospel origins has taken a fresh turn, especially in connection with B. Gerhardsson's *Memory and Manuscript*, which elaborates Riesenfeld's theory. J. G. Davies (ExT, Dec. 1961, p. 71) suggests some far-reaching implications for the synoptic problem, if Gerhardsson's thesis is correct.

themselves that the place where Jesus' body was laid is empty.

The implications are the same as those of Matthew's account: Jesus was raised in the same body in which he was buried, whatever changes that body might have undergone at the resurrection.[96]

Much more elaborate and of very special importance for our subject are Luke's narratives of Jesus' resurrection.

First we find again the story of the empty grave and of the message from heaven proclaiming that Jesus was raised from the dead (24:1-7). This time we hear of two messenger angels instead of one, as in the other Synoptics. Plummer explains the difference very plausibly by remarking: "Where, out of two or more, only one is spokesman, he is necessarily remembered. The other or others may easily be ignored or forgotten. It is an exaggeration to call such differences absolute discrepancies" (ICC).

There is also a marked difference between the statements made by the angels as Luke reports them and those recorded by Matthew and Mark. It is obvious, however, that the message as such is the same. The difference between the accounts is easily explained if we suppose that the angels said much more than is recorded in any of the gospels, which is very probable. "Each evangelist merely records those words that were necessary for his form and scheme of proclaiming the resurrection of Jesus."[97] It is not easy to explain why the words "He is not here, but is risen" are lacking in manuscript D and in some important Latin authorities. Apart, however, from the strong evidence that can be adduced to defend their authenticity, it is obvious that the words say nothing new, nothing that is not implicitly stated in the other words of the message.

There is no doubt that the truth proclaimed by Luke is the same as that of the other Synoptics: the Crucified One has been raised in the same body which was buried.

Luke's account of Jesus' post-resurrection appearances (24:

---

[96] Since the authenticity of Mark 16:9-20 is controversial, the discussion is limited to vv. 1-8. Furthermore, no attempt is made here to explain or harmonize alleged contradictions between Mark's account and those of the other synoptics. Apart from the fact that the differences do not directly bear on our subject, the inspiration of Scripture excludes the possibility that the Evangelists contradicted each other, even though we may not be able to show how certain seemingly contradictory statements can be harmonized.

[97] N. Geldenhuys, *Commentary on the Gospel of Luke.*

13ff.) adds important evidence that Jesus' body was a body of flesh.

We have, first, the narrative of Christ's appearance on the way to Emmaus. C. H. Dodd calls it "a highly finished literary composition."[98] This does not imply that it is historically unreliable, as Alan Richardson suggests, who calls the narrative "a superb parable."[99] Why cannot what actually happened be described in a most beautiful way? There is no reason to disagree with Plummer (ICC) when he conjectures that Luke obtained his information directly from one of the disciples mentioned in the narrative, probably from the one whose name (Cleopas) he records.

The whole narrative depicts the risen Lord as a real person with a physical body, but particularly these words from verses 30 and 31: "When he had sat down with them to meat, he took the bread and blessed; and breaking it he gave to them. And their eyes were opened, and they knew him." The text implies not only that Jesus was physically present, but that his risen body was identical with his crucified body. For it was when their visitor took bread, blessed, broke and distributed it, that the two disciples identified him as their crucified Master. They may have been present at previous occasions when Jesus acted as host, and his characteristic manner of taking the bread, blessing and distributing it may have been the means by which Jesus opened their eyes so that they recognized him.[100] Or it may be that during the meal they saw the scars in Jesus' hands after the Lord had opened their eyes, so that they were able to see what they previously could not see when their eyes had been "holden" (v. 16).[101]

However it may have been, they recognized Jesus as their Master who had been dead, rose from the dead, and was now

---

98 In Nineham, op. cit., p. 13 (cf. S. M. Gilmour, IB: "a story of singular grace and charm").

99 An Introduction to the Theology of the New Testament, p. 194.

100 K. H. Rengstorf (NTD) refers to Luke 9:11ff.; 10:38ff.; 22:14ff. Similarly Geldenhuys, Plummer (ICC), et al. There is no reason to find here a reference to a Eucharist of the risen Christ with his disciples, as S. M. Gilmour suggests, claiming that the language "is too solemn to be easily understood as referring to an ordinary meal" (IB). How weak this ground is appears from the same scholar's remark on Luke 9:16, where the same "solemn" language is used: "rabbinical notices show that a Jewish host observed much the same ritual at any common meal."

101 V. 35 has: ". . . how he was known to them in the breaking of the bread," which may mean either "by the way he broke the bread" or "while he broke the bread" (NEB: "at the breaking of the bread").

bodily present in their midst and having a meal with them, breaking bread with the hands they knew so well. It is obvious that only a resurrection in a body of flesh can account for what happened there in Emmaus as Luke relates it.

The strongest evidence, however, that Jesus' resurrection-body was a body of flesh is provided by Luke's account of the appearance to the disciples on the evening of that great Easter Day (vv. 36ff.). When Jesus suddenly stood in their midst they were terrified, thinking they saw a spirit, i.e., the incorporeal spirit of a dead person.[102] It is not clear whether they recognized Jesus; either they did recognize him but could not believe that he was *physically* present (because of his mysterious, sudden appearance),[103] or they did not recognize him because his glorified resurrection body was so different from the body in which he died (cf. Greydanus, KNT). The former interpretation seems to suit the context better, though the latter is also possible.

Jesus removed all uncertainty by identifying himself to the disciples; moreover, he showed that he was *physically* present in the *same* body that he had previously possessed. He invited them to look at his hands and feet, implying that the scars left there from the nailing on the Cross were visible — for otherwise Jesus would have drawn their attention to his face.[104] The scars made it clear, more than anything else could do, that the crucified and buried Master was standing before them in the very same body in which they had seen him suffer. Then, to give them proof that the body they saw was not something immaterial, but real and solid, Jesus invited them not only to see but also to handle, to touch his body: "for a spirit hath not flesh and bones, as ye behold me having" (v. 39).[105]

There is no indication that the disciples actually did touch the body of the Master, since verse 41 says that they "still disbelieved for joy, and wondered." A. Plummer (ICC) and G. C. Berkouwer (*De Persoon van Christus,* p. 172) suggest that the disciples did touch Jesus. They appeal to I John 1:1, where the Apostle says that he and the other disciples "handled" Christ with their

---

[102] Cf. 1 Pet. 3:19, where *pneuma* has the same sense. Manuscript D has *phantasma*, a ghost, which word also occurs in Mark 6:49 and parallel passages.

[103] So, e.g., Geldenhuys, Godet, *et al.*

[104] B. Weiss, in Meyer's *Kritisch exegetisches Kommentar über das Neue Testament.* Similarly A. Plummer, *et. al.*

[105] The causal meaning of *hoti* is to be preferred with a view to the context.

hands. But the context shows that John is not speaking there of what happened after the resurrection, but of Jesus' whole life. If the disciples touched Jesus at the occasion mentioned above, John *may* have thought of that "handling," too. But it cannot be proved. Moreover, in Jesus' words the emphasis is on seeing, not on handling, and verse 40 states "he *showed* them his hands and his feet." Even if the disciples did not actually touch Jesus' body, the fact that our Lord declared it to be a body of flesh and bones and invited the disciples to make sure by touching it surely proves the point in question.

An important question is, Why did Jesus use the expression "flesh and bones" and not "flesh and blood"? According to B. F. Westcott the latter was the common formula, which in this case was replaced by "flesh and bones" because for the Jews the blood was the symbol and seat of corruptible life. Jesus' resurrection-body had put on incorruption, and to indicate this Jesus spoke of "flesh and bones" instead of "flesh and blood."[106] According to K. Bornhäuser the Jews expected the resurrection to start from the bones, as the imperishable element of the human body. The apostolic tradition must have been influenced by this conception, he suggests.[107]

Such interpretations, however, seem rather far-fetched. It is true that "flesh and blood" was a common formula, but it did not denote the substance of man's body but man himself in the totality of his existence.[108] In Luke 24:39 it is very particularly the *substance* of Jesus' body which is in dispute. Therefore the most natural explanation seems to be that Jesus referred to his flesh and bones because they are the most solid parts; they give shape to the body, can be seen, touched, and handled, whereas the blood cannot.

It follows that the expression "flesh and bones" does not exclude the possibility that Jesus' resurrection-body had blood also. W. Milligan remarks rightly that there is no reason why glorified flesh and bones should be possible but not glorified blood (*op. cit.,* p. 241).

---

[106] B. F. Westcott, *The Gospel of the Resurrection*, p. 137. Similarly N. Geldenhuys, *op. cit.,* and W. Milligan, *The Resurrection of our Lord,* p. 241. Milligan, however, rejects rightly the idea that Jesus' body was bloodless.

[107] Cf. quotations from Bornhäuser's work, *Die Gebeine der Toten*, by W. Künneth, *op. cit.,* pp. 74ff.

[108] E. Schweizer, TWNT, VII, 128.

Jesus' statement (v. 39) that he "has" (Greek *echein*, to possess) a body of flesh and bones is significant. It implies that such a body is an *essential* part of the risen Lord[109] and excludes Westcott's accommodation-theory, which claims that the risen Lord was usually a spirit, but on occasion took a resurrection-body solely for the purpose of making himself visible to men.[110]

When the disciples still doubted and wondered, Jesus asked them for something to eat. After they gave him a piece of a broiled fish he ate it before their eyes (vv. 41-43).

Textual critics have pondered these verses because certain ancient manuscripts contain additions to what is now considered the authentic text. This problem, however, has no special significance for our subject. The "authentic" text shows abundantly that Jesus' body was *capable* of receiving food and, indeed, *took* food.

This does not imply that Jesus' body *needed* food, which would be inconsistent with Paul's statement in I Corinthians 6:13. It is evident from the context that Jesus ate only to convince the disciples that his body was "flesh and bones." It was meant as a last and decisive demonstration.[111]

There was nothing deceptive in Jesus' taking food which he did not need, for as A. Plummer rightly says: "The alternative 'either a ghost, or an ordinary body needing food' is false. There is a third possibility: a glorified body, capable of receiving food. Is there any deceit in taking food, which one does not want, in order to place others, who are needing it, at their ease?" (ICC).

Moreover, we must also reject the suggestion that Jesus' eating

---

[109] So S. Greydanus (KNT), who also makes the interesting remark that the appeal of Jesus to the disciples' senses of sight and touch as means by which to ascertain the reality of his presence, implies the trustworthiness of these senses, which is of great importance also with regard to the Transsubstantiation doctrine.

[110] E. Sauer (*op. cit.,* p. 107) rightly remarks that in this case Christ would have misled his disciples by what he said. A. M. Ramsey, who is more or less in favor of some "vision-theory," admits: "there may not be a great deal of difference between temporary accomodations to the former mode of existence (Westcott's view) and visions granted to the disciples" (*op. cit.,* p. 124).

[111] K. H. Rengstorf (NTD) remarks that fish was nothing unusual in Jerusalem, as already appears from Nehemiah 13:16. In pious Jewish circles it was a much appreciated element of the Sabbath meal. We need not assume, therefore, that this part of the narrative is a later addition speaking of what happened in Galilee (John 21:9ff.), as S. M. Gilmour (IB) seems to suggest.

was merely a sham, as is sometimes ascribed to angels.[112]   The
context (vv. 39, 40) is flatly against it.

We conclude that Luke's witness with regard to the nature of
Jesus' resurrection-body is clear and forthright.   It was a body of
flesh, essentially identical with that in which Jesus was buried,
bearing the scars of the wounds inflicted upon it at the crucifixion
and capable of taking food.   Luke's minute study and precise description of its characteristics are appropriate for a medical man,
from whom one may expect "something like the fullness of a medical diagnosis."[113]

Turning now to the Gospel according to John, we find that
Chapter 20 begins with an account of the empty tomb — an account which "is undoubtedly that of an eyewitness."[114]   The narrative provides various particulars not found in the Synoptics, but
these need not be discussed here.

An important feature of John's account, however, is the stress
that he lays on Jesus' graveclothes.   The disciples who visited the
grave came to believe in Jesus' resurrection when they saw what
the risen Master himself had left behind in the tomb.   Although
Mary Magdalene had told them that Jesus' body was stolen, seeing
the cloths in which Jesus had been buried and the napkin carefully
rolled up convinced at least one of them (v. 8) that Mary was
mistaken.   No grave robber, he probably reasoned, would first
strip the body, then neatly roll up the napkin and lay it in a place
by itself (E. Hoskyns).   "He saw and believed," viz. "that Jesus
had actually risen from the dead" (IB).

W. F. Howard (IB) supposes that Jesus' body "had been swiftly
dematerialized, leaving the swathing cloths as they were. . . . It
was their position that made the disciple leap to the conclusion
that the material body had been transformed into a spiritual body."
According to this scholar "the interpretation that thinks of the
linen cloths as merely having been 'rolled up' is too jejune for the
context."[115]

Against this theory we may raise the following objections:

1. It makes John contradict Luke, for according to Luke Jesus
declared that he had flesh and bones.   Such a contradiction is also
suggested in Howard's interpretation of John 20:20, where we

[112] B. Weiss, op. cit.
[113] V. McNabb, The Resurrection of the Body, p. 7.
[114] A. T. Olmstead, Jesus in the Light of History, p. 248.
[115] Similarly G. H. C. MacGregor (MNTC), et al.

read that Jesus showed the disciples his hands and his side. Here this scholar remarks that John does not, like Luke, speak of the risen Lord as eating or being touched. But contradictions like these are incompatible with the inspiration of the Scriptures.

2. Our survey of John's conception of flesh in the previous chapter has shown that a "dematerialization" of Jesus' body (which according to Howard "best fits the Johannine view of the mode of the Resurrection") does not agree with John's view of the Incarnate Word, who has become flesh and still is flesh.

3. On Howard's theory that Jesus' resurrection-body was a spiritual phenomenon which could "appear and disappear at will" (p. 796, IB), it is impossible to interpret naturally John's account (chs. 20, 21) of the appearances that Jesus made to Mary Magdalene and to the disciples.[116] We think particularly of Jesus' word to Mary, "touch me not"; of the fact that Jesus showed the disciples his hands and his side; and of Jesus' having a meal with the disciples at the Sea of Galilee. The latter episode, Howard suggests, is an allegory, but this is incompatible with John's obvious intention to describe historical facts. Howard interprets the other events along the lines of the accommodation-theory, which is incompatible with the character of Jesus, as we have seen.

4. Howard supposes that Jesus' napkin was lying where his head had been, and that it kept its annular shape when Jesus' body dematerialized. These conclusions fit his conception of the resurrection, but they are not warranted by the text. The text says only that the napkin was in a place by itself; where that place was is not stated. While the Greek participle for "rolled up" might have the meaning Howard attaches to it, it need not have that meaning. As Bernard admits: "it cannot be regarded as certain." The only thing that John makes absolutely clear is that in Jesus' empty grave everything was in perfect order, as the graveclothes showed, and hence the body could not have been

---

[116] John 21, which many regard as written by one of John's disciples, is completely Johannine in style and character. There is no trace in the tradition that this Gospel was ever in circulation without Chapter 21. We believe, therefore, that if one of John's disciples or helpers wrote this chapter (as is probably the case with vv. 24, 25) he recorded what the apostle himself had often told his friends, so that in this chapter, too, we have the fully reliable account of an eyewitness (cf. S. Greydanus, *Bijzondere Canoniek*, I, 244; and F. W. Grosheide, *Het Heilig Evangelie volgens Johannes* (KNT), I, par. 4-8, 10; II, 549-51).

stolen or otherwise hastily removed.[117]   With Jesus himself gone
from the grave, the only conclusion remaining to be drawn was:
he is risen, and has purposely left these graveclothes behind in
perfect order as a sign that he has conquered death.   A living person does not need the apparel of the dead.

To avoid unnecessary repetition of matters discussed in connection with Luke, we will touch only briefly on the following
passages.

In John 20:17 Jesus says to Mary: "Touch me not; for I am
not yet ascended unto the Father."   The rendering "Touch me
not" (KJV, ERV, ASV, et al.), however, seems hardly correct.
We take the present imperative with me in its usual meaning,
signifying "the breaking off of an action already in progress"
(C. K. Barrett).   With R. C. H. Lenski we probably should translate: "Stop clinging to me," or as several modern versions have it:
"Do not cling to me" (BV, NBG, NEB, Weymouth, et al.; RSV:
"Do not hold me").

Jesus did not mean to say that his resurrection-body was too
glorious to make touching permissible,[118] which would conflict
with Matthew 28:9, Luke 24:39, and John 20:27.   It is also
difficult to see how the fact that Jesus had not yet ascended to the
Father could be the reason (Greek: gar) why Mary was not allowed even to touch him.

Various interpretations of Jesus' statement, some of which include conjectural emendations, have been offered.[119]   We cannot
discuss them here.   Most probably, Jesus' words were based on the
way in which Mary clung to him; he discerned that she would not
let him go again, that she wished everything to continue as before.
In this respect her laying hold of Jesus was different from that of
the other women (cf. Matt. 28:9).   Hence Jesus tells Mary that
she is mistaken.   She must cease clinging to him, trying to keep
him always with her.   Jesus is about to ascend to the Father[120] and
from then on the fellowship with him will be of a different sort.[121]

117 Cf. J. Calvin, F. W. Grosheide (KNT), W. Hendriksen (NTC), et al.
Grosheide refers in a note to Crysostom's remark (510 A) that the
orderly condition of the cloths is the more miraculous, since the spices
used at the burial made the cloths stick to the body like lead.

118 Thus P. Benoit, Revue Bibl. 56, 2 April 1949, p. 483, quoted by
Grosheide.

119 A brief survey may be found in J. H. Bernard's Commentary (ICC),
ad loc.

120 We understand the present tense as denoting what is about to happen
and is already in preparation during these great forty days.

121 Cf. J. Calvin, F. W. Grosheide (KNT), E. L. Smelik (PNT), et al.

The implication for our subject is that the risen Lord had a body that *could* be touched, namely a body of flesh and bones, as Luke says.

In John 20:20 we read that Jesus showed his disciples his hands and his side. Luke speaks of his hands and feet. There is no contradiction between the two statements. Both evangelists mention parts of Jesus' body upon which wounds had been inflicted while he was hanging on the cross. The tradition as it came to Luke probably placed more emphasis on the hands and the feet, whereas John must have been particularly impressed by the hands and the side. Neither of them denies any of the three features.[122]

Despite the slight difference in detail, the evangelist John, like Luke, teaches the identity of Jesus' resurrection-body with the body in which he died, and also that it was physical, not immaterial.

John 20:24-29 brings to a climax all that the Gospels tell us concerning the nature of Jesus' resurrection-body. We hear Thomas declare that he will not believe in Jesus' resurrection unless he see the scars in the Master's body and feels Jesus' wounds with his hands. We are told that Jesus invited Thomas to do what he had said he wanted to do. Commentators differ on the question whether Thomas actually put his hand into the wounds of Jesus' body. It makes no difference in connection with our subject. The truth stands out that Jesus himself convinced this doubting disciple of the glorious fact that the Crucified One has become the Risen One, in whose very flesh death has been overcome by life and immortality victoriously brought to light.

Even radical critics like H. J. Heering and A. Oepke admit that John detracts nothing from the corporeality of Jesus' resurrection.[123] To escape the inevitable conclusion that Jesus' resurrection-body was one of flesh, these scholars suggest that the Christian community added these "massive conceptions" to the original tradition for apologetic reasons. No evidence, however, can be adduced to support this suggestion which, again, degrades the biblical records into documents full of pious fraud.

After all we have found in John's Gospel it cannot surprise us when we are told in John 21:1-14 that the risen Lord had a meal

---

[122] C. K. Barrett suggests that Jesus possibly was never nailed to the cross, but tied to it with ropes. He writes: "Belief that wounds were inflicted by nails might have arisen out of the theological significance ascribed to the blood of Christ. . . ." This, however, degrades the Gospel narratives into pious fraud, without any evidence to support the suggestion.

[123] H. J. Heering, *op. cit.*, p. 122; A. Oepke, TWNT, II, 334.

with his disciples, he himself acting as host, taking bread and fish and giving it to them with his own hands (v. 13).

The question whether Jesus himself partook of the food is doubtless to be answered in the affirmative. It is most naturally implied in Jesus' question, "Children, have ye aught to eat?" (v. 5), and in the way John depicts the meal itself. Even though John does not explicitly state that Jesus ate together with the disciples, the conclusion is unwarranted that he "only presided at the meal" (J. H. Bernard, ICC, p. 701). It was a matter of course that Jesus, being host to the disciples, joined them in the meal. There are things that need not be stated because they are self-evident.

This interpretation is confirmed by Peter's words to Cornelius (Acts 10:40, 41): "Him God raised up the third day, and gave him to be made manifest, not to all the people, but unto witnesses that were chosen before of God, even to us, who ate and drank with him after he rose from the dead." We agree with O. Cullmann that Peter must have been thinking here of what happened at the sea of Galilee and maybe also of what Luke 24:30 describes.[124]

Undoubtedly, then, the early apostolic tradition spoke of a risen Jesus whose body is truly physical and even capable of taking food, even though it did not necessarily need that food. Moreover, this testimony of Peter proves that it is completely unwarranted to dismiss narratives like that of John 21:1-14 as allegories, legends, etc., with little or no historical value. Such criticism amounts to breaking away the very foundations of Christianity.

In the Book of Acts we have already discussed 13:34ff. and 10:41; we turn now to Peter's words spoken on the day of Pentecost, which are of great importance for our subject. In 2:26, 27 Peter quotes a passage from Psalm 16: "Therefore my heart was glad, and my tongue rejoiced; moreover my flesh also shall dwell in hope: because thou wilt not leave my soul unto Hades, neither wilt thou give thy Holy One to see corruption." Peter declares that David spoke these words with reference to Christ, and that they have been fulfilled in Christ's resurrection. For David died, was buried and saw corruption, but Christ was not "left unto Hades, nor did his flesh see corruption" (v. 31).

E. Schweizer remarks that "flesh" here, as in the Old Testament, denotes the whole man (TWNT, VII, 124), and admittedly

---

[124] O. Cullmann, *Early Christian Worship*, pp. 15-16; cf. also J. Pickl, *Messias-Koning*, pp. 254ff., and various commentators.

the flesh is never to be separated from man as a person. But in this passage the emphasis is very strongly on the fact that the person is a man *of flesh*. F. W. Grosheide rightly points to the fact (already discussed in this study when we dealt with Psalm 16) that first the inner, immaterial side of man is mentioned, the *kardia* (heart), which implies that *sarx*, in distinction from *kardia*, denotes the material side. Moreover, the fact that *sarx* is preceded by the expression *eti de kai* (even . . . also) shows that "flesh" must be understood here as the physical side of man, in distinction from his "heart" or soul.

It is evident, therefore, that in Acts 2:27 Peter is referring to Jesus' flesh in the literal sense of the word: it was Jesus' body of *flesh* which did not see corruption.

Some have concluded from Peter's statement that Jesus' body did not suffer any dissolution while it was lying in the grave.[125] But this is probably pressing the language too far. The meaning can very well be that dissolution, though immediately starting after Jesus died, was interrupted and overcome when Jesus was raised to immortal, incorruptible life.

There is reason to prefer this interpretation. Jesus' death was very real, and there is no real death without dissolution. Moreover, as Grosheide suggests, in Acts 13:34 the word *meketi* (no more, no longer) is used in the same context, which suggests that there was dissolution and corruption up to the moment of the resurrection.

Whether or not there was dissolution in Jesus' buried body, one thing is beyond doubt: the apostolic *kerygma* recorded in Acts proclaims that the body of our Lord was delivered out of the clutches of death and brought to glorious, incorruptible life.

In this respect there is complete agreement between Acts, Paul's witness in I Corinthians 15:1ff., the Synoptics, and John's Gospel. This, we may say, is the unequivocal teaching of the New Testament.

In the light of all the statements discussed it is utterly unwarranted to use the so-called "mysterious elements" in the resurrection-narratives as evidence that the resurrected Jesus had no body of flesh, or only "in some sense" a body of flesh.[126]

Against those radical critics who see in these narratives many

---

[125] So, e.g., J. Calvin; Bishop J. Pearson, *An Exposition of the Creed*, ed. Nichols, p. 537; *et al.* (Cf. SB, II, pp. 618ff., for quotations from Rabbinic literature bearing on the expression.)

[126] Thus W. Barclay, *Crucified and Crowned*, p. 154.

irreconcilable contradictions, W. Barclay remarks: "the men who wrote the New Testament were not fools."[127]   We may also apply this statement to the New Testament teachings concerning Jesus' resurrection-body.   W. Barclay's statement is highly appropriate when some modern scholars speak of "confusion" in the resurrection records and of "an obvious conflict in the involved ideas of body."[128]

When the evangelists ascribe "mysterious" features to Jesus' resurrection-body, they cannot possibly be regarded as implicitly annulling their own statements that the Lord had a body of flesh. The only legitimate inference to be made is that our Lord in his risen body of flesh was able to act in a mysterious, miraculous way.

The mysterious elements are mainly the following.

1. The risen Lord could mysteriously appear and disappear at will. In Luke 24:31, for example, we read that when the men of Emmaus recognized the Master, "he vanished out of their sight." The word *aphantos,* which the Greek uses in this clause, occurs frequently in Greek literature to denote "a supernatural disappearance" (J. M. Creed, *ad loc.*).   Most commentators agree that in Luke 24:31 it suggests that Jesus mysteriously vanished: suddenly he left, though the two men did not see him go.

Luke 24:36 tells us that Jesus himself stood in the midst of the disciples as they were gathered together in Jerusalem. It is clearly implied that this was a sudden and miraculous appearance. Those assembled did not see or hear him coming; he just was there, standing in their midst. Especially this manner of appearance may have caused the disciples to suppose that they saw a spirit (v. 37).

John 20:19 certainly speaks of the same appearance, but here the description is more circumstantial. Luke has only *este* (he stood), whereas John also mentions Jesus' arrival: "he came and stood." Moreover, John informs us that Jesus came "when the doors were shut." In verse 26, where the narrative of the appearance to Thomas begins, John writes again, "Jesus cometh, the doors being shut." It is obvious that a miraculous coming is suggested, a sudden appearance notwithstanding the fact that the doors were shut.

Many scholars interpret this as meaning that Jesus' body passed right through the closed doors,[129] which of course creates the prob-

---

127 *Ibid.,* p. 157.
128 So, e.g., H. E. Fosdick, *A Guide to Understanding the Bible,* p. 284.
129 E.g., C. K. Barrett, *in loc.;* E. Stauffer, *op. cit.,* p. 125; Wilbur M. Smith, in *Baker's Dictionary of Theology, s.v. "Resurrection."*   Dr. Smith

lem of how our Lord could state and prove immediately after this that he had a body of flesh and bones. Barrett suggests that according to John, Jesus "was at once sufficiently corporeal to show his wounds and sufficiently immaterial to pass through closed doors." But a body that is at once material and immaterial seems a *contradictio in terminis.*

The fact is, however, that nowhere in the Gospels is it said that Jesus' body passed through closed doors. The only thing we are told is that he suddenly appeared while the doors were closed. It is certainly implicitly suggested that there was something mysterious and miraculous in his entering the room, but how he did enter is not mentioned at all.

Jesus could not have entered through the closed doors because, according to his own words, he had a body of flesh and bones that could be handled, take food, and the like. Calvin, commenting on John 20:19, calls the idea of Christ's body passing through closed doors a "childish trifling, which contains nothing solid, and brings along with it many absurdities."

How did Jesus enter? Nobody knows, and the numerous suggestions made by commentators are all mere guesses. We do not even know whether "the doors" mean only the outer door of the building itself, or the inner door to the room where the disciples were gathered, though the former interpretation seems more plausible.[130]

According to Lenski it was not even necessary that the doors should be opened, because of "the divine omnipresence of which the human nature of Jesus partakes. . . ." This opinion, however, contradicts the continuous teaching of Scripture that Christ not only was very God but also very man, and that he still *is* man (I Tim. 2:5). As man, in his human body, Jesus was not divinely omnipresent nor could he ever become so. It would mean the annulment of his being very man, and the ascension would become a deceptive sham action, as would his promised visible return from heaven. W. Hendriksen (NTC) rightly remarks that the very words used in John 20:19, "Jesus came and stood in the midst," prove that Jesus' human nature after the resurrection was not omnipresent. One who is omnipresent need not *come,* unless this

---

even goes so far as to say that "Christ's body passed through the grave clothes and through the sepulchre, without the stone having been rolled away, and through the walls of the room in which the disciples were assembled. . . ." There is nothing in the Gospels to justify such statements.

[130] As A-G indicates, the plural is often used of one door (*s.v. thura*).

word is taken in a metaphorical sense, for which the text gives no ground.

On the other hand, Jesus was very God as well, and we have to take this into account when confronted with his mysterious coming and vanishing. What could prevent him from opening closed doors merely by the power of his will and from making his coming and leaving sudden, unusual, and unnoticed actions?

Moreover, his resurrection-body, though a body of flesh, apparently had qualities different from the body of his humiliation. The Spirit, who raised him from the dead, endowed him with extraordinary power (Rom. 1:4). It is not correct to say that he was now beyond space and time, which again would be a denial of his humanity. But with K. H. Rengstorf (NTD) we may say that he was not subject to the laws of space and time or dependent on nature, but above them. This power was not something entirely new, as appears in Mark 6:48ff., where we read of Jesus walking on the sea, and in all the other accounts of miracles as well. The new element is this, that after the resurrection "this miraculous quality completely characterizes and determines Jesus' whole life and being" (Rengstorf). Here we may refer to I Corinthians 15:40ff., where Paul is speaking of the spiritual body, a passage later to be discussed at length. In the risen Christ, who was able to act in a mysterious and miraculous way, we can see already what Paul means by a "spiritual body": a body of flesh completely dominated by the Spirit's powers, living in space and time and yet not enslaved to present laws of space and time, but free with the freedom which characterizes the new humanity.[131]

2. All this applies also to the second mysterious element in the Gospel records of the appearances: Jesus was often not recognized at first sight.

Matthew 28:17 informs us that when Jesus met with his eleven disciples on the hill in Galilee "some doubted." S. E. Johnson (IB) interprets this to mean that they doubted Jesus' resurrection, but with many other commentators we prefer the interpretation that the disciples doubted Jesus' identity.[132] There was apparently something unusual in his figure.

In the Lukan narrative of Jesus' appearance to the disciples at Emmaus we read that the risen Lord joined them on their way

---

[131] So, e.g., B. Kenrick, *The New Humanity*, pp. 70ff.; J. C. Ryle, *Commentary on John;* and K. Schilder, *op. cit.*, p. 230.
[132] So, e.g., F. W. Grosheide (KNT); A. Plummer, *op. cit.;* T. H. Robinson (MNTC); and R. V. G. Tasker (TNT).

home, talked with them, and sat at their table — all without their recognizing him. Only when he took bread, blessed it, broke and gave it, "their eyes were opened, and they knew him" (Luke 24:13ff.).

K. H. Rengstorf suggests that they could not recognize Jesus because the organ of faith was lacking. The way to faith had first to be prepared in their hearts before he could reveal himself to them. This explains (says Rengstorf) why the Lord did not appear to his enemies: they lacked faith in him.

This is contradicted, however, by the fact that Jesus appeared to one of his most hostile enemies, Paul, and also to unbelieving Thomas. In both cases faith was *created* by the appearance.

A. Plummer suggests that the two disciples of Emmaus "were preoccupied and had no expectation of meeting Him, and there is good reason for believing that the risen Saviour had a glorified body, which was not at once recognized." This may be true enough, but it can hardly be the whole truth. Verse 16, "But their eyes were holden (*ekratounto*) that they should not know him," seems to suggest that by a miraculous power their eyes were prevented from recognizing Jesus. The risen Lord apparently wanted first to instruct them from the Scriptures about his resurrection. If they had been allowed to recognize him immediately, they might easily have missed this instruction.[133]

John 20:14ff. describes the appearance to Mary Magdalene. We are told that she saw Jesus standing, talked with him, but did not recognize him. Jesus had to speak her name in a very special way to make her recognize him.

That Mary mistook Jesus for the gardener may have been partly due to the tears which blinded her eyes and to the fact that in the garden she naturally expected the gardener.[134] It is quite possible, however, that the change which the resurrection had brought about in Jesus' body also played a role.[135] Mary did not even recognize Jesus' voice.

In John 21, describing the appearance of Jesus at the Sea of Galilee, we are again confronted with the fact that Jesus was not recognized at first. The disciples in the boat saw him standing on the beach; they talked with him, but did not recognize him. No reason is stated, but the nature and appearance of Jesus' body may certainly have played a role, as well as a supernatural "hold-

---

[133] Thus S. Greydanus (KNT).
[134] So M. J. Lagrange, quoted by F. W. Grosheide, *ad. loc.*
[135] Cf. F. L. Godet.

ing of their eyes" (cf. Luke 24:16): the risen Lord wanted to make himself known by the miracle he was to perform.

The statement of verse 12 is remarkable: "And none of the disciples durst inquire of him, Who art thou? knowing that it was the Lord." The verb *exetasai* means to make investigation. If the body of Jesus had not possessed certain strange features, the disciples would not have desired to ask whether he was really their risen Master. His appearance must have made them uncertain. They did not *actually* ask Jesus who he was because the miracle had convinced them that it was indeed Jesus and nobody else.

There is no reason to deny either these mysterious elements in Jesus' appearances, or the clear testimony of the evangelists that Jesus was raised in a body of flesh. With regard to these things the *kerygma* of the Gospels requires faith, just as the miracles Jesus performed in the days of his humiliation have to be accepted by faith. There is, after all, no fundamental difference between believing on the one hand that Jesus could walk upon the water before the resurrection, despite the fact that he had a real human body of flesh and, on the other, that after the resurrection he could act independently of the laws of time and space, despite the fact that his resurrection body was a real, though glorified, human body of flesh.

To faith may well be added the modesty and caution of the truly scientific mind. To express it in the words of Alan Richardson: "Despite (or rather, because of) the advances of modern physical science, we now know that we know so little about the properties of bodies that we must not dogmatize about what the body of the Lord could or could not have done; and the Christian mind will be slow to set aside the apostolic witness in favor of any changing modern hypotheses."[136]

---

[136] *S.v.* "Resurrection" in *A Theological Word Book of the Bible*, ed. A. Richardson.

CHAPTER FIVE

THE BODY OF OUR EXALTED LORD, THE LIFE-GIVING SPIRIT

1. SPIRITUALIZING VIEWS

There can be no doubt that according to the New Testament the body in which our risen Lord appeared to his disciples *during the forty days between the resurrection and the ascension* was a glorified body of *flesh*. Before a conclusion can be drawn from this fact, however, as to the "substance" of the future resurrection-body of the believer, we must ask whether Jesus' *ascension* brought about such a change that he *no longer* has a physical body of flesh. If the latter is true, there is no ground for expecting that the believers will be raised in a glorified body of flesh. For according to Philippians 3:21, the "body of our humiliation [will be] conformed to the body of his glory."

The question is controversial. A. Kuyper, for instance, believes in a spectacular glorification of Jesus' resurrection-body at the moment of the ascension, but this was a glorification of Jesus' body of flesh, which he retained in heaven.[1] W. Milligan, unlike Kuyper, does not believe in a special glorification of Jesus on the occasion of the ascension. According to him, Jesus' glorification began at his resurrection. But with regard to the "substance" of Jesus' glorified body Milligan's conclusion is the same as that of Kuyper: "There is not a word in the New Testament to favor the idea that the Savior, now exalted in the heavens, has a body different from that which he possessed on earth."[2] A. Edersheim expresses a similar opinion,[3] and so, more recently, does W. Künneth. This scholar claims that the resurrection-body of our Lord during the great forty days already "possessed a heavenly corporeality."[4] Several others holding similar opinions could be mentioned.

---

[1] *Van de Voleinding,* II, 231,239ff.
[2] *The Resurrection of Our Lord,* pp. 14,15.
[3] *The Life and Times of Jesus the Messiah,* II, 664.
[4] *Theologie der Auferstehung,* p. 226.

Many other scholars maintain that Jesus' ascended body is not fleshly. H. Bavinck, for instance, differed from his famous countryman and colleague Dr. Kuyper in that, according to him, the substance of Jesus' resurrection-body was in a state of transition during the great forty days. At the ascension it was changed into a body no longer of flesh and blood, but of some other matter, although the essential identity with the previous body was retained.[5] A similar view is held by Charles Hodge,[6] James Orr,[7] and others.

Other scholars go still further by suggesting that Jesus' resurrection-body underwent a change from the material to the spiritual. H. B. Swete, for instance, speaks of a gradual spiritualization during the great forty days.[8]   Recently W. Barclay has suggested the possibility of such a change with an appeal to Jesus' word to Mary Magdalene in John 20:17: "I am ascending to My Father. . . ," which expression according to Professor Barclay seems to imply that a gradual, increasing spiritualization took place which finally made an end to the incarnation.[9]   A. Oepke also seems to hold such a view, though he expresses himself rather vaguely: "A distinction has probably to be made between the corporeality of the Risen One and that of the Glorified One."[10]   J. A. T. Robinson suggests that Christ had appeared to Paul "not in the manner of the great forty days, but in His Post-Ascension form." The latter was *"The resurrection body of Christ, not as an individual, but as the Christian community,"*[11] "a body out of any direct relation to the material order."[12] It is not clear whether according to Robinson the resurrection-body of the great forty days was one of flesh and blood, which then must have changed into an immaterial "body" at the ascension.   Robinson may as well view the appearances mentioned in the Gospels as accommodations of a Christ who immediately after death was spiritualized.   For according to him Colossians 2:15 states that the dying Jesus divested himself

    [5] *Gereformeerde Dogmatiek*, IV, 775-76.
    [6] *Systematic Theology*, II, 628-29.
    [7] *The Resurrection of Jesus*, pp. 196-97.
    [8] *The Life of the World to Come*, pp. 50ff., 82.
    [9] *Crucified and Crowned*, p. 178.   See also his *The Promise of the Spirit*, p. 35, where we find the significant expression: "So long as the Incarnation lasted. . . ."
    [10] TWNT, II, *s.v. egeiro*, p. 334.
    [11] *The Body*, pp. 58-59 (italics Robinson's).
    [12] *In the End God. . .*, p. 93.

of the flesh as the tool and medium of the powers of death and sin.[13]

2. RESURRECTION AND ASCENSION IN PAUL'S WRITINGS

Closely related to the spiritualizing views just mentioned is another conception which must be studied in this chapter, because if it is correct, the exalted Christ cannot be said to have a glorified body of flesh. It concerns the theory of those who regard Paul's teachings about the exalted Lord as essentially different from those of the Gospels and Acts. According to them Paul, representing the oldest tradition, did not know of a bodily ascension of the resurrected Jesus at the end of forty days. It is claimed that in the earliest *kerygma* Jesus' resurrection and ascension were identical or nearly coinciding. Whatever Paul's conception of the resurrection may have been (there was and is difference of opinion on this point), his Christ, different from the Jesus of the Gospels, is an immaterial, spiritual Lord. Long after Paul had passed away the legend of a bodily ascension was created by the Christian community and found its way into Luke's Gospel and Acts.

This conception was developed under rationalistic influences particularly by the Tübingen School of the first half of the nineteenth century. D. Fr. Strauss presented it in its most radical and consistent form.[14] The Tübingen School died, but E. Earl Ellis remarks rightly that "Tübingen retained a remarkable familiarity with the following generations."[15] Only a few instances can be mentioned here. A. Deissmann wrote that according to Paul "the resurrection of Jesus was the resumption of the spiritual life of Jesus in glory with the Father. It was not fleshly but it gave to the Living One, probably by a process of transformation (so one would conclude from I Cor. 15:51) a spiritual heavenly body."[16] A. Harnack dealt very extensively with the traditions concerning resurrection and ascension. According to him they were originally regarded as identical events, the separate ascension related in Acts being a later legend.[17] In more recent times Kirsopp

---

[13] *The Body*, p. 41. This explanation is rejected by E. Schweizer, who says that in Col. 2:15 Christ's flesh-body is not mentioned (TWNT, VI, 137, n. 292).

[14] *Das Leben Jesu kritisch bearbeitet*, pp. 612ff.

[15] *Paul and His Recent Interpreters*, p. 20.

[16] *Op. cit.*, p. 142.

[17] A. Harnack, *History of Dogma*, I, 201ff. (esp. n. 1 on pp. 203-04). For further evidence from the various publications by Harnack dealing with

Lake has claimed that the writings of Paul "give us the needed correction to the materialism of the Lukan and Johannine accounts of the risen Lord," accounts which were written long after Paul "under the stress of Docetic controversy." According to Paul the resurrection of Christ consisted in the changing of his physical body into an immaterial, spiritual one, which at the same time went to heaven and appeared from there.[18]

Still more recently similar views, though differing in detail, have been promoted by R. Bultmann,[19] E. Schweizer,[20] H. Traub,[21] and others.

In support of the claim that Paul's exalted, spiritual Lord differs from the risen Jesus of flesh and blood as he is depicted in the later Gospel tradition, the fact is adduced that the Gospels say little or nothing about a bodily ascension and that only Acts gives a circumstantial and rather "materialistic" account of it. This is said to prove that a bodily ascension did not belong to the older tradition to which Paul had access. This is allegedly confirmed by the fact that in I Corinthians 15:3ff. several appearances of Christ are mentioned but not a word is said about a bodily ascension after forty days; Paul apparently did not know of it. An appeal is also made to certain significant statements of Paul which seem to give undoubted proof of Paul's spiritual conception of the exalted Lord. To such statements belong, for example, Philippians 3:21, where Paul speaks of "the body of his [Christ's] glory," which is taken as "a body consisting of glory"; II Corinthians 3:17, "Now the Lord is the Spirit"; II Corinthians 5:16, where the Apostle says that we know Christ no more after the flesh; and the many passages where Paul uses his favorite phrase "in Christ," which is interpreted in a spiritualizing way. Very particularly from Paul's description of Christ as the second Adam, as given in I Corinthians 15:44ff., it is argued that Paul's Christ is an immaterial one. Is Christ not called "a life-giving spirit" (v. 45), a spiritual man, who is not of the earth but heavenly (vv. 46-49)? Does the Apostle not exclude flesh and blood from the Kingdom of God (v. 50), so that the body of the believer

---

this problem, see the Free University doctoral dissertation by C. Stam, *De Hemelvaart des Heren in de Godsopenbaring van het Nieuwe Testament,* pp. 76ff., notes 23-28.

[18] *Op. cit.,* pp. 223, 226, 230ff.
[19] ThNT, I, 45.
[20] *Lordship and Discipleship,* p. 38.
[21] TWNT, *s.v. ouranos,* pp. 524, 529.

which is to be raised by Christ will be a spiritual body, which implies that Christ himself has such a body?

Coming now to a closer examination of the various contentions mentioned, we will first discuss whether the ascension belonged to the earliest *kerygma,* and whether it is to be regarded as bringing about a change in the condition of Jesus' body.

The argument that Paul does not mention the ascension in I Corinthians 15:3ff., which allegedly proves that he identified the resurrection with the ascension, is not convincing, as is the case with nearly every *argumentum ex silentio.* The whole fifteenth chapter of I Corinthians deals with the resurrection of the dead, which was denied by some (v. 12). Since Christ's resurrection is the basis of the believers' resurrection, Paul speaks first of the former. He points out (vv. 1-4) that the earliest gospel tradition, as he received it and passed it on to the Corinthians, contained the message of Jesus' resurrection, which was already predicted in the Old Testament. Then he describes (vv. 5ff.) how Christ gave ample proof of his resurrection by appearing in person to various disciples and other believers, of whom the greater part are still living. The last of these appearances was to Paul himself, and is obviously regarded as being like the others. Immediately after this the Apostle starts speaking about the inseparable connection between the resurrection of Christ and that of the believers, all in order to convince the erring Corinthians that there is indeed a resurrection of the dead.

Since the resurrection of Christ and of the believers is thus the only theme Paul is dealing with in this chapter, can it surprise us that he does not mention the ascension? We should have been more surprised if he had mentioned it.

If Paul's silence about the ascension warrants any conclusion, it would be that the Christ of the great forty days was for Paul identical with the exalted Lord who appeared to him. For Paul places all appearances, including the one to himself, on a par. And since the apostle certainly believed that Jesus was raised in the same body in which he had been buried, as we found in the previous chapter, he must have regarded the heavenly Lord who appeared to him as still possessing that body.

Proceeding from the negative to the positive, we find ample proof in Paul's letters that he did know of the ascension.

In Romans 8:34 he declares: "It is Christ Jesus that died, yea rather, that was raised from the dead, who is at the right hand of God, who also maketh intercession for us."

H. Traub (TWNT,V, 523) appeals to this verse as evidence that Christ's being raised is identical with his ascension and being at the right hand of God. Similarly J. Knox (IB) speaks of the love of Christ, manifested "not alone in Jesus' death . . . but also in his being raised from the dead to the right hand of God," thus suggesting that Jesus' resurrection and ascension are identical.

But the construction of the sentence is against such an identification, and particularly Knox's paraphrase, "raised from the dead to the right hand of God," is a misrepresentation of what the text states. As various commentators remark, there is (probably connected with a very early creed) a "stately gradation: died . . . was raised . . . who is at the right hand of God . . . who intercedes for us" (J. A. Beet). "Stroke follows stroke, each driving home the last" (Sanday and Headlam, ICC). Paul is apparently referring to successive events: death, resurrection, and enthronement (ICC). This appears not only from the "stately gradation," but also from the fact that the Greek has aorist participles for "died" and "was raised," whereas what follows is a separate clause with the verbs in the present indicative.

Therefore, though it is true that the ascension is not emphatically mentioned, it is clearly implied, and Sanday and Headlam are right when they call this verse "a great text for the value and significance of the Ascension."[22]

Ephesians 1:20 confirms this interpretation. There Paul declares that God "raised him [Christ] from the dead, and made him to sit at his right hand in the heavenly places." If Paul had identified the resurrection with the ascension, he would not have constructed the clause as he did, using two aorist participles connected with "and"; this construction indicates that "raised" and "made him sit" refer to separate, successive events. F. W. Beare (IB) speaks in this connection rightly of "the great drama of salvation" as a "drama in several acts," among which resurrection and ascension each have their own place and significance.[23]

In Ephesians 4:8-10 the ascension is definitely mentioned. Here the Apostle declares that Christ "ascended on high" (v. 8), "far above all the heavens. . ." (v. 10).

We cannot discuss here all the exegetical details of the passage to which these clauses belong, or the problem connected with

[22] Cf. also H. C. G. Moule (*Comment.*); H. N. Ridderbos (CNT); and C. Stam, *op. cit.*, p. 50.
[23] This does not imply that we agree with the word "drama."

Paul's quotation from the Old Testament. The following remarks may suffice.

J. Schneider declares that the verbs used in this passage (Greek *katabainein* and *anabainein*) are technical terms for the descent of the Redeemer upon the earth and for his ascending from earth to heaven (TWNT, I, 519). There can be no doubt that Paul is referring to the incarnation on the one hand and to the ascension on the other.

According to H. Traub the expression "ascended far above all the heavens" gives strong evidence of Gnostic influences. The heavens, he says, are regarded here as heavenly spheres inhabited by evil spirits. They were not the goal of Christ's ascension; he only passed through them (TWNT, V, 526).

Very recently, however, K. G. Kuhn has convincingly shown that the Epistle to the Ephesians strongly resembles the Qumran literature in language and style; it is therefore no longer possible to claim that Ephesians was written under the influence of the Jewish-Christian "Gnosis."[24] When Paul speaks in Ephesians 4:10 of "all the heavens," we think with R. C. H. Lenski of the three heavens named in II Corinthians 12:2, 4, "which are commonly thought to be the atmospheric, the sidereal and the angelic heavens (Paradise)." That Christ ascended "far above" them does not mean that he went to a place somewhere which is not heaven. Lenski rightly asks: "where would that be?" The expression can only mean that the ascension gave Christ supremacy over all the heavens: "all heaven bows to him."[25]

This supremacy of Christ over heaven is also clearly expressed by Paul in Philippians 2:9-11, where the expression "God highly exalted him" in the light of what follows certainly refers to what happened after the resurrection, when Christ ascended into heaven. The result of this exaltation of our Lord is that "in the name of Jesus every knee shall bow, of things in *heaven* . . . etc."

In I Timothy 3:16, probably a Christian hymn or "a citation or catechism . . . a primitive epitome of Christological instruction. . . ,"[26] we find a description of "the mystery of godliness": "He who was manifested in the flesh, justified in the spirit, seen

---

[24] K. G. Kuhn, "Der Epheserbrief im Lichte der Qumrantexte," in NTS, July 1961, pp. 334ff.

[25] Similarly S. D. F. Salmond, in *The Expositor's Greek Testament*, et al.

[26] E. K. Simpson, *The Pastoral Epistles*.

of angels, preached among the nations, believed on in the world, received up in glory."

Here we are mainly concerned with the last phrase: "Received up in glory." With various modern versions we render this clause: "taken up in glory" (cf. BV, NBG, RSV, *et al.*). The question is, Does this phrase refer to the ascension?

According to some it does not. E. F. Scott (MNTC) and E. L. Smelik (PNT), for example, understand the phrase in an eschatological sense, as speaking of what will happen to Christ after the last judgment. Then he will enter his eternal kingdom. It seems better, however, to take it as referring to the ascension, as the majority of the commentators do.[27] The verb *analambanein* used here occurs as a technical term for the ascension of Enoch, Elijah, and others in Jewish literature.[28] In Mark 16:19 and Acts 1:11 it is employed to denote the ascension of our Lord.

Moreover, it is evident that all the preceding verbs in the aorist tense speak of what happened to Christ in the past. The verb in the last phrase is in the same tense, and it is difficult to see why only the last reference should be to the future.

For all these reasons there can be little doubt that the last phrase of I Timothy 3:16 refers to Christ's ascension. Nor can it be doubted that the ascension occurs here in marked distinction from the resurrection. D. Guthrie says that this verse is probably only part of an early Christian hymn because (according to him) Christ's death and resurrection are not mentioned. It is quite natural that Christ's death should not be mentioned in a hymn that evidently speaks of his greatness, but it would be surprising, indeed, if the hymn contained no reference to his resurrection. With various commentators we hold that the second phrase, "justified in the spirit," contains this reference. Nor does it mean that Christ was raised in a spiritual body (in contrast to his previous flesh-body), as F. D. Gealy (IB) suggests. "Flesh" in this connection probably means the sphere of *human weakness* in which Jesus lived on earth, while the "spirit" refers to the sphere of his *resurrection-life* as *full of the Spirit's* power,[29] a resurrection-life which meant Christ's vindication as the Son of God (cf. Rom.

---

[27] E.g., C. Bouma (KNT), F. D. Gealy (IB), D. Guthrie (TNT), W. Hendriksen (NTC), W. Lock (ICC), and E. K. Simpson.
[28] Cf. G. Delling, TWNT, IV, 8.
[29] Cf. the interpretation of I Pet. 3:18 in Chapter 3 of this study.

1:4).[30]   But that the resurrection is referred to, as Gealy and others claim, can hardly be doubted.

If this interpretation is correct, the ascension and resurrection are indeed mentioned here as markedly distinguished events.

Our study of the Pauline epistles leads to the conclusion that the ascension is mentioned more than once by the Apostle.   The paucity of these references is not surprising.   Paul's writings are not historical books.   They describe the exalted Lord in the work he is doing in heaven for the benefit of his body, the Church, rather than the event which brought him into heaven.   The only historical record in Paul's letters (I Cor. 15:3ff.) deals wholly with the resurrection and hence one should not expect a reference to the ascension there.

Thus Paul's letters do not prove either that the ascension was identical with the resurrection or that it took place in a way other than that described by the later gospel tradition.   No scriptural ground can be adduced for these claims.

3. RESURRECTION AND ASCENSION IN THE GOSPELS

The Gospel according to Matthew provides no record of the ascension.   It ends with the appearance of the risen Jesus to his disciples on a mountain in Galilee.   When the question is asked why we are not told of Jesus' ascension, the answer has to be found in the character of this Gospel.   It is generally recognized that Matthew wrote particularly for the Jews, proclaiming Jesus as the promised great Son of David, the Messiah-King of Israel in whom the Kingdom of God has come.[31]   The genealogy at the beginning of the Gospel gives proof of this, and so does the fact that in 1:20 Joseph is addressed as "son of David," whereas in 2:2 we see the Child of Bethlehem honored and persecuted as "the King of the Jews."   Quite in line with this beginning and with the whole Gospel, in which the conception of the Kingdom of God is so prominent, is the ending (28:18ff.).   Here the risen Jesus declares that all authority in heaven and on earth is given unto him, and he charges his disciples to conquer the whole world for him, the King of heaven and earth.   In recording this, Matthew can be said to have reached the end of what he wanted to say.

---

30 So, e.g., C. Bouma, W. Hendriksen, E. K. Simpson, et al.
31 Cf. Feine-Behm, Einleitung in das Neue Testament, pp. 51ff.; S. Greydanus, Bijzondere Canoniek, I, 84ff.; H. N. Ridderbos, Het Verborgen Koninkrijk, pp. 14ff.; et al.

He could leave it to others to write about the new stage of the Kingdom, which started with the ascension.[32]

As regards Mark's Gospel, if the verses 9-20 of the last chapter are not from the pen of Mark (which problem cannot be further discussed here), then we have to do with an unfinished gospel. For though some modern scholars believe that the Gospel originally ended at 16:9 with the words "for they were afraid," the majority of those who consider the longer ending spurious will agree with B. H. Bramscomb (MNTC) that it is "certain that the Gospel did not end or was not intended to end with verse 8." R. A. Cole (TNT) is right when he remarks: "To end the Gospel with verse 8 is not only abrupt linguistically, but abrupt theologically."[33]

For this reason it is wrong to conclude that the oldest gospel tradition, which usually is regarded to be Mark's, has no reference to the ascension. One cannot solve one problem by appealing to another, in this case to the problem of how the authentic ending (if there ever was one) could be lost, or what might have caused Mark to break off his Gospel in what many regard to be the middle of a sentence.

If, on the other hand, Mark 16:9-20 is the authentic Markan ending, as some still believe to be the case,[34] then verse 19 records the ascension as a distinct event, in complete agreement with the account of Luke in his Gospel and in Acts.

In the Gospel of Luke we find a clear statement about the ascension in 24:51: "And it came to pass, while he blessed them, he parted from them, and was carried up into heaven." The authenticity of the last clause is controversial. It occurs in some important codices (e.g., Codex Vaticanus) but is lacking in others that are also of great significance (e.g., Codex Sinaiticus). Consequently some editions of the Greek New Testament, some English and other versions, and some New Testament scholars consider the words authentic and retain them, whereas others omit the clause.

---

[32] Cf. C. Stam, *op. cit.,* pp. 11ff.

[33] The textual evidence for the so-called "short ending" is so insignificant that it cannot possibly represent the authentic ending.

[34] So, e.g., R. C. H. Lenski; J. Keulers, *De Evangelien Markus en Lukas,* who refers to the Bible Committee of his Church (the Roman Catholic Church) which decided that "the evidences are not sufficient to prove that the ending cannot have been written by Mark"; J. A. C. Van Leeuwen (KNT), who at least deems the authenticity of the longer ending possible; *et al.*

So much seems certain, however, that even apart from these ending words of verse 51 the reference is evidently to the ascension. B. Weiss denies this, claiming that if the last clause of the verse is spurious there is no ground to think here of the ascension. In that case, he writes, Luke records an incidental farewell of Jesus, like that of verse 31. But this interpretation is unacceptable. Verse 31 says simply that Jesus vanished out of the sight of the men of Emmaus. In 50ff., however, we have a complete description of a definite farewell. It is all very solemn and unique. There is not only a farewell blessing from Jesus, but while Jesus is parting from his disciples he holds up his hands to bless them. Then the disciples, left alone, return to Jerusalem "with great joy," a qualification inexplicable if it had followed an ordinary farewell. Similarly, the end of verse 53, stating that they were continually in the temple blessing God, speaks clearly of a final departure and farewell. There are, indeed, "no reasonable grounds for doubting that this is the story of the Ascension that Luke elaborates in Acts 1:6-11" (S. M. Gilmour, IB).

We now raise a further question of greatest importance: Does Luke place the ascension on the same day as the resurrection?

According to W. Barclay, "on any natural reading of the whole chapter it seems to place the Ascension on the same day as the Resurrection."[35] This interpretation, however, is unacceptable for the following reasons:

1. It creates a contradiction between what Luke writes in his Gospel and what he declares in Acts 1:3, where he speaks of forty days elapsing between resurrection and ascension. Apart from the inspiration of Scripture, which excludes such a contradiction, the latter is unthinkable in view of Luke's recognized abilities as an author.

2. At first sight the words recorded in verses 44-49 seem to have been spoken by Jesus immediately after the preceding words, on the evening of the resurrection day, when Jesus came in the midst of his disciples for the first time. Th. Zahn remarks rightly, however, that Luke more than once begins a sentence with "And he said. . . ," as he does in verse 44, where the context makes it clear that there is no chronological connection with what precedes.[36] B. Weiss points out, further, that Luke more

---

[35] *Crucified and Crowned*, p. 171. Similarly S. M. Gilmour (IB), *et al.*

[36] Cf. his *Commentary, ad loc.*, n. 77, where reference is made to Luke 6:39; 9:23, 59, 61; 13:6; 18:1. Similarly A. Plummer, *et al.*

than once connects his accounts of certain events with "and" (Greek *de*) where there is no direct chronological sequence.[37]

So far as Luke's style is concerned, then, the events recorded in Luke 24:44ff. could have taken place on another day than that of the resurrection.

3. The events mentioned in Luke 24 could hardly have happened on the same day. It was nearly evening when Jesus entered the house in Emmaus (v. 29). After his stay in this house the men of Emmaus made the journey to Jerusalem. There they met with the disciples before Jesus stood in their midst. The appearance of Jesus, with all that happened in connection with it (vv. 36-43), must have taken considerable time. If after all this the walk from Jerusalem was made to the place "over against Bethany," the ascension must have been a hurried midnight affair. But Luke's account in verses 50-51, however brief, points in a quite different direction.

4. Greydanus (KNT) points to the fact that in verse 13 ("that very day") and in verse 33 ("that very hour") there is a clear chronological indication. To these two passages a third may be added, viz. verse 36, which begins: "And as they spake these things." Obviously in chapter 24 Luke takes some care to designate which events happened on the resurrection day. The fact that the beginning of verse 44 contains no such indication makes it very likely that what follows took place on another day.

5. The preceding arguments also hold for verses 50ff. Here the passage starts with "And he led them out. . . ," which may refer to quite another day from that on which the words of verses 44-49 were spoken.

For all these reasons there can be no doubt that Luke speaks of the ascension at the end of his Gospel and that his words give no ground for the assumption that he places the ascension on the same day as the resurrection.

In the Gospel according to John there is no special record of the ascension. Undoubtedly, however, the Evangelist knew about the ascension, and in his characteristic way he even throws light upon it in the many passages where he records Jesus' sayings concerning his return to heaven, whence he had come.[38]

Space does not permit us to discuss the various exegetical prob-

---

[37] Weiss refers to 20:27, 41, 45; 21:1.
[38] E.g., John 6:62; 7:33; 8:14, 21; 12:32; 13:1-2; 14:2, 3, 12, 28; 16:5, 7, 10; 17:5, 11; 20:17.

lems connected with most of these passages.[39]   An exception must
be made for John 20:17, where Jesus is recorded as saying to
Mary: "Touch me not; for I am not yet ascended unto the Father;
but go unto my brethren, and say to them, I ascend unto my
Father and your Father, and my God and your God."

The first half of this verse has been discussed in the preceding
chapter. Now the second half requires consideration.

The fact that Jesus says to Mary "I ascend unto my Father,"
using the present tense, has sometimes been interpreted as meaning: at this moment I am going to heaven. The ascension took
place, it is claimed, on the day of the resurrection, between the
appearance to Mary and that to the disciples on the evening of the
resurrection day.[40]   All the other appearances must then have
taken place from heaven, to which Jesus returned after every appearance.[41]

This, however, is unacceptable. It is obviously in conflict with
the record of the ascension in Acts 1, which leaves no room for a
plurality of ascensions but speaks of it as one unique event. We
have seen that Luke 24:50-53 presents the same view.

The theory under discussion stretches the meaning of the present
anabaino, "I am ascending," too far. The present is sometimes
used in Greek to denote what is about to take place after a short-
er or longer period.[42]   C. K. Barrett (Comm.) points to I Corinthians 15:32, "let us eat and drink, for tomorrow we die,"
where "we die" is in the present but denotes a future event.
No less striking is Revelation 1:7, where it is stated that Christ
"cometh [present tense] with the clouds," which doubtlessly has
future meaning since the text continues, "and every eye shall see
[future tense] him."

Therefore with Barrett and others we would translate Jesus'
word to Mary as follows: "I am about to ascend. . . ."

That the present is used instead of the future is certainly not

[39] A very able discussion of these passages may be found in C. Stam's dissertation, *op. cit.,* pp. 24-36.

[40] So, e.g., G. H. C. Macgregor (MNTC) and W. F. Howard (IB). Many
others in favor of this interpretation are mentioned in the article on this
subject by F. F. Bruce, C. A. Phillips, and W. G. Essame in ExT, July
1939, pp. 478ff. Cf. also C. Stam, *op. cit.,* pp. 100ff.

[41] An interesting discussion on the question where Jesus stayed during the
great forty days took place between W. Tom and C. J. Goslinga, *Gereformeerd Theologisch Tijdschrift,* 1938, pp. 404ff.; 1939, pp. 303-06; 519ff.

[42] Cf. F. Blass, A. Debrunner, *Grammatik des neutestamentlichen Griechisch,* pp. 144ff.

without significance, especially in the context of John 20:17. It means that the forty days are a period in which Christ is preparing for the ascension. As the risen and glorified Jesus he belongs in heaven, on the throne. That is why Mary must not try to retain him as if he were going to stay on earth.

We may conclude then that the Gospel of John speaks several times of the ascension and that there is no ground to assume that, according to John, resurrection and ascension were identical or took place on the same day.

4. THE ASCENSION IN ACTS

In Acts we find an extensive and unequivocal record of the ascension in 1:6-11. As this is generally recognized, the following remarks may suffice:

1. There is no ground for doubting the accuracy of the phrase "forty days," as W. Barclay and others suggest.[43] The appeal to heretical writings by Valentinians and Ophites who spoke of a period of eighteen months and even eleven or twelve years instead of forty days is quite unconvincing. The tradition of the Church was certainly safer in the hands of the historian Luke and the Christian community than in those of Gnostic sects.

2. The modern mind is apt to revolt against the "materialistic" description of the ascension, as the theories of scholars like those mentioned in footnote 43 show. Macgregor understands the cloud that intercepted Jesus before the eyes of the disciples metaphorically, and places the word "ascension" in quotation marks. The ascension, according to him and other scholars, was merely a "vanishing from sight," as it happened at the end of the appearance to the men of Emmaus. Karl Barth even more or less ridicules a literal ascension: "like going up in a balloon . . . embarking upon a wonderful journey into space" (CD, III/2, 453).

But here, again, the trustworthiness of Scripture is at stake. There is simply no evidence, textual or otherwise, to prove the modern theory that a later, materialistic embellishment altered the original tradition. This theory gratuitously impugns the veracity either of Luke or the Christian community, solely because the modern mind cannot make sense of the events as Scripture describes them. The "spiritualized" version of Jesus' appearances and disappearances is presumably more intelligible.

---

[43] W. Barclay, *op. cit.,* p. 174; K. Barth, CD, III/2, 452ff.; G. H. C. Macgregor (IB); E. Schweizer, *Lordship and Discipleship*, p. 38; *et al.*

3. Related to all this is the question whether heaven is to be regarded as a place.   Many would deny this on the ground that we can no longer accept the three-storied universe in which, according to them, the apostles believed.[44]   They regard heaven not as a local place but "a state of blessedness . . . with God."[45]

Such a contrast, however, cannot be accepted.   Admittedly, the three-storied universe can gladly be abandoned, together with the rabbinical conceptions of three or more heavens, higher and higher up in the skies.   Though the apostles, as children of their age, may personally have cherished certain popular ideas of this kind, in their inspired writings they do not intend to teach astronomy or any scientific world-view.   They proclaim God's mighty acts of salvation in Jesus Christ.   Nowhere in Scripture is there a biblical scientific world-view which claims acceptance in faith, and "all counting of heavens we can leave to the rabbis."[46]

This, however, does by no means imply that heaven is no place at all.   If Jesus disappeared from the earth at the ascension, he must have gone somewhere, unless his disappearance meant his total annihilation (which is absurd) or the complete and absolute deification of his human nature.   The latter idea is flatly against Scripture, which speaks of the glorified Christ as the *man* Christ Jesus (e.g., Acts 13:38; 17:31, I Tim. 2:5).   Even if the ascension meant a complete spiritualization of Jesus' human nature (for which there is no ground in Scripture, as we shall see), as a spirit he should be *somewhere*.   Only God is beyond space in the absolute sense of the word, as far as his Being is concerned, though he is immanent in all creation: nobody can ever escape his presence (Ps. 139:7ff.; Acts 17:28).

Creatures, however, cannot exist but in space and time.[47]   Even spirits, who have no physical body that can be measured, cannot be omnipresent.   As creatures they must necessarily be somewhere in space, though they do not occupy a measurable part of space.   According to Scripture their usual dwelling place is heaven, which is part of God's creation (Gen. 1:1).   There they worship God, whose throne is in heaven and who, from there, rules the universe

---

[44] So, e.g., W. Barclay, *op. cit.*, p. 175, and A. M. Ramsey, *op. cit.*, p. 123.
[45] W. Barclay, *The Acts of the Apostles* (DSB). See also J. G. Davies, *He Ascended into Heaven*, pp. 56ff.
[46] K. Schilder, *Wat is de Hemel?*, p. 110.
[47] A. Kuyper, *op. cit.*, pp. 202ff.; cf. K. Schilder, *op. cit.*, pp. 100ff.; see also K. Barth, CD, II/2, 521: "Time was created simultaneously with the universe as its form of existence."

and blesses his people (e.g., Ps. 103:19-21; Isa. 6:1ff.; Heb. 8:1; 12:2; Rev. 4:2ff.).

The fact that terms like "God's throne," "God's right hand," and the like are anthropomorphic and figurative does not in the least justify the denial of heaven as a place, where the angels are, where Enoch and Elijah went, where Jesus Christ is, and "the spirits of just men made perfect" (Heb. 12:23). Though God's throne is not a material phenomenon, it is certainly to be understood as the created, glorious center of God's dominion. And when Christ is said to sit at the right hand of God we must think of that same localized center of God's dominion.[48]

Since heaven, in the theological sense of the word, is outside the earth, and nobody here below is able to locate it, it must necessarily be *above* the earth. If Jesus, as the Book of Acts tells us clearly, left the earth and went to heaven before the eyes of the disciples, then he could do so only by going up. Not only is there nothing laughable in the ascension story of Acts, but it describes faithfully what could not have happened in a different way.

There are two other passages in Acts which prove that the ascension as a separate event was part of the earliest tradition of the Church. According to Acts 2:24ff., Peter, on the day of Pentecost, spoke first of Jesus' resurrection (vv. 24-32) and then of his ascension (vv. 33-36). Verse 32, "This Jesus did God raise up, whereof we all are witnesses," is apparently the conclusion of the argumentation in verses 24-31, where it is shown that David's prophetic utterances in Psalm 16 were fulfilled in Jesus: David's flesh saw corruption, that of Jesus did not; David's tomb is still there, with David himself among the dead; Jesus' tomb is empty, for God raised him from the dead as the apostles can witness who met him after the resurrection.

Verse 33, which reads, "Being therefore by the right hand of God exalted, and having received of the Father the promise of the Holy Spirit, he hath poured forth this, which ye see and hear," is not a conclusion from what precedes but the opening sentence of what follows, beginning with "For David ascended not into the heavens. . . ." Obviously now the ascension of Jesus comes under discussion, and the argument which follows, making an appeal to Psalm 110, "is similar to that in Ps. 16 . . . the words cannot apply to David, they must apply to the Messiah;

---

48 H. Traub speaks of "the in-a-way localized dominion of God" (TWNT, V, 523). On the question whether heaven is a place, see also A. Kuyper, *op. cit.,* pp. 477ff., and K. Schilder, *op. cit.,* pp. 98ff.

Jesus did in fact ascend into heaven, and so satisfied the terms of Scripture" (F. F. Bruce).

There is, finally, Acts 3:21, where Peter says that "the heaven must receive (Jesus) until the times of restoration of all things." Whatever exegetical problems may be involved here, there can be no doubt that the reference is to Jesus' ascension into heaven, where according to God's plan he must remain for a certain period until the prophetic Scriptures are fulfilled.

In the Book of the Acts, indeed, Jesus' resurrection and ascension are presented as two different events, the latter taking place forty days after the former and having its own theological significance.

5. The Ascension and the Alleged Change in the Substance of Jesus' Body

We must now ask whether Jesus' body underwent a substantial change at the ascension, so that it ceased to be a glorified body of flesh.[49]

The first important passage to be discussed in this connection is Acts 1:10-11: "And while they were looking stedfastly into heaven as he went, behold two men stood by them in white apparel; who also said, Ye men of Galilee, why stand ye looking into heaven? this Jesus, who was received up from you into heaven, shall so come in like manner as ye beheld him going into heaven."

Ignoring exegetical details which are irrelevant to our subject, we may make the following remarks.

1. The message of the angels leaves no doubt that Jesus is in heaven, that he will return from there, that he will be the identical Jesus, in his resurrection-body of flesh (*this* Jesus), and also that he will return in the same manner as he went, i.e. visibly, with the clouds of heaven.

T. P. Ferris (IB) claims that this statement, which Acts ascribes to angels, originates from the mistaken belief of the early Christians that Jesus would return just as he went. According to this scholar, and many others, the early Christians did not know that Jesus will return only in a spiritual way throughout history, but never as

---

[49] To the references made earlier in this chapter may be added J. G. Davies, *op. cit.*, who pictures the resurrection and ascension as two parts of a single process of glorification by which Christ's body became "a heavenly body of shining ethereal substance, which was revealed . . . to Paul" (p. 59).

promised in Acts.   As we said before, this critique of the biblical record has no foundation whatsoever.

2. E. M. Blaiklock (TNT) suggests that the angels did not mean that the Lord would literally emerge downward from "a cloud." Rather, they meant that he would once more break into this world from the other, out of eternity into time and history. But there is no more reason to accept this judgment than to suppose that Jesus did not literally ascend upward, or that there was no real cloud.

Admittedly, many unanswerable questions can be raised about the manner of Christ's second coming.   It is not possible to form any adequate conception of it, especially in the light of the fact that according to Scripture the second coming will concern all inhabitants of the earth.   It will be the greatest act of divine revelation and manifestation that ever took place.

But we do injustice to Scripture if for these reasons we deny the reality of what is clearly stated.   According to Daniel 7:13 the Son of Man will come with the clouds of heaven, and Jesus himself applied this prophecy to his second coming (Matt. 24:30; 26:64; Mark 13:26; Luke 21:27).   Moreover, throughout the history of revelation and salvation we see clouds appearing as signs of God's coming and presence.[50]   Why then rule them out in connection with the final and decisive act of divine revelation and salvation in the second coming of Christ which, also according to Revelation 1:7, will be a coming "with the clouds"?

There is, indeed, no reason to doubt the message of the angels that this Jesus will return "in like manner" as the disciples saw him go to heaven.[51]

The identity of the pre-ascension Jesus of flesh and blood with the Jesus in heaven who is to come appears also from other Scripture passages.   Some of these which refer to the glorified Jesus as the one who has come (and still is) *in the flesh* (I John 4:2; II John 7) have already been discussed in another connection.

Here we may point particularly to a passage in the Book of Revelation, *viz.*, 5:6, where John writes that in heaven he saw "a Lamb standing, as though it had been slain."

There can be no doubt that the Lamb is Jesus Christ, for the

---

[50] E.g., Exod. 19:16ff.; 24:15ff.; Num. 11:25; I Kings 8:11; Matt. 17:5; Mark 9:7; Luke 9:34.

[51] For the visible return of Jesus in his resurrection-body see also K. Barth, CD, III/2, pp. 448, 452-54, 502, 508ff.

word "lamb" is used twenty-nine times in the Apocalypse, "as a designation of the crucified Messiah" (R. H. Charles, ICC).

That the Lamb is standing and has seven horns and seven eyes (v. 7), occupying a central place in heaven is generally recognized as a symbol of the power and glory given to Christ as the reward for his sacrifice on the cross.

Remarkable, however, is the fact that the Lamb stands "as though it had been slain." The word *hos* (as though) indicates that at this moment the Lamb is not dead but alive. It connects the two characteristics of the heavenly Christ: he is (on the one hand) the Lamb that has come to glory and power, and still (on the other hand) he bears visible signs of his sacrificial death. He stands there "as one slain." In the Greek text the perfect participle *esphagmenon* is used, indicating that the Lamb is "still retaining the appearance of the death wounds on its body."[52]

Though all this is seen in a vision, we are not to think here only of invisible, spiritual realities. Particularly in the light of John's record of the risen Christ, showing his disciples the scars of the death-wounds in his resurrection-body (John 20:20, 27), we may see in the vision of Revelation 5:6 an indication that our Lord still has the same body in heaven. So he appears there before the Father, praying for his Church as one who bears the marks of his all-sufficient sacrifice in his glorified body, and whose intercession is therefore effective (Rom. 8:34). So do the saints in heaven see him, bearing in his glorified body the marks of his love for them, a love unto death; and seeing him so they adore him with the new song, recorded in this same vision: "Worthy art thou to take the book, and to open the seals thereof: *for thou wast slain*" (Rev. 5:9), and again: "Worthy is the Lamb *that hath been slain* to receive the power. . . ." (5:12).

In addition to the passages discussed, there is another reason for believing that Jesus' body did not undergo a change of substance after the ascension. The theological place of the ascension in the New Testament also points in this direction, and that place is *subordinate* to the resurrection. In the New Testament it is the resurrection which is the decisive event in the history of salvation. This is seen in Peter's preaching on the day of Pentecost (Acts 2:22ff.), in that of Paul in Antioch (Acts 13:29ff.) and in Athens (Acts 17:30ff.), as well as in that of all the apostles (Acts 4:33). The resurrection of Jesus with its implications is given the main emphasis.

[52] R. H. Charles (ICC); similarly H. Alford, S. Greydanus (KNT), *et al.*

The resurrection provides the glorious evidence that Jesus is the Son of God (Rom. 1:4); it means the abolishment of death and the victory of life and incorruption (I Tim. 1:10); it is the basis of the Christian faith and hope (I Cor. 15:14ff., I Pet. 1:3) and the guarantee of our future resurrection in glory (Rom. 8:11; I Cor. 15:20, 49; I Thess. 4:14).

This being the case, it is not in the least surprising that the Gospels say much more about the resurrection and the appearances of the risen Lord than about his ascension.

Hence it is theologically unwarranted to make the ascension virtually the great turning point in Jesus' ministry, instead of the resurrection. This is done when the ascension is said to inaugurate a complete change in Jesus' existence, from being the *incarnate Word,* the Word-become-*flesh,* into a person without any flesh at all, a person who is either a mere spirit or one possessing a body of some different, spiritualized matter.

In the earliest preaching of the apostles, Paul included, we hear the declaration that Jesus' flesh did not see corruption (while David's flesh did) but was raised up, never to see corruption any more (Acts 2:30-32; 13:34ff.). So the Scriptures had been fulfilled. But what could be the value of such triumphant declarations if this incorruptible flesh of Jesus was eliminated after forty days, to make place for something quite different?

According to I Corinthians 15:54 God's purpose with the believers will be accomplished when "this corruptible shall have put on incorruption, and this mortal shall have put on immortality." Jesus' *resurrection* brought him this incorruptibility and immortality. What else can we conclude but that in Jesus as the last Adam (Man!) and "the firstfruit of them that are asleep" (I Cor. 15:20, 45), God's purpose with man has been accomplished in principle, and that in the *flesh*?

There can be no doubt, then, that Jesus' glorious resurrection-body of the great forty days is definitely the body which he has in heaven and in which he is to return in glory.

The ascension certainly brought about important changes for Jesus and for his Church. It removed him from this hostile earth where sin and death have their sway, to heaven where all adore him as the conqueror of sin and death (Rev. 5:8ff.). It meant his enthronement at the right hand of the Father, to exercise all authority in heaven and on earth, an authority given to him as the reward for his sacrifice on the cross (Matt. 28:18; Acts 2:34-36;

Rev. 5:12). It enabled him to do his high-priestly work in behalf of his Church in the heavenly sanctuary (Rom. 8:34; Heb. 7:24, 25; 9:11, 24-26). It placed at his disposal the Spirit with all his comforting, sanctifying, enlightening powers and gifts, the Spirit through whom he as the Head has communion with the Church as his body, making her God's temple (John 14:16; 16:7; Acts 2:33; I Cor. 12, etc.).

But all these and other changes which the ascension brought about have nothing to do with a change in Jesus' resurrection-body. It is in his risen, incorruptible, and immortal body of flesh that Jesus Christ in heaven exercises his all-embracing authority and performs his heavenly ministry as the exalted King, Priest and Prophet of the Church.

Undoubtedly, his exalted position in heaven implies the possibility that he can display supernatural glories and appear in a splendor of light. So he appeared to Paul on the Damascus road (Acts 9:3), and so he will come at the end of the ages (Mark 8:38; 13:26; Matt. 24:30). But this gives us no right to regard the body of our risen and exalted Lord as being changed into a body consisting of some light-substance or glory. Much less does the manner in which he revealed himself to John in a vision (Rev. 1:13ff.) give any ground for such a conclusion.

How unwarranted such conclusions are appears clearly from Jesus' transfiguration on the mountain (Matt. 17:1ff.; Mark 9:2ff.; Luke 9:28ff.).

R. Bultmann, with the old liberal school, regards this event as an unhistorical, misplaced resurrection story.[53] This interpretation cannot be accepted. It denies without solid evidence the trustworthiness of a historical record found in all the Synoptic gospels and later confirmed by one of the eyewitnesses, Peter (II Pet. 1:17).[54] C. H. Dodd, moreover, has shown that even on form-critical grounds the record of the transfiguration cannot possibly be regarded as a misplaced resurrection story.[55]

We take the transfiguration of our Lord as a historical event and with most commentators we consider it to be of an eschatolo-

---

[53] ThNT, I, 26ff. For other more or less similar interpretations see the brief survey by S. E. Johnson, IB, VII, 458.

[54] Further reasons why the historical character of this account cannot be doubted are given by A. Plummer, *An Exegetical Commentary on the Gospel according to St. Matthew, ad. loc.*

[55] In D. E. Nineham, *Studies in the Gospels*, p. 25.

gical nature.   In it the three intimate disciples of Jesus were given "a glimpse of the future glory of the Messiah, whom they had confessed."[56]

We need not enter upon a discussion of the many interesting and important exegetical problems involved.   What concerns us here is whether Jesus ceased to have a body of flesh during the transfiguration.

Some answer in the affirmative.   S. E. Johnson, for example, compares Jesus' metamorphosis to the shining of Moses' face (Exod. 34:29-35) as described by Philo (*Moses,* II, 51, 288). God had changed Moses' body "into a mind-substance like the radiance of the sun" (IB, VII, 459).

The text, however, gives no ground for such interpretations.   It declares that Jesus' *appearance* changed, and that this happened "before them": Jesus' outward appearance as the disciples saw it was now different from his normal appearance.   We are also told what the change consisted in, for the *kai* that follows after *metemorphothe* is certainly explanatory: the change consisted in the two elements mentioned in Matthew 17:3 and Luke 9:29, namely that Jesus' face shone like the sun and his garments became glistering.[57]

We cannot agree with A. Richardson when he says that "the reflection of the divine glory with which the face of Adam (man) was once radiant, God's *eikon* (Gen. 1:26ff.), is now visible again in Christ" (*op. cit.,* pp. 66-67).   According to I Corinthians 15: 45ff., the last Adam possesses and grants a glory which was not yet attained by the first.   But the implication of Richardson's statement that in the transfiguration Jesus (like Adam) was still a man of flesh and blood is certainly correct.

Calvin rightly speaks of the transfiguration as taking place under *symbols* of Christ's heavenly glory, which gave the disciples a *taste* of that glory (cf. A. Richardson: "a glimpse").

Seen in this light, what happened on the mountain in that great hour contains a warning *not* to conclude that Jesus' body has ceased to be a body of flesh when the New Testament speaks of bright glory for the exalted Lord.   At the transfiguration, heavenly glory shone in and through and from Christ's body of *flesh,* and even in, through, and from the *garments* in which it was clothed.

---

[56] A. Richardson, *An Introduction to the Theology of the New Testament,* p. 183.

[57] So F. W. Grosheide (KNT) and Th. Zahn (ZK), both on Matt. 17:2.

6. PAUL'S TEACHING ON THE BODY OF THE EXALTED CHRIST

We turn now to the question: Is Paul's Christ, the exalted Lord, a spiritualized Christ who (unlike the risen Christ of the Gospels and Acts) has no body of flesh?

Some claim, as we saw before, that this question must be answered in the affirmative.

Before discussing the statements in Paul's writings to which these scholars appeal, we may make the following general remark.

On the standpoint of faith in Scripture as the inspired Word of God, the claim that Paul's Christ differs essentially from the Jesus of the Gospels and the Acts cannot possibly be considered valid. It is incompatible with that unity of the New Testament which results from a single inspiring Spirit. The Spirit whom Jesus promised to the apostles to guide them into all the truth (John 15:26; 16:13) is the same Spirit who filled Paul and inspired him when writing (Acts 9:17; I Cor. 7:40). The Spirit does not contradict himself.

Rather than entering into a general discussion of Paul's Christology,[58] we will confine ourselves to the most important passages that play a part in the controversy.

1. In II Corinthians 3:17 Paul declares: "Now the Lord is the Spirit. . . ." According to many scholars Paul declares here that Christ and the Spirit are completely identical. Paul's Christ is a Spirit-Christ, mystical and pneumatic.[59]

Careful exegesis of the text shows, however, that this is a misrepresentation of Paul's meaning.

There is, to begin with, the fact that "Spirit" has the article. If it were anarthrous the emphasis would be on spirit as a quality, and Paul would declare that the Lord is (a) spirit, with all the emphasis on the last word. As the statement reads now the emphasis is not on "Spirit" but on "Lord": the *kyrios* is the Spirit. In other words, Paul does not give here a description of our exalted Lord's ontological nature and essence, saying that it is spiritual not physical. The question whether Christ in heaven has a

---

58 Of the many recent works that deal with this subject we mention only a very few: J. Gresham Machen, *The Origin of Paul's Religion;* H. N. Ridderbos, *Paul and Jesus;* and G. Sevenster, *De Christologie van het Nieuwe Testament,* Ch. 3.

59 Thus, e.g., W. Bousset, *Kyrios Christos;* A. Deissmann, *op. cit.,* p. 138; H. J. Heering, *op. cit.,* pp. 120, 217; J. Knox, *Christ the Lord,* p. 66; and Paul Tillich, *op. cit.,* II, 157.

body, and if so what kind of body, does not enter the picture at all.

This appears also from the context. In this chapter Paul is discussing how as an apostle of Jesus Christ he has been entrusted with the ministry of the new covenant (v. 6). The old covenant had Moses as the mediator and was characterized by the killing letter of the law, while the new covenant is that of the Spirit, who gives life (vv. 3, 6). The Jews do not understand the law (the revelation of the Old Testament) because they lack spiritual insight as a result of the hardening of their mind. The veil of unbelief and disobedience makes it impossible for them to see God's revelation in the right light (vv. 14, 15). Everything becomes clear, however, when a man turns to the Lord (v. 16), i.e., to Christ (v. 14). "In Christ," i.e., where there is true fellowship with Christ in faith, the veil is taken away (vv. 14, 16): Christ grants the right understanding of the Old Testament.

When Paul has come to this point he continues: "Now the Lord is the Spirit." In the light of the preceding context this statement can only mean that the Lord Jesus Christ and he alone (*kyrios* is emphatic, as we saw) gives the true, spiritual, and life-giving understanding of God's revelation in the Old Testament. He, being himself full of the Spirit, works this understanding through the Spirit in those that are his.[60]

It is certainly significant that Paul expresses this truth by declaring that the Lord *is* the Spirit. This makes it clear that Christ and the Spirit cannot be separated. He possesses the Spirit in his fullness and has all the gifts of the Spirit at his disposal.[61] Only in fellowship with him can the blessings of the Spirit be experienced. In the "experience of the Christian life the work of the Spirit and the work of the risen Lord are one and the same" (W. Barclay, DSB).

This, however, does not in the least imply that they are identical. F. V. Filson rightly calls this "an unreasonable assertion."[62] Not

---

[60] N. H. Waaning, *Onderzoek naar het Gebruik van Pneuma by Paulus* (Diss. Free University), pp. 29ff. Similarly many commentators.

[61] Cf. H. D. Wendland (NTD), *ad loc.* W. C. Van Unnik in his article "Jesus the Christ" (NTS, Jan. 1962) points out that the name *Christos,* which Paul uses three times in II Cor. 3, denotes Jesus as the Anointed One, who is possessed by the Spirit.

[62] F. V. Filson, *op. cit.,* p. 73. Cf. also the same author in IB, *ad loc.,* and H. N. Ridderbos, *Paul and Jesus,* pp. 86-87.

only does Paul time and again distinguish between Christ and the Spirit (e.g., in Rom. 15:18; II Cor. 3:3; 13:14), but in the very verse under consideration he shows that they are not identical by continuing: "and where the Spirit of the Lord is, there is liberty" (i.e., freedom from sin and condemnation, which the Mosaic law could not provide).

Many problems involved in this verse, as for example whether or not the Spirit must be understood as a mere spiritual power exercised by Christ,[63] cannot be discussed here. For our purpose it is sufficient to know that in II Corinthians 3:17 Paul does not identify Christ and the Spirit, and that this verse does not provide the slightest evidence that to Paul Christ is a Spirit-Being without physical body.

2. Another statement by Paul that has been adduced as evidence of the apostle's conception of a spiritualized Christ is II Corinthians 5:16: "Wherefore we henceforth know no man after the flesh: even though we have known Christ after the flesh, yet we know him so no more." According to some the apostle declares here that the Christ as he knows him, the Christ who appeared to him on the Damascus road, is quite different from the historical Jesus. Since the resurrection there is only a Spirit-Christ, whose authority is more than the word of the historical Jesus. The latter is of no importance any more.[64]

New Testament scholars, however, are increasingly convinced that, against the background of Paul's writings in general, such a contrast between the historical Jesus and a pneumatic Pauline Christ cannot be reasonably inferred from II Corinthians 5:16. The Epistles are crowded with evidence that the apostle was profoundly interested in the words and works of the historical Jesus. Moreover, his concentration on the cross and on Christ crucified (I Cor. 2:2), despite the fact that such a Christ was a stumbling-block for the Jews and foolishness to the Greek (I Cor. 1:23), shows clearly how much the historical Jesus and the exalted Lord were one in Paul's preaching.[65]

[63] So, e.g., A. M. Hunter, op. cit., p. 39, and E. Schweizer, TWNT, IV, 416.

[64] Thus, e.g., H. J. Heering, op. cit., pp. 109-217. Cf. also W. Bousset, Die Schriften des neuen Testaments, II, 195, and many other scholars of the Religions-geschichtliche school.

[65] So H. Anderson, "The Historical Jesus," in Scottish Journal of Theology, June 1960.

In contemporary discussions Paul's statement in the verse under discussion is more often explained as expressing not a repudiation of this historical Jesus as such, but "of the historian's (or disciple's) reconstruction of the historical Jesus."[66]

Apart from various theological aspects of the alleged difference between the "historical Jesus" and the "Jesus of faith," which cannot be discussed here, it seems completely unwarranted thus to make Paul a partisan in our modern philosophical discussions, fighting with Bultmann and others against what J. M. Robinson calls "an abstraction," namely "the historical Jesus . . . who is . . . an earthly phenomenon among others, to be objectively discovered. . . ."[67]

We can agree with Bultmann (ThNT, I, 238) and many others that the expression "after the flesh" is best taken as modifying the verb "to know." As regards the meaning of the statement, which is very controversial, we would prefer to believe that Paul is here denouncing the unspiritual, sinful, and distorted view concerning Jesus Christ which is characteristic of the unconverted man. Such was Paul's own "fleshly" knowledge of Jesus before his conversion, when he regarded Christ as dangerous to the spiritual well-being of Israel. Now, i.e. after his conversion, when his eyes had been opened by the Spirit, he knows Jesus in a spiritual way, as he really is: the Lord and Redeemer.[68]

Even if one would prefer a different interpretation there can be no doubt, especially in the light of the context, that in this statement Paul is not contrasting an earthly Jesus of flesh and blood with a heavenly Spirit-Christ. The question whether the exalted Lord has a body, and if so what kind of body, is not under discussion here.

3. Philippians 3:21 is also often adduced as evidence for the theory that according to Paul our exalted Lord has no body of flesh. Paul declares here that Christ, when he returns from heaven, "shall fashion anew the body of our humiliation, that it may be conformed to the body of his glory. . . ." Several authors take the phrase "the body of his glory" as meaning "his body

[66] J. M. Robinson, *A New Quest of the Historical Jesus,* p. 87. Cf. also J. Reid (IB), *ad loc.,* and E. Schweizer, TWNT, I, 238.

[67] J. M. Robinson, *ibid.*

[68] Thus P. Bachmann (ZK); F. V. Filson (IB); A. E. J. Rawlinson, *The New Testament Doctrine of Christ,* p. 90; G. Sevenster, *op. cit.,* p. 197; *et al.*

that consists of glory." "Glory," they claim, stands for a kind
of matter that forms the substance of Christ's body in heaven.[69]

This exegesis, however, is untenable, as a careful reading of
the text shows. Paul contrasts our present body with that of our
exalted Lord. After both instances of "body" he adds a noun in
the genitive case, first the word "humiliation," then "glory."
The parallel in this verse implies that both genitives must have
the same nature. In the phrase "the body of our humiliation" the
genitive cannot possibly describe the substance of our present
body, but is obviously a genitive of quality: our present body is
characterized by "humiliation." This means: "it belongs to the
state of humiliation caused through sin" (R. P. Martin, TNT).
Perhaps Paul was also thinking of the sufferings for Christ's sake
that the Christian must endure in his body (J. H. Michael,
MNTC).

E. F. Scott's interpretation, that for Paul "man is essentially a
spiritual being, and his present condition as earthly creature,
clothed in a body of flesh, is alien to him" (IB), is incompatible
with Paul's high view of the body of flesh as we have discovered it
in his writings. Michael rightly rejects the KJV rendering "our vile
body" because it might lead one to suppose that Paul expresses a
Stoic contempt for the body. In the Greek text he writes, "there
is not the least suggestion" of such contempt.

Since, then, the genitive in the first half of Paul's statement
doubtless speaks of the condition of our present body, so must
the second genitive ("of his glory") be a genitive of quality stating
the glorious condition of our exalted Lord's body, irrespective of
its substance. The contrast in Paul's statement is not between
a body of flesh and a body of glory, but between a body in a
state of humiliation (whatever its substance may be) and a body
in glory (whatever its substance may be).

It is evident that Philippians 3:21 does not contradict what we
have found earlier, that Christ's heavenly, glorious body is a body
of glorified *flesh.*

Of great importance with regard to Paul's conception of the
body of our exalted Lord is his Adam-Christ parallel, found particularly in Romans 5:12ff. and 1 Corinthians 15:21ff.

Most of the aspects of the Adam-Christ relationship are not

---

[69] So H. W. Robinson, *The Christian Doctrine of Man,* p. 131. More
recently also R. Bultmann (ThNT, I, 192); O. Cullmann, *Immortality . . . ,*
pp. 46-47; A. M. Hunter, *Interpreting Paul's Gospel,* pp. 55; and E. F. Scott
(IB).

directly relevant to our subject and need not be discussed here. This applies to such subjects as the historicity of Adam as the first man, the father and representative of the human race; the legal and forensic element in the Adam-Christ relationship, including the doctrine of original sin as taught in Romans 5; Karl Barth's "Christo-monistic" interpretation of Romans 5:12-19 (in *Christ and Adam*); and other problems.

We are concerned with one special aspect of the Adam-Christ parallel, that of 1 Corinthians 15:45-48, where we find the two "Adams" contrasted as follows: the first Adam was a living soul, natural, of the earth and therefore earthy, while the last Adam, Christ, is a life-giving spirit, spiritual, of heaven and therefore heavenly.

Several scholars suggest that Paul's argumentation in this passage points to Philo's distinction between a heavenly and an earthly man. The background of this distinction is to be found in Platonic philosophy and Hellenistic Gnostic mythology with its figure of the *Urmensch*.[70]

If these scholars are right, Paul's exalted Lord appears in this passage as a Spirit-Being. Philo's heavenly man is essentially contrasted with man on earth, in the Platonic manner. He is a "miniature heaven . . . altogether without part or lot in corruptible and terrestrial substance."[71]

There are, however, such striking contrasts between Paul's conception of the heavenly second Adam and the heavenly man (or *Urmensch*) of Philo and the Gnosis, that there is more reason to believe that Paul is here *opposing* Philo's ideas than to assume that he is influenced by them. For Philo's heavenly man is not the second Adam, as is the case with Paul, but the first. The Adam of Genesis 1:27 and 2:7 is Philo's second Adam.

In Philo's conception the first or heavenly Adam is the divinely created Idea, of whom the Adam of clay is but a poor picture; in Paul's parallel the heavenly Adam follows after the earthly in time. In Philo's conception the spiritual (the Idea) is first and is followed by the natural; Paul says that the natural is first and then the spiritual (v. 46). There is no certainty that Paul *intended* to refute Philonic ideas, which may have influenced

---

[70] Thus, e.g., R. Bultmann, ThNT, I, 174; E. Käsemann, *op. cit.*, pp. 166ff.; G. Kittel, TWNT, I, 143; and E. Schweizer, *Lordship and Discipleship*, p. 46.

[71] E. Earle Ellis, *Paul's Use of the Old Testament*, p. 64. Cf. Philo, *Leg. Alleg.*, I, 12, 31; *Op. Mundi*, 46, 69, 82.

the Corinthian errorists, but it is certain that in fact he teaches the opposite of what Philo taught.[72]

As regards pagan, Gnostic myths which allegedly may have contributed to Paul's Christology, the latter stands in the greatest contrast to the ideas of any known Gnostic myth, as various scholars have shown.[73] Referring to their studies we may say with J. Moffatt (MNTC, *ad loc.*): "For Paul, Christ is not the primal Man of Iranian or Philonic speculation on the Cosmos. . . ." Though the apostle sometimes uses philosophical or religious terms common in his Hellenistic surroundings, this by no means implies that he was influenced by pagan philosophy or Gnostic myths. "A God-fearing Jew did not defile himself by contact with heathen cults."[74]

As to the positive teaching of I Corinthians 15:45-48, an elaborate and detailed exegesis of this controversial passage lies beyond the scope of this study.[75]

The following remarks may suffice.

1. In the first part of verse 45 Paul quotes Genesis 2:7 from the LXX, adding the words "first" and "Adam." We agree with those commentators who interpret this addition as indicating that Paul wants to speak not of man in general but of the historical Adam in Paradise.

2. This first Adam, according to Genesis 2:7, became "a living soul." This cannot be understood as meaning that in Adam's body there was a living soul (so Calvin; Lenski; and J. Short, IB). The text says that Adam *became* a living soul. The whole Adam, body and soul, by God's creating, life-giving power, became a living "soul."

3. The expression "a living soul" stands in contrast to "a life-giving Spirit," which characterizes Christ. This implies that the qualification "living" must emphasize the fact that Adam had

---

[72] C. T. Craig (IB); Ellis, *op. cit.,* pp. 64-65; H. D. Wendland (NTD); *et al.*

[73] See, e.g., Ellis, *op. cit.,* p. 65; A. Oepke, TWNT, II, 334; H. Traub, TWNT, II, 528ff., 537; and H. N. Ridderbos, *Paul and Jesus,* Ch. 5.

[74] Tresmontant, *op. cit.,* p. 21. Cf. E. Schweizer, TWNT, VI, p. 419: "Paul reasons actually in a Jewish way, though he uses Hellenistic terminology."

[75] Karl Barth's peculiar interpretation of this passage (in *Die Auferstehung der Toten*) cannot be discussed either. A critical review of Barth's standpoint may be found in G. J. Streeder's doctoral thesis, *Een Beoordeling van Barth's Exegese van 1 Corinthen 15,* Ch. 4. Streeder arrives at the conclusion that Barth's interpretation of our passage is "philosophical, not literary-exegetical. . . . He gives an 'ontology' of Adam and Christ. . ." (p. 98).

received life and actually lived, but did not possess life-creating power. He "just lived," constantly dependent on God's life-sustaining power.

4. As to the contrast "soul" and "spirit," G. J. Streeder holds that here "soul" has a more or less ethical connotation. It speaks of Adam as a *sarx*-being without God's Spirit and his workings, and in this Streeder sees why Adam's body became perishable (*op. cit.,* p. 94). We cannot agree here, because it is hard to see how this conception can avoid blaming God for Adam's sin and its consequences. *God created Adam as a living soul.* If Adam as a living soul was without the Spirit of God and his working, how could God blame Adam for not standing the test?

With Grosheide (CNT, KNT, NLC) and others we take "soul" in this verse in its ethically neutral connotation of "being."[76]

The contrast between "soul" and "spirit," characterizing respectively Adam and Christ, indicates that Adam, though not without the Spirit of God, had not yet reached the stage to which God wanted him to come and to which Christ brings those that are his: the stage of being filled to capacity, in body and soul, with the Spirit of God and consequently possessing eternal life in all its fullness and imperishable glory.

5. Since it is obvious that "soul" does not denote the substance of Adam's body, it follows that "Spirit" cannot possibly denote the substance of Christ's glorified body. As in 2 Corinthians 3:17, Christ is called a spirit because God, who during Jesus' earthly ministry already gave him the Holy Spirit "not by measure" (John 3:34), gave him the fullness of the Spirit when he raised him from the dead and made him sit in glory at his right hand (Acts 2:33). The exalted Lord is so full of the Spirit and so glorious through the Spirit, in body and soul, that he is called "Spirit" or "the Spirit."

As we saw in connection with 2 Corinthians 3:17, this statement in no way implies that the exalted Christ did not have a glorified body of flesh.

Moreover, the fact that Acts 2:33 declares that Jesus *received* the promised Spirit (i.e., the fullness of the Spirit's gifts and power) from the Father, confirms our finding that Christ did not change into a spirit at the ascension.

6. Though the "life-giving" work of Christ, as the Spirit-filled

[76] Cf. Gesenius-Buhl, *s.v. Nephesh;* Trench, *Synonyms,* p. 267f.; E. de Witt Burton, *Spirit, Soul, Flesh,* pp. 62-67; and G. Ch. Aalders on Gen. 2:7 (KV).

last Adam, includes spiritual regeneration, it is certainly contrary to the context to interpret the word solely in this way, as does J. Short (IB). With most commentators we may also see here, in particular, the power of Christ to raise the dead to new and glorious life, changing the "natural body" into a "spiritual body" in conformity with the body he possesses himself (John 5:21; 6:33ff.; Rom. 8:10, 11).[77]

7. Verse 46 states emphatically that the "natural" precedes the spiritual. The rendering "natural" for the Greek *psychikon* (KJV, ERV, *et al.*) may not be adequate, but it is preferable to "physical" as found in RSV, BV, *et al.* Grosheide rightly remarks: *"psychikos* is not *physikos"* (NLC, n. 39). The rendering "physical" in contrast to "spiritual" suggests a contrast between man's physical body and the Holy Spirit, which we found to be foreign to the teachings of Paul.

The word *psychikon* must be understood in the light of the preceding statement that Adam became a living soul (*psyche*). *Psychikon* therefore denotes Adam's life as he received it at creation and as it is reproduced by natural procreation and birth.

Bultmann (ThNT, I, 251) takes "natural" in the loaded sense of 1 Corinthians 2:14, denoting the "unspiritual man . . . who has no possibility whatever of perceiving God's will. . . . Adam must have been sinful by nature." This idea is completely unscriptural, as is shown in Genesis 1:27, 31.

It is certainly true that after the Fall being "natural" implies being "natural" in the loaded sense of the word, much the same as is the case with man being "flesh." But in the passage under consideration Paul is speaking of the first Adam before the Fall, in contrast to Christ as the last Adam.

Therefore *psychikon* in verse 46 must denote Adam's life and condition, in body and soul, *as God created it.* This was a "natural" kind of life, in contrast to the spiritual life of the risen Christ. Adam was not yet immortal. Though he did not necessarily have to die, because he was created in a state of innocence, he could sin and *become* death's prey under the judgment of God, as actually happened. He was not yet *spiritual,* as the risen Christ is. This does not mean that Adam had a body of flesh: the risen Christ has a body of flesh, too, and yet is spiritual. The point is that Adam was not yet full of the powers of the spirit to such an extent that he possessed immortal, glorious, in-

---

[77] Thus J. Calvin, F. W. Grosheide, R. C. H. Lenski, G. J. Streeder, *et al.*

corruptible life in body and soul, while the risen Christ did possess this life. The way of obedience would, however, have led Adam to that stage (Gen. 2:17; 3:22).

8. When verse 44 says that the "natural" precedes the "spiritual," we must take this as a general statement which applies to Christ as well, since he became true man "in all things . . . like unto his brethren (Heb. 2:17).

At the incarnation Christ did not adopt human nature as Adam would have attained it if he had not sinned. Christ was not *born* as a "life-giving spirit" in the sense of verse 45. The Word became *flesh* (John 1:14), i.e., he adopted human nature as Adam possessed it to obey God in that nature as Adam should have done, and to merit in that nature immortality, glory, and spiritual power, as Adam would have received them had he not sinned.

For that reason it says in verse 45 that Christ *became*[78] a life-giving spirit. It happened when, as the reward for his atoning death, he *received* the promised Spirit in his resurrection and ascension (Matt. 28:18; Acts 2:33). He became a life-giving spirit as *the last Adam,* i.e., the last *man*: the unique and exclusive representative of those whom the Father gives him (John 6:37; 17:9), who leads them to that glory which Adam should have obtained for the human race as its first representative (Rom. 5:12ff.; 1 Cor. 15:20ff., 49.[79]

With the resurrection and exaltation of the last Adam, the age to come (which is the age of the Spirit) has victoriously invaded this present "natural" (*psychikon*) age. Christ conquered death, and as the life-giving Spirit he has been crowned the actual ruler of world and history. The ruler of the old age was Satan; in this age the "natural" had become the sinful. But Satan, together with his accompanying forces of sin and death, has been vanquished. He leads a defeated army on the retreat, and still retains some power and influence; this is the "not yet" side of the age to come. But the age to come is already present, here and now, in that the last Adam, the life-giving Spirit, reigns with all the powers of the Holy Spirit, breaking the resistance of the defeated enemy, preventing his reorganization, protecting all who are "in Christ,"[80] and preparing the enemy's final destruction in the great consummation when immortality and glory, which the last Adam

---

[78] The verb *egeneto* of v. 45a has to be supplied in 45b.
[79] Cf. W. Milligan, *The Resurrection of the Dead,* pp. 170ff.; E. Sauer, *op. cit.,* pp. 14-15; and K. Schilder, *Wat is de Hemel?,* pp. 51ff., 123ff.
[80] See the discussion of this expression in an Appendix to this chapter.

merited for those who are his, will be their eternal possession (Matt. 28:18; 1 Cor. 15:24, 25, 53-57; Heb. 2:19-15; Rev. 6:2, 20:11ff.; 21:1ff.; etc.).[81]

9. In verse 47 we read of the *origin* of both Adams. The first Adam is said to be "of the earth" (*ek,* out of) and therefore "earthy." The apostle is doubtless referring here to Adam's creation out of the dust of the ground (Gen. 2:7). This origin made his whole existence "earthy," i.e., "bound to the earth" (Grosheide). Lenski says that this refers to Adam's *body* only, whereas Paul's statement about Christ refers to his *person.* But the text does not warrant such a distinction between Adam's body and Christ's person. Grosheide rightly remarks that in both cases the whole man is characterized. Adam was earthy in his whole existence. His life depended on food from the earth, and his place was on earth; the distance between earth and heaven, which Christ removes (Eph. 2:6; 1 Thess. 4:17; Rev. 21:1-3), was fully real for him.

In contrast, the origin of Christ is heavenly: "the second man is of heaven" (again *ek,* out of). Some interpret this as referring to Christ's second coming, which will be from heaven (IB; Godet; Robertson-Plummer, ICC), but the comparison with Adam's origin points in a different direction. With Grosheide, Lenski, Wendland, and others we take "from heaven" as referring to Christ's coming to earth at the incarnation. The man Jesus Christ, born in real human flesh, is the heavenly *Word*-become-flesh (John 1:14), conceived in Mary's womb by an act from heaven (Luke 1:35) and as such descended from heaven (John 3:13).

Paul does not add the word "heavenly," as for Adam he added the word "earthy," but it is doubtless implied, as the following verse shows. Calvin comments rightly: "He is the Son of God, who came down to us from heaven and brings with him, therefore, ✶ a heavenly nature and influence." With him the new *aeon,* that of the Kingdom of Heaven, has come (Wendland).

It is evident, as Grosheide remarks, that Adam and Christ are not contrasted here as to the substance of their bodies. Both are called "man" and thus depicted as having the same kind of body. But whereas Adam's humanity was characterized by his ✶ origin from the earth, Christ's humanity is characterized by his heavenly origin: he is *the heavenly in the flesh.*

[81] Cf. K. J. Popma, *Eerst de Jood maar ook de Griek,* pp. 17ff.; *Inleiding tot de Wijsbegeerte,* pp. 84ff.; O. Cullmann, *Christ and Time,* pp. 140-41; and *Immortality . . . .* pp. 41-43.

Again, Paul does not say explicitly here that this heavenly origin and character of Christ's humanity has revealed itself most fully in his resurrection and sitting in glory at the right hand of the Father. But it is implied, for the second man, of whose origin Paul speaks here, is the Christ of whose resurrection and glory he has spoken in this same chapter (15:1-28). It is the risen and *glorified* Christ whom Paul calls the second man.

Well might this heavenly origin (and nature) of the Word-become-flesh be emphasized by Paul over against Adam's earthy origin and nature. For only as the *Heavenly Man* (God revealed in the flesh) could Jesus Christ become the life-giving Spirit. Only so could he be the second *man,* the new representative of the human race, who is so full of the Spirit who raised him up from the dead that he is able to raise up those that are his through the same Spirit.

10. Reviewing the Adam-Christ parallel in 1 Corinthians 15: 45-48, we may claim that this passage does not in the least deny that the glorified Christ has a body of flesh. Not the substance of Christs' glorified body as compared with that of Adam's body is under discussion here, but Christ's whole person and work compared with Adam's. In this passage "Spirit" does not denote the immaterial, but that which is Spirit-filled, qualified and empowered by the Holy Spirit. Nor does "heavenly" denote that which is immaterial. It characterizes the second *man,* as *God* in the *flesh,* and therefore able to lead those whom he represents to the same glory that he himself has received.

The final conclusion to be drawn from all the passages discussed in this chapter can be none other than this: the New Testament in general and Paul's epistles in particular provide no ground for denying what is clearly implied by Jesus' own words: "a spirit hath not flesh and bones, as ye behold me having" (Luke 24: 39).

The exalted Lord is still the Word *incarnate,* who retained his flesh when he was raised from the dead and became a life-giving Spirit. In and through him the age of the "natural" was transformed into the age of the Spirit. For he has retained his body of flesh and bones, but it is no longer a body such as Adam possessed.

Adam's body was earthy, in every respect bound to the earth, dependent on food provided by the earth, destined to propagate by natural birth the human race on earth, not yet immortal, not yet glorified, still capable of becoming an instrument of sin (before the Fall) and an actual instrument of sin (after the Fall), and therefore subject to death under the wrath of God.

The body of flesh of our exalted Lord, quite differently, is the glorious body of the life-giving Spirit. It is a spiritual body, a body not *qualified by* the flesh and bound to the earth as Adam's body was. The body of flesh of our exalted Lord is qualified by the Spirit, who dwells in it with all his fullness and through whom it is a center of heavenly, imperishable life, an inexhaustible source of heavenly energies. It is not in the least dependent on food, but it can take food if the Lord wants it to do so. It can be seen and touched, if he deems it desirable, but it is able to vanish and withdraw in a miraculous way. It can walk all the way from Jerusalem to the Mount of Olives, a traveler on earth, and then suddenly leave the earth, ascending into heaven, its true home. It still wears the scars of the wounds inflicted on it at the crucifixion, but it is so glorious that when the Lord appears in it to Paul the latter falls down as struck by lightning. It is rejected as a reality even by a great many that call themselves Christians, but at the consummation of the world, when Christ appears, every eye shall see it, even the eyes of those that pierced him (Rev. 1:7).

Such is the body of flesh of our exalted Lord, according to the Scriptures.

Such is the spiritual body of the second *man,* who became a lifegiving spirit.

APPENDIX

THE EXPRESSION "IN CHRIST"

The expression *en christo* and its equivalents, which are frequently used by the apostle Paul, has often been interpreted in a spiritualizing, mystical way.

A. Deissmann regards it as the central term of Paul's Christianity, which may be called Christ-mysticism. According to this scholar Paul viewed Christ as identical with the Spirit. Statements like 2 Corinthians 3:17, "Now the Lord is the Spirit," are adduced as evidence. Deissmann understands the expression "in Christ" in a more or less local sense: as we live "in" the air that surrounds us, and as the air is "in" us, causing us to live, so the believers live in Christ and Christ lives in them.[82]

[82] A. Deissmann, *Paul,* pp. 137ff., 147ff.; *The Religion of Jesus and the Faith of Paul,* p. 171.

A. Schweitzer also views Paul's Christ as a Spirit-Christ. According to this scholar Jesus abandoned his flesh-body when he died, and so sin and its power were destroyed. The expression "in Christ," according to this scholar, denotes a mystical oneness with the Spirit-Christ. This mystical unity implies a deliverance from sin and its power. This spiritual deliverance from sin is declared to be the main line of Paul's teaching, with forensic justification a secondary line of thought.[83]

J. Weiss, with other members of the *Religions-geschichtliche* school, views Christ as a kind of "energy" or "fluid" and interprets the expression "in Christ" in the light of the Hellenistic mysteries by which Paul was allegedly influenced.[84]

From our previous study of II Corinthians 3:17 and various other Christological statements of Paul, it is already evident that any spiritualizing conception of Paul's Christ is unacceptable in the light of the apostle's clear teachings. To avoid a needless repetition the following additional remarks may suffice.

1. All theories that interpret the expression "in Christ" in a mystical way fail to do justice to the main line in Paul's thought: the redemptive-historical line.

In Paul's writings Christ is predominantly the representative of his Church, as Adam was for the whole human race (Rom. 5:12ff.; I Cor. 15:20ff., 45ff.). In that capacity Christ did his redemptive work in history, his death and resurrection being at the center of that work.

The expression "in Christ" stands parallel to "in Adam" (I Cor. 15:22), and since the latter cannot possibly be understood in a mystical way, neither can the former. "In Adam" is generally interpreted as denoting the corporate idea of all-in-one and one-for-all; "in Christ" must have the same meaning.

"In," therefore, does not refer here to any mystical fusion, but speaks rather of "belonging to," "being represented by."

2. How impossible it is to view "in Christ" in a mystical way appears also from the fact that Ephesians 1:4 declares: "he [God] chose us in him [Christ] before the foundation of the world." Before any believers came into being they were already "in Christ." This, again, can only mean that they were chosen as those that "belong to," "are represented by" and "reckoned in" Christ.

3. Only in this way is it possible to explain satisfactorily the various statements in which Paul declares that the believers died,

---

[83] A. Schweitzer, *Die Mystik des Apostels Paulus*, pp. 215ff.
[84] Thus, e.g., J. Weiss, *Earliest Christianity*, II, 463ff.

were raised from the dead, and placed in heaven in and with Christ; when he died, was raised, and was placed at the Father's right hand, the same happened to them (Rom. 6:8-11; Eph. 2:4-6; Col. 3:1-4). Particularly II Corinthians 5:14 shows that such expressions do not merely mean that believers here and now experience the consequences of Christ's death, resurrection, and ascension, for we read: "we thus judge, that one died for all, therefore all died." Here the death of Christ as the representative of the Church is doubtless proclaimed to be the death of those belonging to him: on the cross the believers of all ages died in and with Christ.[85]

4. These once-for-all redemptive, historical events certainly affect believers through the operation of the Holy Spirit, who dwells in the Church. But there is nothing mystical here either. In Ephesians 3:16-17 Paul prays that Christ through his Spirit may dwell in the inward man (in the hearts of the Ephesians) *"through faith"*; and in Colossians 2:12 the apostle declares that the Colossians were buried with Christ *in baptism* and raised with him *through faith* in the working of God, who raised him from the dead. It is by *reckoning* themselves to be dead unto sin and alive unto God in Christ Jesus that the believers must fight sin (Rom. 6:11, 12).

5. The actual experience, therefore, of life "in Christ" has nothing to do with some mystical fusion with a Spirit-Christ. It is a matter of *faith* in the historical Jesus in whom the believer died, was raised, and was placed in heaven when all this happened to Christ. The Spirit of Christ, by whose indwelling and operation the believer experiences his being "in Christ," is the Spirit *of faith* (II Cor. 4:13).[86]

---

[85] Cf., e.g., J. Denney, *The Death of Christ*, p. 84.

[86] For discussions of the expression "in Christ," see also H. N. Ridderbos, *When the Time Was Fully Come*, pp. 53ff., and G. Sevenster, *op. cit.*, pp. 182ff.

CHAPTER SIX

THE NATURE OF THE BELIEVER'S
RESURRECTION-BODY ACCORDING TO THE
NEW TESTAMENT

1. RESEMBLANCE BETWEEN THE BODY OF THE GLORIFIED LORD AND THE BELIEVER'S RESURRECTION-BODY

The question as to what kind of body the believer will receive at the end of the ages has already been answered in principle. According to Philippians 3:21 Christ "will change the fashion of our humiliated body so as to resemble his glorious body" (BV). Since this glorious body of our Lord, as we have found in the previous chapters, is a glorified body of *flesh,* the resurrection-body of the believer can be none other than a similar body of *flesh.*

Paul's statement in I Corinthians 15:49, "as we have borne the image of the earthly, we shall also bear the image of the heavenly," leads to the same conclusion.[1] L. Morris (TNT), G. Kittel (TWNT, II, 395), and others interpret this statement as meaning that the believer's *whole life* and not simply some parts of it will reproduce the original, viz. the glorious life of the heavenly Christ. True as this may be, F. W. Grosheide remarks rightly that according to the context there is special reference here to the body. Christ's glorified body in heaven is the original to which the resurrection-body of the believer corresponds. As in his whole existence, so also in his future glorified body of flesh, the believer will resemble his heavenly Lord.

This great resemblance is also suggested by I John 3:2b: "We know that, if he shall be manifested, we shall be like him; for we shall see him even as he is." It is true that this statement is gen-

---

[1] Though the aorist subjunctive ("let us bear") is better attested than the future ("we shall bear"), the latter, which has the support of, e.g., Codex Vaticanus, is to be preferred with a view to the context. (Cf. A. Souter's *Greek Testament;* E. Nestle and G. D. Kilpatrick in the *Greek Testament of the British and Foreign Bible Society,* 2nd ed.; G. Kittel, TWNT, II, 395, n. 100, *et al.*) F. W. Grosheide (KNT) prefers the aor. subj., but adds that in the Koine this tense and the future do not differ much. He suggests the translation: "we may (or, must) bear the image of the heavenly."

182

eral, containing no special reference to the body. On the other hand, the resemblance to Christ referred to in this verse can hardly be envisaged as excluding the body.

II Corinthians 3:18 may also point in the same direction, since we read there that all believers "beholding the glory of the Lord, are being changed into his likeness from one degree of glory to another" (RSV).

The interpretation of this verse is very controversial and cannot be discussed here at length. With a view to our present subject the main question is, What kind of change into the likeness of the glorified Christ is meant?

J. A. T. Robinson supposes that it is a physical-metaphysical change: in the bodies of believers the powers of the age to come are released, "just as they were in the healing miracles of the incarnate Jesus."[2] According to this scholar there is a progressive resurrection starting at baptism and gradually transforming and glorifying the body, until at the *Parousia* this transformation becomes complete.[3]

But this interpretation is foreign to the Pauline conception of the resurrection. Nowhere does the apostle speak of resurrection as a process now going on.[4]

There are two other main lines of interpretation. Some claim that the transformation of believers must be understood in a moral and spiritual sense, and that it happens here and now.[5] It cannot be denied that this is quite in conformity with the context and the use of the present tense ("we are daily being transformed," A.

---

[2] *The Body,* p. 73. O. Cullmann seems to hold a similar view (cf. "Proleptic Deliverance of the Body" in *The Early Church,* pp. 167ff.; cf. also *Immortality of the Soul or Resurrection of the Dead?,* p. 45). From I Cor. 11:28-30, which speaks of sickness and death as the result of the Corinthians' partaking of the Lord's Supper in an unworthy manner, Cullmann concludes that if all the members of the community were to partake of it in a completely worthy manner, "even now there would be no more sickness or death" (*Immortality* . . ., p. 45). Cullmann seems to overlook the fact that not sickness and death *as such* are declared to be the punishment of God for the sinful practices at Corinth, but the *abnormally high rate* of mortality and illness. This would certainly be reduced to normal if the Corinthians repented of their "heinous offense" (Moffatt, *ad loc.*). This, however, is something quite different from saying that death and sickness would cease altogether. No such idea can be validly inferred from this or any other Scripture passage.

[3] *The Body,* pp. 72, 79ff.

[4] Cf. E. E. Ellis, *Paul and His Recent Interpreters,* p. 39.

[5] So, e.g., W. Barclay (DSB), J. Calvin, F. W. Grosheide (KNT), and J. Reid (IB).

Plummer). Others, however, without denying what has been said, hold that this verse contains an eschatological element. They point, relevantly, to the expression "from glory to glory," which most commentators understand as meaning: "the Christian advances from one stage of glory to another" (R. V. G. Tasker, TNT). Here is "the bridge between the present and eschatology."[6] If this is correct, which we do not doubt, Paul declares here that the spiritual and moral change which is now taking place will be followed by, and result in, the final glorification of the believer's body in the resurrection.[7]

This, again, implies that the believers will receive a glorified body of flesh, for the transformation of which Paul speaks here is one "into the same image," i.e., into the image of Christ himself.

2. ON THE SCARCITY OF DIRECT REFERENCES TO THE SUBSTANCE OF THE RESURRECTION-BODY

All of the many *indirect* references we have found and discussed in previous chapters point in one direction: the resurrection-body will consist of glorified flesh. Now, when we wish to consider the *direct* New Testament references to the nature of the resurrection-body, we find hardly any. Only in I Corinthians 15 is the subject touched upon directly. There it is stated repeatedly that the *body* will be raised (which is something quite different from the "immortality of the soul").[8] But no other clearcut statement concerning our subject can be found.

This remarkable fact allows for only one interpretation: when the New Testament books were written there was no doubt in the minds of their authors nor in the minds of most of their readers as to the substance of the resurrection-body. Except for Luke all the authors were Jews, and Palestinian Jews at that, as was our Lord. Even Paul, though born in the Hellenistic world, was brought up in Jerusalem and theologically trained there by Gamaliel, "according to the strict manner of the law of our fathers" (Acts 22:3).

The orthodox Jews of those days, as is generally recognized, believed strongly in the resurrection of the body of *flesh*, even to such an extent that the most crude conceptions were propagated.

---

6 G. Kittel, TWNT, II, 254.
7 So, to mention only a few, C. Hodge, *Comm.*; G. Kittel, *ibid.*; F. J. Pop (PNT); and H. D. Wendland (NTD).
8 Cf. the Appendix to this chapter.

Consequently, when Jesus spoke of the resurrection of the dead and the apostles taught the resurrection of the body, there was no sense in emphasizing the fact that the resurrection-body would consist of flesh. For themselves as orthodox Jews and for their Jewish hearers or readers this was to be assumed. Even their Hellenistic, gentile hearers could think of nothing else when they heard these Jewish apostles speak of the resurrection of Christ and of the future resurrection of the dead.

The truth of this appears from Acts 17:18ff., where Paul's encounter with the Athenian intellectuals, including their "Epicurean and Stoic philosophers," is described. When the apostle has announced that God will judge the world by the *man* Jesus Christ, whose divine appointment is proved by the fact that God has raised him from the dead (v. 31), these Greek intellectuals can stand it no longer. Some mock at the whole idea of "a resurrection of dead men,"[9] while others, equally unwilling to continue the discussion, back out of it by politely saying: "We will hear you on this subject some other time" (NEB).

What caused these Greek hearers to react this way? Certainly not a proclamation of the immortality of the soul. The Epicureans might deny such immortality, for they regarded the soul as made out of fine atoms which are dispersed at death,[10] yet they would not have thought of sneering at the preaching of an after-life for the soul, which was integral to most philosophic systems and mystery-religions of the Greek and Roman world.[11] Nor would any Greek intellectual have reacted as the Athenians did if Paul had preached a "resurrection" of the kind which is often taught today: a man living after death in a more or less spiritualized "body." Many Greeks regarded the soul and even the gods as consisting of refined matter,[12] so that there could be nothing against the idea of a soul having some "body" after death.

What caused the learned men of Athens to sneer at Paul's preaching was something quite different, viz. that according to the apostle God raised the *man* Jesus from the dead (*ek nekron,* out of the dead).[13] This statement, coming out of the mouth of a

---

[9] "A generalizing plural," F. F. Bruce, *ad loc.* "More correctly, a resurrection of dead men" (G. H. C. Macgregor, IB).

[10] Cf. K. O. Brink in *The Oxford Classical Dictionary,* p. 325.

[11] Cf. the article "After-life" by F. R. Walton in *The Oxford Classical Dictionary.*

[12] Cf. K. O. Brink, *op. cit.,* p. 325, and F. F. Bruce on Acts 17:18.

[13] Grosheide (KNT) paraphrases: "out of the group of corpses."

Jew,[14] could have only one meaning for them: Jesus' body, his corpse, which lay in the grave, was resuscitated and as a body of flesh came to life again, and in that risen body the man Jesus was to be the judge of the world. To the Greek mind such a "resurrection of dead men," as it is generalizingly called in verse 32, was an impossible and ridiculous idea held only by Jews.

Indeed, the reaction of the Athenians shows clearly what "resurrection" meant in the Jewish vocabulary in general and in that of Paul in particular: the resurrection of the body of *flesh.*

Can it surprise us, then, that in the New Testament there is hardly any direct reference to the nature of the resurrection-body?

3. DENIAL OF THE RESURRECTION IN CORINTH

As previously noted in I Corinthians 15 Paul deals with the nature of the believer's resurrection-body.

In this chapter Paul is refuting certain objections against a future resurrection, as these were expressed by some members of the Corinthian community. According to verse 12 these Christians said that there is no resurrection of the dead. C. Hodge's assumption that they may even have denied the resurrection of Christ[15] seems to be unwarranted. These people were Christians, who according to verse 11 *believed* the apostolic preaching about a Christ who was buried and raised again from the grave (v. 4). Paul's argumentation in verses 12ff. also seems to take its starting point in the generally agreed fact that Christ was raised from the dead.[16] Moreover, denial of Christ's resurrection would have made Paul's reaction much more fierce than it actually is.

The future resurrection of deceased believers is the issue upon which Paul focuses in this chapter. We do not know the positive ground for denying this doctrine among the Corinthians. As Christians they could not have believed in a total and final destruction of man at death. Rather, in Greek fashion, they must have believed in an after-life for the human soul or spirit and in eternal bliss for the spirits of the believers. This is implied in Paul's

---

[14] J. De Zwaan (TU) argues that all Paul's thoughts in the Areopagus address are thoroughly Jewish, despite the neutral or philosophic tone of the wordings, and that Luke accentuates the Jewish element very much in Acts 18:18; 21:21-26; 22:17, 18; 23:1, 6 (cf. also N. B. Stonehouse, *Paul before the Areopagus,* Chapter 1).

[15] So also J. Short (IB, *ad loc.,* p. 223).

[16] Cf. F. W. Grosheide (KNT, CNT); A. Schlatter (Erl.); W. G. H. Simon (TBC); *et al.*

statement (v. 18) that if Christ is not raised, then also those that are fallen asleep in Christ have perished. Apparently they did not doubt that their deceased brethren enjoyed a blessed condition.

J. Moffatt (MNTC), H. D. Wendland (NTD), and others suggest that these men may have been precursors of the errorists denounced in II Timothy 2:18, who taught "that the resurrection is past already": they believed only in a *spiritual* resurrection in this life, to be followed by spiritual bliss for the soul in the hereafter. They may have appealed to Paul's own teaching that Christians have already been raised with Christ to newness of life.

At any rate, these erring Christians in Corinth denied that there is a resurrection of the dead (literally, of corpses)[17] at the end of the ages.

They must have taken offense at what A. Oepke calls "the materialism of the Jewish hope"[18] and denied, to use the words of Grosheide, "the resurrection of the *flesh*" (KNT). Moffatt finds a parallel in the denial of the resurrection by some Christians a century later, of whom Justin Martyr writes that he heard them declare: "There is no resurrection of the dead, but as soon as we die our souls are taken up in heaven." Justin rejects such teaching as unorthodox: "I and all other Christians of orthodox belief know that there will be a resurrection of the flesh. . . ."[19]

To combat this denial of the resurrection Paul appeals to the resurrection of Christ as he had preached it to the Corinthians and as they had come to believe in it when they were converted, *viz.* as the resurrection of one who was buried and then raised again, i.e., who was raised in the same body as that in which he had died and was buried.[20]

In the light of this resurrection (so Paul argues in vv. 13ff.) it is impossible to deny the resurrection of dead men, either because dead human bodies cannot possibly be raised again, or because the human body is not fit to share in the future life.[21]

If resurrection of dead men is not possible or not suitable, then Christ has not been raised either. This in its turn would imply not only that the apostolic preaching in the name of God is a lie, but that the very foundation of the Church's faith and hope has vanished.

---

17 F. W. Grosheide, KNT.
18 TWNT, I, 371.
19 *Dial.*, 80 (Moffatt's transl.).
20 Cf. our earlier explanation of I Cor. 15:1ff.
21 Either of the two may have been in the mind of these Corinthians.

For Christ did not die just as "a man," like all others. He is the new Man, the new representative of mankind instead of Adam (v. 22). As such he died "for our sins, according to the Scriptures" and was "buried" and "raised on the third day according to the Scriptures" (vv. 3, 4).

If Christ is not risen, i.e., if his body is still in the power of death, then he has failed as our representative. Then there is no forgiveness of sins because he did not really atone for sin. Nor is there any victory, in any sense of the word, over death. Then our faith in him is of no avail in this life (v. 17), and there is no hope for a blessed future for those that died in faith (v. 18). Without his atoning death and his victorious resurrection Christianity is a complete delusion, because our present as well as our future is decided by what our representative did and underwent.

However, Paul argues, Christ was raised indeed, as even the erring Corinthians know. But then that devastating conception that dead men are not raised is untrue and must be abandoned. One dead man has already been raised from the grave, body and all: Christ, our representative. Therefore as certainly as our relation with the first Adam brings death to us, so certainly does our relation with Christ guarantee our victory over death: the resurrection of our bodies at Christ's coming (vv. 20-23).[22]

When we view this argumentation of I Corinthians 15:12ff. against the background of what the errorists denied (the resurrection of this body of flesh) and against the well attested fact of Christ's resurrection (the raising of his *buried* body from the grave, v. 4), then we cannot escape the following conclusions: (a) Paul is proclaiming here that the dead bodies of believers will be raised in the flesh; (b) the denial of such a resurrection cuts at the heart of Christianity, which stands and falls with the bodily resurrection of Christ.

This does not exclude the fact that this resurrection will cause a great change in the body, as is clear both from what Scripture teaches concerning the resurrection-body of Christ[23] and from Paul's own teachings in the second part of I Corinthians 15.

---

[22] We understand the "all" in v. 22 in both cases as referring to the believers, of whose resurrection this whole chapter speaks. The future state of the unbelievers is not dealt with here (cf. Grosheide, Lenski, and others). That Paul is speaking of the *future* resurrection of believers is obvious from the future tense *zoopoiethesontai*.

[23] Cf. Chapter 4 of this study.

4. Interpretation of I Corinthians 15:35-44

Of particular significance for our subject is the passage I Corinthians 15:35-44. Here Paul replies to the questions: "How are the dead raised? And with what manner of body do they come?" (v. 35).

It does not make much difference whether these questions had actually been raised in Corinth and were reported to Paul, or that the apostle himself is formulating questions that he feels someone is likely to ask. The former, however, is to be preferred because it seems obvious that the questions are to be regarded as coming from one who objects to the resurrection of the body on rationalistic grounds. If, in Paul's opinion, it was merely a matter of asking for further information, he could not possibly have begun his reply with *aphron* (fool), i.e., "Fool thou art!"[24]

It should be noticed that the two questions of verse 35 do not have the same meaning, contrary to what many commentators say. According to these scholars the second question is merely explanatory of the first, and the only point of both is the form or nature of the resurrection-body.[25] This interpretation is also suggested by versions that leave out the conjunction "and" (Greek *de*), rendering: "How are the dead raised? In what kind of body?" or similar translations (Moffatt, NEB, RSV, *et al.*).

F. L. Godet rightly points out, however, that the Greek conjunction *de,* connecting the two questions, shows clearly that the questions, though closely related, refer to different matters. This appears also from what follows, since verse 36 obviously gives the answer to the first question and verses 37ff. contain a reply to the second.

The first question, "How are the dead raised?"[26] concerns the very possibility that a dead man can be raised. It "queries the mechanics of the process" of the resurrection (L. Morris, TNT), the "hidden working whereby the awakening of the body which has been given over to death is accomplished" (Godet). In this question we hear the Corinthian rationalist ask in a more or less sneering way: Resurrection of dead men? Corpses being brought

---

[24] Cf. F. W. Grosheide (CNT, KNT), R. C. H. Lenski, *et al.*

[25] So, e.g., H. Alford, W. Barclay (DSB), R. C. H. Lenski, J. Moffatt (MNTC), A. Schlatter (Erl.), *et al.*

[26] J. Moffatt, R. F. Weymouth, and others translate incorrectly: "How do (can) the dead *rise?*" The passive form in the Greek text points to *God's* action in the resurrection.

to life again? Decomposed flesh quickened and restored? How can this ever be? It is simply impossible![27]

The second question has the same background of rationalistic unbelief, but approaches the problem from a different angle. Now the reference is not so much to the impossibility of a decomposed body being raised as to the *kind* of body which the dead are supposed to possess when they are raised.[28] We may suppose the Greek sceptics to be laughing the whole idea of resurrection out of court by querying: What kind of body would arise from a heap of decomposed rubbish? (L. Morris, TNT).

Quite likely (as J. Moffatt suggests) there is a reference here to those crude Jewish conceptions which made belief in the resurrection doubly difficult for the Greek mind. The inquirer seems to ask sneeringly, Do you really mean that the particles of the decomposed body will be put together again so that the body will be precisely the same as it was before death and its life resumed in the same way as before?

We know that such ideas were commonplace in Jewish eschatological literature. Sometimes the blind, lame, and dumb were depicted as being raised in the same condition in which they died, though later they were to be healed. There were some who believed that even conjugal intercourse, etc., was to continue after the resurrection, at least during a certain period.[29]

Against such a background, indeed, the second question is quite understandable, and Paul's answer in 37ff. is fully in conformity with it, as we shall see.

In verse 36 Paul answers the first question of verse 35 with the words: "Thou foolish one, that which thou thyself sowest is not quickened except it die."

There is no trace of rationalistic argumentation here. The apostle does not try to prove that dead and decomposed bodies can be raised by adducing philosophical and logical grounds, thus attempting to justify the doctrine before the judgment seat of human reason. Paul points simply to the *power of God,* who be-

---

[27] Cf. P. Bachmann (ZK), J. Calvin, F. L. Godet, F. W. Grosheide (CNT), C. Hodge, L. Morris (TNT), *et al.* R. F. Weymouth renders: "How can the dead rise?" thus also emphasizing the impossibility according to the inquirer.

[28] The fact that a different verb is employed here also indicates that a new point is being raised.

[29] A striking example is the description given in the Syriac Baruch Apocalypse, 50:1-51:10. See also A. Oepke, TWNT, II, 336, and particularly SB, III, 473-74.

fore the very eyes of the errorists[30] daily brings to life that which had died, giving new life to that which has fallen prey to decomposition.

Some versions obscure the meaning of the verse by rendering the Greek verb *zoopoieo* with the phrase "come to life" (BV, Moffatt, NEB, RSV). The verb, however, has the passive form here, which KJV, ERV, and ASV render correctly: "is not quickened" (cf. v. 22). Paul is not referring to vital energy already present in the seed, but to the quickening, reviving power of God, as also verse 38 proves: "But God giveth. . . ."[31]

Paul's argument runs along these lines: you doubt the possibility of decomposed corpses being raised? How foolish you are! You are forgetting that in the resurrection the power of *God* will reveal itself. What does God do as often as you yourself sow your seed? He quickens your seed by causing it to decompose in the earth. He brings it to new life *through death*. Without dying and being dissolved in the earth it cannot be quickened. Such is the power of God. Are you not a fool when, with this divine power daily revealing itself before your eyes, you dare ask: How can what is dead and decomposed ever be revived?[32]

This analogy of the seed has two sides, as P. Bachmann (ZK), Godet, Lenski, and others rightly emphasize. One side is this: the power of God brings forth not merely a copy of that which was sown, but a much richer and in many respects quite different form of life. The apostle elaborates this point in the following verses, which will be discussed below.

Here we stress the other side, namely that there is an essential *continuity* and organic relation between that which dissolves in the earth and that which God causes to sprout forth from it.

P. Althaus rejects any continuity between our present body and the resurrection-body, claiming that according to Paul, as he speaks in this verse, the present body of flesh must vanish to make place for something of a completely different substance.[33] But here Althaus mistakes Paul's point. The objector questions whether a body of flesh can be raised into *any* sort of body after it is

---

[30] In the Greek text there is special emphasis on the personal pronoun *su*: "What *you* (yourself) sow. . . ."

[31] Cf. Godet, Grosheide, Morris, *et al.*

[32] Noticeable is the resemblance to Jesus' words, spoken to the Sadducees who denied the resurrection: "Ye do err, not knowing the scriptures, nor *the power of God*" (Matt. 22:29).

[33] *Die Letzten Dinge,* pp. 125-26.

dead.   It would therefore be quite irrelevant for Paul to show
that our bodies of flesh will become bodies of another *substance*.
For the Greek mind all kinds of matter are alike opposed to spirit.

The point under discussion is: Can a dead body that was buried
and has fallen prey to decomposition be revived?   Is the resurrection of a dead body of flesh possible?

To this question Paul replies by pointing to God's power to
bring seed to new life through death and dissolution.   His answer
to this question is so much in the affirmative that he calls the
doubter a fool.

Paul's reply implies that there is an essential continuity between
this present body of flesh and the resurrection-body; at the resurrection God will bring this body of flesh to new and richer life.
The substance and essential nature of the seed that was sown is
not changed when it sprouts out in a new and richer life.   No
more may we expect the substance of our bodies to be changed
at the resurrection.   If this body of flesh were not raised "death
would not be vanquished; it would keep its prey" (Godet).

E. Käsemann and R. Bultmann, both rejecting the possibility
of the resurrection of the flesh, realize what is at stake in I Corinthians 15:35ff.   Käsemann is of the opinion that Paul's general
teaching describes the resurrection-body as a spirit-body.   He admits, however, that in I Corinthians 15:35ff. the apostle speaks
differently.   According to Käsemann the only solution lies in
assuming that Paul makes a mistake here.   The parallel of the seed
is not a sound one: the seed does not die at all!   Seed corn and
corn plants are actually of the same substance and only the forms
differ.   Paul's whole argumentation is a failure and contradicts his
general teachings.[34]   R. Bultmann declares that Paul "lets himself
be misled into adopting his opponent's method of argumentation."[35]

Such theories, however, cannot be accepted for the following
reasons.

1. In the many Pauline passages discussed in this study not a
trace has been found of a spiritualizing tendency.   Paul's general
teachings certainly do not point in the direction that Bultmann,
Käsemann, and others suggest.

2. There is no chapter in all of Paul's letters in which he deals
so extensively with the nature of the resurrection-body as I

[34] *Op. cit.*, pp. 135-36.
[35] ThNT, I, 192.

Corinthians 15. To exclude this part of his teaching from his "general teaching" and discard it as a mistake is utterly unwarranted.

3. That in nature seed sown into the ground does not actually die is true only from the standpoint of the laboratory. It is equally true that the seed must completely dissolve in the ground to make the way free for the germ in it. The seed, as it is before the sowing, has to vanish, to die, never to be seen again in its original state (cf. Grosheide, CNT).

After the apostle has shown that even in nature God makes alive what had died (v. 36), he goes on to make it clear that this does not imply that the resurrection-body will have the same manner of existence as the present body. Here, too, what happens in the realm of nature provides an analogy with the resurrection. The sower, Paul argues in verse 37, does not sow "the body that shall be," i.e., the plant that springs from the seed. He sows something quite different in form and appearance, namely "a bare grain" of some kind.

In the light of the context, the word "bare" or "naked" (*gumnon*) should not be pressed to denote the naked state of man's dead body. The fantastic idea of some rabbis that the righteous will rise clothed with garments as the seed comes up clothed[36] has nothing to do with Paul's intention. Nor is there any reference here to the possibility of being found "naked" as Paul speaks of it in II Corinthians 5:4. In the latter passage the word "naked" denotes a possible condition of man *after* death, whereas the "naked" grain of I Corinthians 15:37 is naked *before* it dies.

"A naked grain" means, as most commentators understand it, a small, insignificant kernel, which in appearance is as nothing compared with the "body," the plant which God causes to grow out of it. Yet however great the difference may be, the "body" which God gives to that bare seed is "as it pleased him, and to each seed [he gives] a body of its own" (v. 38).

For the clause "as it pleased him" the Greek text has the aorist *ethelese* (as he willed), which refers to a decision (or planning) of God's will in the past. We may think with Lenski of God's creative word that each plant should yield "seed after its kind" (Gen. 1:11), which G. Ch. Aalders explains as referring to the diversity of plant forms as God created them (KV).

---

36 Cf. SB.

C. T. Craig (IB) takes the words "as he has chosen" (RSV for: "as he willed") out of their context, as if they expressed the thought that God may give to a seed *any* kind of plant "body" that pleases him. Craig infers that "it is not legitimate to argue the same continuity between the physical body and the resurrection-body that we know to exist between a seed and the plant growing from it."

This is surely unsound exegesis. Not only does Craig obscure the meaning of the aorist tense, but he ignores completely Paul's subjoined explanation (v. 38): "and to each kind of seed its own body" (RSV). Here we are told emphatically that there will be continuity: each kind of seed receives, in conformity with God's decision and fixed purpose, the body that belongs to it: out of a grain of wheat he brings a wheat plant, out of a grain of rye a rye plant, etc.

The implications of verses 36-38, taken as a whole, are obvious. They teach on the one hand the substantial continuity between our present body (the seed) and the resurrection-body (the plant "body," growing from the seed): *this* body of flesh will be raised. This continuity extends to the individual person: as each kind of seed develops into the kind of plant God chose for it, so the individual body will be raised in such a way that its individuality is preserved. There is no such thing as a mass produced resurrection-body.

On the other hand, our passage proclaims the great difference between our present body and the resurrection-body as regards form, appearance, and manner of existence. The resurrection-body will be like a full-grown plant compared with the bare grain of seed from which God raised it: it will excel our body as we possess it now in every respect. The change will be beyond our imagination.

It is significant that verse 38 speaks of *God* who in nature *gives* the seed its new "body." To Paul the processes of nature, however regular and self-evident, are acts of God. The "miracle" of the seed, dying in the ground and bringing forth a new, richer, and more glorious life, is caused by God's almighty power.

This emphasis on God's activity in nature shows that we may not press the biological analogy too far by supposing that our bodies contain an indestructible kernel or immortal germ which God keeps after death and which he uses as a "nucleus" for the resurrection-body. E. Sauer claims that only in this way can we conceive how the old body can actually be the "seed" of the future body.[37]   With Berkouwer,[38] Grosheide, Lenski, and K. Schilder,[39] we are of the opinion that no such biological conclusion may be drawn from Paul's sowing parallel.   An immortal germ in the human body implies a natural immortality of that body, which is against the scriptural teaching that our bodies are *mortal* and return to *dust* (Gen. 3:19).   Moreover, in the sowing parallel Paul does not point to biological laws operating in the seed but to *God's power*.   It was the errorists in Corinth who pointed to biological laws, saying that a dead body, dissolved in the earth, cannot possibly be raised again.   Paul appeals, against the biological laws, to God's miraculous power to raise what is dead and dissolved.

Something quite different is H. Bavinck's suggestion that there may well be some material connection between the present body and that of the resurrection.[40]   In I Corinthians 15:52 Paul declares that the believers who live on earth when Jesus returns will be *changed,* and his description of that change in the following verses does not point in the direction of a complete new creation. This is confirmed by Jesus' use of the word "regeneration" to describe the eschatological renewal of all things (Matt. 19:28).

There is certainly no ground for the crude conceptions held by some church fathers and later theologians, namely that God will call together the scattered dust of each man's dead body to restore that body's peculiar substance.[41]

Since, however, the resurrection brings about a renewal and glorification of *this* body, Bavinck's suggestion that God may use some of the decomposed matter of the present body as the *substratum* for the resurrection-body is certainly worth considering. To say that it is implied in Paul's parallel of the seed would be unwarranted.   Here Paul answers different questions.   And though he proclaims the essential continuity and identity of our present body with the resurrection-body, he does not say *how* God

---

[37] *Op. cit.,* p. 108. Similar theories are held by K. Dijk, *Over de laatste Dingen,* III, 102; Canon C. H. Robinson, *Studies in the Resurrection of Christ,* pp. 13-17; *et al.*

[38] *De Wederkomst van Christus,* I, 238.

[39] *Op. cit.,* p. 292.

[40] *Gereformeerde Dogmatiek,* IV, 776.

[41] Thus, e.g., Tertullian, *De Resurr. Carn.,* Ch. 63; Rufinus, *Comm. in Symb.,* 42; Zach. Ursinus, *Commentary on the Heidelberg Catechism,* p. 312; and Bishop J. Pearson, *Exposition of the Creed,* ed. Nichols, p. 531.

preserves them. Despite Bavinck's suggestion, the "how" remains God's secret.

In verse 39 the apostle refers to the various kinds of flesh that we find in the world: flesh of men, beasts, birds, and fishes, all of them differing in structure, quality, functions, etc. Yet they all are flesh, differing not in essence but in degree (Grosheide, NLC).

According to Grosheide (CNT, KNT, KV) Paul is not comparing the above differences with the difference between our present body and the resurrection-body. He is only illustrating and expanding his previous assertion that God can give every seed its own body; the whole creation, he says, shows God's power to build bodies out of different kinds of substance.

It is difficult to see, however, why the apostle should use so many words to explain what everyone can see before his eyes, namely that each seed receives its "own body" in the plant that grows from it. Therefore, with Calvin, Hodge, Lenski, Morris, Wendland, and others, we read in verse 39 an indication of God's power to give the dead *human* body a new structure with new qualities and functions.

The objectors in Corinth had asked how *this* body of flesh can ever be raised from the dead in a different form and endowed with different characteristics. Paul replies by reminding them that many sorts of fleshly bodies already exist, each having its distinctive structure. Can it then be considered impossible for God, who created this variety, to change the present body of flesh into a resurrection-body consisting of flesh but nevertheless greatly different from the present body?

The argumentation continues along the same lines when Paul says in verse 40 that there are "celestial bodies, and bodies terrestrial: but the glory of the celestial is one, and the glory of the terrestrial is another." In Verse 41 the apostle describes the difference in glory among the celestial bodies themselves: sun, moon, and stars.

It is significant that Paul does not use the word "flesh" here, as he did in verse 39, but speaks of "bodies." This finds its natural interpretation in the fact that all four classes of verse 39 (men, beasts, birds, and fishes) *are* of flesh, whereas verse 40 compares creatures of fleshly substance with others of a different substance. Moreover, Paul no longer desires to contrast substances as such, but (as v. 40b shows) the different kinds of glory that God is able to create, whatever the substance of the creature may be. Hence now the common name "bodies."

Some scholars take the "celestial bodies" as living creatures in heaven (angels, the blessed), or suppose that Paul believes the stars themselves to be angelic beings. These scholars base their interpretation on current conceptions in Jewish apocalyptic and other literature.[42]

This, however, seems unwarranted. Granted that such ideas were commonplace in certain writings of Paul's day, this does not prove that he held them too, as appears from the fact that he deviates from the crude Jewish conceptions of the resurrection-body. Some say that the word "bodies" in Paul's vocabulary cannot possibly denote sun, moon, and stars, but these people forget that the apostle even uses the word "body" for the plant which grows from seed (v. 38).

Furthermore, the context allows no reference to angels and deceased saints. For it is clearly Paul's intention to compare different kinds of glory that are *visible,* which is not the case with the alleged heavenly bodies of angels and deceased saints.

For these and other reasons[43] we agree with P. Bachmann, F. L. Godet, F. W. Grosheide, Robertson-Plummer, A. Schlatter, and others, that the "celestial" or "heavenly" bodies must be understood in the normal, astronomical sense.

In verse 40 the different glories of terrestrial and celestial bodies as two distinct classes are mentioned first. Though all bodies on earth, human, animal, or plant bodies, have some glory as creatures of the glorious Creator (Ps. 8), the glory of sun, moon, and stars with their bright radiancy is of a quite different kind.

In verse 41 the apostle points out that even within the second class, that of the celestial bodies, there is a great variety in glory: sun, moon, and stars vary greatly among themselves. Just as it was stated in verse 39 that there are different kinds of flesh on earth, so we are here reminded of the variety of brightness with which the celestial bodies shine.

Some scholars say that the glory of the celestial bodies is their

---

[42] So, with some differences as regards details, C. T. Craig (IB), J. Moffatt (MNTC), L. Morris (TNT), H. Traub (TWNT, V, 542), H. D. Wendland (NTD), *et al.*

[43] Cf. Lenski, who points also to the graduation in Paul's argumentation (vv. 36, 39, 42). See also Bachmann's extensive comments on the subject (ZK, p. 459).

"substance," in contrast to the flesh-substance of the terrestrial bodies.[44] H. Clavier even suggests that Paul makes this contrast to pave the way for the idea of a spiritual body not consisting of flesh, which he mentions later in this chapter.

But Paul ascribes glory not only to celestial bodies, but also to terrestial. If Clavier and others are right, then Paul would be declaring that terrestrial bodies also consisted of glory, which is certainly not so.

Within the framework of Paul's argumentation we understand him to be stating simply that God is here and now draping his creatures on earth and in the skies with various kinds and grades of glory.

The implication for the resurrection is obvious. Paul has emphasized the power of God to bring dead bodies to a new and richer life, and here he points particularly to the power by which God glorifies the resurrection-body. All creation shows that God is a glory-creating God, whose power to create different grades of glory manifests itself on earth and in the skies. Should it be impossible for such a God to turn our present, mortal, earthly body of flesh into a heavenly, immortal, glorious resurrection-body of flesh?

Is there also an indirect reference here to the difference in glory that the believers will show after the resurrection, along the lines of Daniel 12:3, where we read that the wise shall shine as the brightness of the firmament, and they that turn many to righteousness as the stars?

Calvin, Hodge, Lenski, Berkouwer,[45] and others are of the opinion that such a reference is completely absent.

Grosheide would accept the idea but declares that it is more application than exegesis; Godet calls it "a purely secondary illusion."

In view of the context it seems best to deny any reference in this direction. The next verse declares, "So also is the resurrection of the dead," which introductory words are followed by a description of the difference between the present body and that of the resurrection. We read there of a change from "dishonor" to "glory,"

---

[44] E.g., H. Clavier in his article, "Breves Remarques sur la Notion de *soma pneumatikon*," in *The Background of the New Testament and its Eschatology,* ed. W. D. Davies and D. Daube, p. 348; C. T. Craig (IB), *et al.*
[45] *De Wederkomst van Christus,* I, 239.

but nothing is said about a difference in glory among the saints that are raised. That difference is not denied, but it is not under discussion.

In verses 42-44, beginning with "So it is with the resurrection of the dead" (NEB), it becomes clear that Paul in the preceding analogies has been referring to the power of God to raise the present body of flesh in a condition different from the present. Here the apostle continues to state in greater detail what will happen to our bodies at the resurrection.

Carrying on the metaphor of the grain being sown and raised, he contrasts this present body with that of the resurrection by repeating four times: "It is sown in . . . it is raised in. . . ."

There is difference of opinion here regarding the time when "it" (i.e., the "seed") is sown. Some take it as referring to the human seed being sown when a man is born into the world. Then, according to them, the body is sown.[46]

The analogy, however, with the seed that is sown *into the ground* (vv. 36-37) points undoubtedly to the interment of the body after death, as most commentators interpret it. Moreover, as Godet rightly remarks, the qualifications "in dishonor" and "in corruption" cannot be meant to characterize the life of the child, "full of freshness, at the moment when it begins to unfold its powers."

Therefore, this present body is to be considered the "it," "the seed" that is buried in the ground and raised by God's power. Paul probably does not mention explicitly the subject of "it is sown" because he wishes to place all the emphasis on the different characteristics of the present body in comparison with those of the resurrection-body.

It should be noticed that the conditions and characteristics that follow apply to this present body in general, not especially to the *dead* body that is buried. In verse 44 the body that is sown is called a "natural" (*psychikon*) body, which proves that the apostle is not thinking only of a corpse. Paul evidently means that the condition of our present body, which *after it has died* is "sown," is one of corruption, dishonor, weakness, and being "natural." Death and burial only make explicit what has been present all along.

It is of the greatest significance for our subject that no *change of substance* is mentioned. If Paul had meant by "spiritual body"

---

[46] Thus, e.g., C. T. Craig (IB), J. Moffatt (MNTC), and T. T. Shore (in *Layman's Handy Commentary*).

a body not consisting of flesh but of spirit, his argumentation in this passage would be most unsatisfactory and hard to explain. For in our chapter the apostle is dealing, as we have seen, with objections raised under the influence of Hellenistic thought, which strongly denied the possibility and suitability of a resurrection of this present body of *flesh*. If Paul had believed that the resurrection-body would not be a body of flesh, he should have said so here, where he discusses its differences from this present body. The erring Corinthians would gladly have accepted the idea that some phenomenon, which might be called a "body," would be raised, but that certainly would not be *this body of flesh*.

Instead, Paul continues the analogy of "sowing" and "being raised," which undoubtedly points in the direction of "a material connection between the two bodies" (Bachmann). The four contrasting characteristics of both bodies have nothing to do with a difference in substance, as appears also from the fact that Paul uses the expressions "sown *in* . . . ," "raised *in* . . . ," followed by nouns that state *conditions* of the bodies concerned, not the "material" they consist of. Corruption, dishonor, and weakness do not denote "substances" any more than do incorruption, glory, and power.

Particularly the contrast of verse 44, "it is sown a natural body; it is raised a spiritual body," is most striking in this respect. For here the word "body" is used, and the resurrection-body is contrasted in the most direct way to the present body.

We need not repeat what has been said in the previous chapter about the words "natural" (*psychikon*) and "spiritual," as not referring to different kinds of substances.

What should be noticed now is that Paul, contrasting the two bodies, uses particularly the words "natural" (*psychikon*) and "spiritual." If Paul wanted to teach that the resurrection-body will not be a body of flesh, he would certainly have used another word than *psychikon*. In Paul's writings the most common counterpart of "spirit" is "flesh," and if he meant to say that this present body is a flesh-body in distinction from the resurrection-body as a spirit-body, the apostle would have used his favorite words "carnal," "fleshly," or "fleshy" (*sarkikon* or *sarkinon*). The fact that Paul avoids all of these adjectives and instead uses *psychikon* proves that he wants to prevent the Corinthians (and the Church of all ages) from thinking that there is no resurrection hope for this present body of flesh.

5. "Flesh and Blood Cannot Inherit the Kingdom of God"

The words heading this section, taken from I Corinthians 15:50, require careful consideration with a view to our subject.

Already in the early Church, all who denied the resurrection of this body of flesh fell back upon this passage, as Irenaeus writes: "This [passage] . . . is adduced by all heretics in support of their folly. . . ."[47]

In recent times, too, a great many of the works quoted in this study as denying the resurrection of the flesh adduce this verse as proof that Paul also denied it. Some pay hardly any attention to the context in which Paul's statement occurs, or to the significant fact that the apostle does not speak of the "flesh" but of "flesh and blood," which as we hope to show has a quite different meaning. H. H. A. Kennedy, for example, simply declares: "Here is one of the Apostle's axioms. Flesh is, of course, the material substance of the earthly life. . . ."[48] To prove that Paul did not believe in a resurrection of the flesh O. Cullmann quotes our statement without any further interpretation.[49] C. T. Craig (IB), though giving some further interpretation, claims that these words show not only that Paul denied the resurrection of the flesh, but that he denied that the risen Christ had a body of flesh as Luke speaks of it.

The explanation, however, is not as simple as that.

The expression "flesh and blood" occurs in four other passages in the New Testament, viz. Matthew 16:17, Galatians 1:16, Ephesians 6:12, and Hebrews 2:14. In the latter two passages it is used with inversion. The words form "a single conception . . . a semitic wordpair."[50]

In all the passages just mentioned, it is obvious from the context that "flesh and blood" does not denote the substance of the human body. When Jesus says to Peter after his great confession (Matt. 16:17), "Blessed art thou, Simon Bar-Jonah: for flesh and blood hath not revealed it unto thee. . . ," Jesus cannot possibly have thought that the substance of flesh and blood could give a man any revelation. Reading the expression "flesh and blood" within the context of the other passages leads to the same conclusion: the substance of the human body is not meant.

[47] *Against Heresies,* V, 9 (ANF, p. 534).
[48] *St. Paul's Conceptions of the Last Things,* p. 238.
[49] *Immortality. . . ,* p. 46.
[50] J. Jeremias, NTS, Feb. 1956, p. 152.

E. Schweizer shows convincingly that the expression belongs to the Rabbinic vocabulary. The Rabbis never used it for the flesh-substance or for the human body. The latter they named with increasing frequency *guph,* which can also mean "person." "Flesh and blood" always denoted the whole man with all his functions, with particular emphasis on man's earthly condition as a frail and perishable creature, in contrast to the eternal and almighty God.[51]

There is no ground for interpreting the expression "flesh and blood" as it occurs in I Corinthians 15:50 in a different way. On the contrary, here again the whole man is meant, particularly in his frailty and perishableness, as appears from the fact that the verb in Greek is in the singular and in the parallel clause (50b) the word "corruption" is used for "flesh and blood": "neither doth corruption inherit incorruption."[52]

J. Jeremias and Robertson-Plummer view the parallelism in this verse as synthetic, so that "flesh and blood" and "corruption" are interpreted as referring to different groups of men. "Flesh and blood," according to them, denotes those that will be alive when the end comes, whereas "corruption" refers to those that died before the Parousia and whose bodies have suffered corruption in the grave.

With E. Schweizer and most commentators, however, we regard the parallelism as synonymous, so that "flesh and blood" in 50a is called "corruption" in 50b, "corruption" denoting that which is perishable and a certain prey of death and destruction. This interpretation is in perfect accordance with the meaning of the expression "flesh and blood" in Rabbinical literature and in the New Testament.

Here the question arises, however, What does Paul mean when he says that "flesh and blood cannot inherit the Kingdom of God?"

According to Grosheide and Lenski Paul declares in this statement that to obtain the blessings of God's Kingdom in Jesus Christ man must be born again, as Jesus taught Nicodemus (John 3:3, 6). This means that our passage does not speak of the resurrection of the dead.

It is difficult to see how this can be the correct interpretation, since Paul immediately after verse 50 continues to speak of the resurrection. It also seems incongruent with what the scholars

---

[51] TWNT, VII, 115-16. Similarly many commentators. F. W. Grosheide (CNT) and Robertson-Plummer (ICC) also point out negatively that "flesh and blood" does not denote man in his sinfulness.

[52] E. Schweizer, *op. cit.,* p. 128.

concerned declare, that "flesh and blood" does not denote man in his sinfulness.   It is because of his sinfulness that man needs a spiritual regeneration, not because he is a frail and perishable creature, a certain prey of death and corruption.   Also the parallel clause, "corruption does not inherit incorruption," points in a different direction, as does the word "inherit," which in the context of I Corinthians 15 decidedly seems to speak of the eschatological entering into God's completed kingdom, which will be a kingdom of "incorruption," i.e., of immortality, imperishability, and glory.

With the majority of commentators we understand verse 50a as declaring that "flesh and blood" cannot possibly have a place in the glorious realm of the new heaven and the new earth, which Christ will establish at his second coming.

Does this mean that the body of the resurrected saints cannot be a body of flesh, as many scholars claim?[53]

We answer in the negative for the following reasons:

1. If this is the correct interpretation, Paul's statement in this verse contradicts what Scripture says about Christ's resurrection-body of "flesh and bones," a body which he has in heaven and in which he will come again to enter with all the saints into the eternal kingdom.

2. If Paul declares here that a body of flesh is incapable and unworthy of partaking of the future glory, he contradicts his general teachings on the subject, which, as we have seen, point in a quite different direction.

3. The interpretation under discussion misrepresents the expression "flesh and blood" as if it meant the physical body, and in particular the "substance" of that body, whereas in the New Testament in general and in Paul's writings in particular (Gal. 1:16; Eph. 6:12) "flesh and blood" undeniably denotes the *whole man* in his weak, perishable, corruptible *human nature,* as we have seen.

4. The context excludes this interpretation.   In verses 51ff., which immediately follow our passage, Paul explains what *kind* of change is necessary for man to enter the new world.   This change is *not* the annihilation of our present body and its replacement by a completely new body of a different substance.   On the contrary,

---

[53] Thus, to mention only a few by way of example, C. T. Craig (IB), F. Godet, Jean Hering (*The First Epistle of Saint Paul to the Corinthians*), and H. D. Wendland.

the apostle declares in verse 53 that *this* corruptible and mortal body will be endowed with the glorious gifts of incorruption and immortality.   This means that the *condition* of our present body will be changed, precisely as we found Paul saying earlier in verses 42ff.

For all these reasons the clause "flesh and blood cannot inherit the kingdom of God" must be interpreted along different lines. In the light of all we have found, the only correct and natural interpretation seems to be that *man, as he is now, a frail, earthbound, perishable creature,* cannot have a place in God's glorious, heavenly kingdom.   His human nature must first be changed so that he will be able to live in a world which is completely different from this present world: a new world in which sin, weakness, and death are unknown, where procreation of the human race is no longer needed, where there is no marriage, where the continuation of life depends no longer on eating and drinking and digestion, where heaven and earth are united as never before, and God dwells among and in his people with all the fullness of his Spirit (Isa. 33:24; Matt. 22:30; 1 Cor. 15:28; Rev. 7:16; 21:1-4).

To live in such a world man need not be deprived of his body of flesh, in which resides the image of God, any more than Christ needed to abandon his body of flesh.   What man needs is a change in the *conditions* of his body and of his *whole humanity;* a change from corruptibility, perishability, dishonor, and all that belongs to this earth-bound life, to indestructibility, immortality, glory, and all that is characteristic of a world which indeed may be called heaven on earth, and where the Spirit of God fills man's body and soul to the brim, as he does the new Adam, the life-giving Spirit.[54]

It is obvious that such a body of flesh is beyond adequate human understanding, just as is the glorious body of our Lord. The change of which Paul speaks is a divine miracle.   When Paul speaks of this change in Philippians 3:21, he adds emphatically that it will take place "according to the working whereby he is able even to subject all things unto himself."   Miraculous power is necessary. For this reason no scientific verification and understanding is possible.   God's miracles require *faith.*   To deny the possibility of a body of flesh which has all the character-

---

[54] Thus, in the main, J. Calvin, R. C. H. Lenski, *et al.*

istics described above, just because our scientific mind cannot conceive of such a body, amounts to thinking lightly of the power of that God for whom there is nothing impossible (Luke 1:37).

To say it with the words of H. Bavinck: "Almighty God who during this life, despite the constant flux of all the particles of our body, is able to preserve its identity from childhood to old age, possesses without doubt the power to do something similar through death."[55]

Paul's statement in 1 Corinthians 15:50, understood as we have suggested, is a most suitable conclusion to what has preceded. The NEB rendering: "What I mean, my brothers, is this . . ." is well chosen, for what follows is a further explanation and conclusion of the sowing parallel (vv. 35-44) and the Adam-Christ parallel (vv. 45-49).

In the first parallel Paul has spoken of God's power to raise dead bodies to new and richer life. In the Adam-Christ parallel the apostle has shown that in Christ's glorious resurrection as the last Adam God's plan with the first Adam and his offspring has been realized in principle. In the future resurrection of believers the latter will be renewed after the image of the risen Christ.

Now here, in verse 50, Paul states in conclusion that a tremendous change must come about. This change has been already implicitly announced in verses 35-49. In verse 50, however, it is explicitly stated to be absolutely necessary. If the erring Corinthians thought that Paul taught a resurrection which was a mere repetition and continuation, they were now undeceived: "flesh and blood," man in his present condition, is not able to enter the new world.

Therefore, Paul continues (vv. 51ff.), *because* "flesh and blood cannot inherit the kingdom of God," not only those who are dead but also those who are alive when Jesus returns from heaven will be changed: "we shall *all* be changed" (v. 51). This change is an absolute necessity for every believer: "For this corruptible *must* (Greek emphatic *dei*) put on incorruption and this mortal *must* put on immortality" (v. 53).

We may conclude from our study of the relevant passages of 1 Corinthians 15 that, in conformity with his general teachings, the apostle Paul speaks here in an unambiguous way of the resurrection of this body of flesh in a glorified condition.

---

[55] *Geref. Dogmatiek,* IV, 776.

6. THE ALLEGED DEVELOPMENT IN PAUL'S ESCHATOLOGY

According to many scholars we do not find Paul's final and mature teachings on the future state of the believer in 1 Corinthians 15. They assert that there was a development in the apostle's eschatology, especially with regard to the resurrection.

His earliest view, they claim, is found in 1 Thessalonians 4:13ff., where he follows the ancient Jewish tradition of a physical resurrection on the great day at the end of the ages, which Paul then regarded as imminent. This whole apocalyptic expectation, according to H. W. Robinson, was "a failure" and "led to the more spiritual development of Paul's thought."[56]

In 1 Corinthians 15 Paul allegedly still expected Christ to return very soon,[57] but instead of a physical body the believer would then receive a non-physical, spiritual body, for "flesh and blood cannot inherit the kingdom of God."

The last stage of the development, it is claimed, is to be found in 2 Corinthians, where as a result of Hellenistic influences Paul discards the whole idea of a visible return of Christ with a coinciding resurrection of believers. Here Paul teaches a Christ-mysticism in which the eschatology is already realized and which has replaced the "futurist eschatology" of the apostle's earlier phase.[58] Here the resurrection of the body is not regarded as taking place at the end of the world but at death. Particularly 2 Corinthians 5:1ff. is said to teach that a heavenly, non-physical body is waiting in heaven for each individual believer, who will assume that body immediately after death.[59]

To this theory we offer the following remarks in rebuttal:

1. What is called a development of Paul's views involves such a complete transformation that it would render all of Paul's eschatological teachings unreliable. An apostle who twice changed

---

[56] *The Christian Doctrine of Man*, p. 129. Similarly C. H. Dodd, *New Testament Studies*, p. 108; C. E. Raven, *op. cit.*, p. 130; *et al.*

[57] So, e.g., C. H. Dodd, *op. cit.*, p. 110; A. M. Hunter, *Interpreting Paul's Gospel*, pp. 54ff.; and many others. See against the idea of an "unforeseen delay in the *parousia*" K. Barth, CD, III/2, 497, 509.

[58] Thus, among many others, C. H. Dodd, *The Apostolic Preaching and its Development*, pp. 62ff. In his *The Coming of Christ*, Prof. Dodd has somewhat mitigated the rejection of "futurist eschatology" (p. 8), but Christ's coming as a future event in history is still denied (p. 16).

[59] With difference of opinion as regards details, this conception is held by P. Althaus, *Die Christliche Wahrheit*, II, 478; A. Deissmann, *op. cit.*, p. 218; C. H. Dodd, *New Testament Studies*, p. 110; C. E. Raven, *op. cit.*, p. 110; H. W. Robinson, *op. cit.*, p. 130; *et al.*

his mind on such vitally important issues as the second coming of Christ and the future life of the believer could not possibly be trusted for his allegedly final and mature teachings. This is candidly admitted by C. E. Raven, who, after discussing the expansion of Paul's thought, concludes that as Christians of the western world we must adopt "a very different attitude from that of Paul."[60]

All this is incompatible with Paul's claim to be an apostle, miraculously called, who knows the truth through special revelation and is authorized to proclaim it with divine authority (Gal. 1:11,12; 1 Thess. 2:13; 4:1,2; 2 Thess. 3:12,14; 1 Cor. 14:37; 2 Cor. 1:18ff.; 4:1ff.; 13:3,10, etc.). These claims, if they mean something more than just sinful boasting, exclude any possibility that Paul's teachings are inconsistent and contradictory.

2. Paul's so-called mature eschatological teaching contradicts that of the Gospels and particularly that of Jesus himself.

R. H. Fuller, among others, has provided ample proof that Prof. Dodd's "realized eschatology" fails to do justice to various synoptic sayings of Jesus which contain "an obvious future reference,"[61] whereas D. E. Holwerda has carefully examined and contested Bultmann's "present eschatology" with regard to John's gospel.[62] This Gospel also contains many sayings of Jesus which undeniably point to the future.

Paul cannot possibly be regarded as contradicting his Lord.

3. Paul himself was convinced that his "earliest" eschatological teaching in 1 Thessalonians 4:13ff. was derived from Jesus, as appears from his emphatic statement: "For this we say unto you by the word of the Lord. . ." (v. 15).

It makes no essential difference whether Paul is referring here to one or more unknown sayings of Jesus, or to a special revelation given to him by Christ, or to various recorded sayings of Jesus that he is restating in his own formulation. What is undeniable is that Paul claims divine authority for his "Jewish, materialistic, futurist" eschatology of 1 Thessalonians 4:13ff. If we attribute to Paul the idea of a "resurrection" of the "body" immediately after death, then we are not only depriving 1 Thessa-

---

[60] *Op. cit.,* p. 113.
[61] *The Mission and Achievement of Jesus,* Ch. 2.
[62] *The Holy Spirit and Eschatology in the Gospel of John, passim.* This book is a doctoral dissertation presented at the Free University in Amsterdam.

lonians 4:13ff. of any meaning,[63] but we implicitly declare that the apostle is capable of denying in the name of the Lord (2 Cor. 5:1) that which he elsewhere (1 Thess. 4:13ff.) proclaimed as divine truth in the name of the same Lord. This is completely unacceptable.

4. There is no difference between Paul's teachings in 1 Thessalonians 4:13ff. and those in 1 Corinthians 15, as far as the resurrection-body of the believer is concerned. This has been shown in the present and previous chapters of this study, when the "spiritual body" and the "exclusion" of "flesh and blood" from the kingdom of God were discussed. This implies that the alleged profound change in Paul's view, under Hellenistic influences, must have taken place during the short period which elapsed between the writing of 1 and 2 Corinthians.[64] This is highly improbable.

5. If Paul indeed changed his mind between 1 Corinthians 15 and 2 Corinthians 5, his failure to explain this change to the same congregation is unaccountable. This holds true particularly because in this same epistle we hear Paul defending himself against the accusation of showing "fickleness" and being a man whose word is "yea and nay" (2 Cor. 1:17). If 2 Corinthians 5:1ff. contradicts 1 Corinthians 15, Paul's self-defense in 2 Corinthians 1:17 is rendered invalid immediately after he has given it. The apostle was not the man to do such a foolish thing.

6. 2 Corinthians itself proves that Paul has not changed his mind but is consistent in his eschatological teachings. In 2 Corinthians 1:14 the apostle declares that the Corinthians are his glorying "in the day of our Lord Jesus."

Though this statement includes the present situation,[65] there can be no doubt that Paul is speaking here of "the Day with a capital D, the day when Jesus will come to judge."[66] R. Bultmann is right when he places this statement on a par with all the Pauline statements concerning Christ's Parousia, including those of 1 Corinthians 1:8, 5:5, and 15:23.[67]

In 2 Corinthians 4:14 we have another striking evidence. In

---

[63] Cf. O. Cullmann, "The Proleptic Deliverance of the Body," in *The Early Church*, p. 165.

[64] According to F. W. Grosheide (KNT on II Corinthians, p. 20), about one year; Feine-Behm (*op. cit.*, pp. 156, 161) reckons from Spring to late Autumn of A.D. 57, about seven months.

[65] Grosheide, *ad loc.*, points to the present tense *esmen*, "we are," and takes "*in* the day of . . ." as "*up to* the day. . . ."

[66] R. Hanson, *II Corinthians*, p. 31; F. V. Filson (IB), *et al.*

[67] ThNT. I, 346.

the preceding passage Paul speaks of the sufferings he has to endure for the gospel, sufferings which mean a constant dying (vv.
7ff.). Amid these sufferings it is his comfort that "the life of
Jesus," i.e., the supernatural power of the Lord, manifests itself
in his mortal body, enabling him to carry on his apostolic task:
though permanently dying, the apostle may still live to the
benefit of the Church and to God's glory (vv. 10ff.).

Meanwhile, Paul realizes that some day his sufferings may
result in death. Does that mean that the victory will ultimately
be to death? In verse 14 Paul declares that this will not be so.
The victory will be to life, not to death, for God who raised up
the Lord Jesus will raise up Paul and all believers, presenting
them together with Jesus before his throne in glory.

There can be no doubt that Paul is speaking here of the
resurrection of the body at the Parousia. The future verbs
egerei and *parastesei* point in that direction, but significant also
is the reference to God having raised up the Lord Jesus. That
means that the resurrection Paul is mentioning here, is viewed
as a resurrection similar to that of Jesus and requiring the same
almighty power of God. All this is in complete agreement with
Paul's eschatology in other epistles, especially with such statements as 1 Corinthians 6:14, Romans 8:11, and 1 Thessalonians
4:16.

To complete the picture: in the very passage, 2 Corinthians
5:1-10, which is said to contain Paul's new eschatological insight, the statement of the last verse (v. 10) contradicts the
alleged change: "For we must all be made manifest before the
judgment seat of Christ; that each one may receive the things
done in the body, according to what he hath done, whether it be
good or bad." The metaphor "judgment seat" shows clearly
that Paul is dealing here with the last judgment, to be held at
Christ's second coming.[68] It is then that everyone will reap what
he has sown in this life.

The three statements combined (2 Cor. 1:14; 4:14, and 5:10)
prove beyond all doubt that Paul's eschatology in 2 Corinthians
does not differ in any way from that in 1 Thessalonians and in
1 Corinthians: the apostle proclaims the coming of Christ at the
end of the ages to judge the living and the dead, bringing this

---

[68] Cf. D. H. Wendland and most commentators. With E. E. Ellis we reject the interpretation of those who take this verse as referring to a judgment at death, as fully foreign to Paul's teachings ("The Structure of Pauline Eschatology" in *Paul and His Recent Interpreters,* p. 46, n. 9).

present life to its final close in a body which (as regards the believer) is like the body of our risen Lord.

7. On the basis of what has been stated we must reject as contrary to Paul's mind and his explicit statements any exegesis which explains 2 Corinthians 5:1ff. as speaking of a spiritual body waiting in heaven and to be assumed immediately after death.

It is not difficult to read such a concept into this passage, because of the terminology and metaphors employed, but sound hermeneutics requires something different. It requires an explanation which does strict justice to Paul's eschatology, which in all his letters is invariably the same.

8. We need not discuss the interesting question whether in 2 Corinthians 5:1ff. the apostle is speaking of what the believer may expect immediately after death in an intermediate state between the moment of death and the Parousia, or whether he is discussing the Christian's hope as it will be fulfilled at the end of the ages.[69] This question, together with various other exegetical problems involved in this passage, has no special bearing on our quest for the nature of the believer's resurrection-body.

7. THE RESURRECTION-BODY IN THE LIGHT OF MATTHEW 22:30 AND I CORINTHIANS 6:13

There are two other statements in Scripture which are often adduced as evidence that we cannot expect a resurrection of this body of flesh.

The first statement is Jesus' answer to the question of the Sadducees, who asked which of the seven men, married in succession to the same woman, should have her as wife in the resurrection. Our Lord replied: ". . . in the resurrection they neither

[69] Many recent commentators declare that in II Cor. 5:1ff. Paul is not speaking of an intermediate state. If this be true, as this author is inclined to believe, it does not imply that this concept is foreign to Paul's mind or to Scripture in general. Although there is a growing tendency to reject an intermediate state (for the believer a state of conscious existence in blessed fellowship with Christ and the heavenly congregation), certain passages seem definitely to point in that direction as, e.g., Luke 16:22ff.; 23:43; Phil. 1:23; Heb. 12:23; and Rev. 6:9. Attempts to explain the intermediate state away from these passages (as, e.g., in the very recent study by B. Telder, *Sterven en Dan?*) are not convincing because they fail to do justice to the statements concerned. On the other hand it cannot be denied that in the New Testament not the intermediate state but the resurrection of the body is of paramount importance. I Cor. 15:32 proves, e.g., that to Paul an intermediate state would count for nothing if the resurrection of the body were not to follow.

marry, nor are given in marriage, but are as angels in heaven" (Matt. 22:30; cf. Mark 12:25). In Luke we read: "for neither can they die any more: for they are equal unto the angels" (20: 36).

Some conclude from these passages that "in the life hereafter" we will have no body and consequently will be "freed from the limitations which necessarily belong to bodily existence."[70] Others suggest that Jesus ascribes to those that enter the resurrection-life "angelic bodies, made from the light and glory of God."[71] There are also some who interpret Jesus' words as implying that the sexual difference between male and female will cease to exist.[72] Schleiermacher went even so far as to declare that Jesus teaches here the future cancellation of the difference between male and female *souls*.[73]

But Jesus' words do not allow for such interpretations.

In the first place, it should be noticed that Jesus spoke these words to the Sadducees, who denied *the raising up of dead bodies from the graves*. Their question would have made no sense if they were not thinking of a resurrection body fit for marriage and reproduction and actually employed in both.

Against this background Jesus' answer is remarkable because he actually confirms this supposition of the Sadducees. They deemed it impossible, but Jesus states only that they err, "not knowing the Scriptures, nor the power of God." That means: What you, Sadducees, erringly deny, namely the raising of dead bodies from the graves, is promised in the Scriptures and will be accomplished by the power of God.

This is confirmed by the fact that our Lord then states: "For when they shall rise from the dead . . ." (Mark 12:25), and: "But as touching the dead, that they are raised . . ." (v. 26). With a view to the issue under discussion between the Sadducees and Jesus, these words can only mean that according to Jesus

[70] E.g., W. Strawson, *Jesus and the Future Life,* pp. 207, 227; Dorothy L. Sayers renders Jesus' words as follows: "Blessed spirits neither marry nor are given in marriage" (*The Man Born to be King,* p. 224).

[71] J. Baillie, *And the Life Everlasting,* p. 136; S. Barton Babbage in *Reformed Theological Review,* IX, 4, 23.

[72] So, for example, K. Dijk, *Over de Laatste Dingen,* III, 106; P. Eudokimoff, "The Mystery of Marriage" in *The Student World,* XLV (1952), 151ff., quoted by A. Hijmans in *Bezinning,* Kampen, 1958, pp. 218ff.; and P. Althaus, *Die Letzten Dinge,* p. 126.

[73] Quoted by P. Althaus (*op. cit.,* p. 126, n. 1), who disagrees with Schleiermacher on the ground that if the latter were right personal identity would be lost.

dead men will indeed rise up in their own physical bodies. "What else could rise up thus?" we may ask with Lenski.

This excludes the possibility that we shall be raised as spirits, or that we shall receive an "angelic body" consisting of some heavenly "glory-matter," without any physical connection with our present bodies.

Second, though our Lord defends the scriptural doctrine of the resurrection of believers[74] in their physical bodies, he makes it clear that he disagrees with the popular Jewish conceptions of his day and with the teachings of the Pharisees, who pictured the future life as a mere continuation of this life. According to the Rabbis "the world to come would not differ essentially from the present, but only be more beautiful and glorious, with greater fertility, etc."[75]

Jesus, in contrast to all such theories, declares that those that are raised from the dead "neither marry, nor are given in marriage; but are as angels in heaven" (Mark 12:25).

It is notable that the text does not read that they *become* angels, but that they are "angel-like."[76]

This being "angel-like" must not be taken as implying more than the context clearly indicates. In the context, for instance, not a word is said about a future cancellation of the difference in sex, either in body or soul. Any such inference is therefore invalid.

One thing is emphatically stated by Jesus: in the world to come there will be no marriage, just as there is no marriage among the angels. *In that respect* the risen saints will be "angel-like."[77]

---

[74] Plummer and many other commentators point out that Christ is speaking of the resurrection of believers, using the words *ek nekron* (out of the dead). This expression differs from *ton nekron* (of the dead) which as a rule is used to denote the resurrection of *all the dead* (John 5:28, 29; Acts 17:32; etc.). Greydanus adds that although all the dead will receive their bodies back and so far forth may be said to rise again, yet only the believers will rise in the proper and full sense of the word, namely to eternal life. The others will be in the power of "the second death," under the punishment of God (Rev. 20:6, 13-15).

[75] K. II. Rengstorf (NTD), *ad loc.* Rengstorf adds that Mohammed's sensualistic pictures of the future life have their closest counterpart in these Jewish conceptions.

[76] Luke has the unusual word *Isaggelos,* which is better rendered "like angels" (NEB) or "angel-like" (Kittel, TWNT, I, 87) than "equal to the angels" (ASV, ERV).

[77] W. Manson (MNTC) on Luke, *ad loc.,* interprets: "Their mode of life is like that of angels."

Jesus' words by no means imply that the resurrection-body will have no sexual qualification, as appears from the fact that Luke, whose account is more elaborate than that of the other Synoptics, immediately subjoins the reason for there being no marriage. This reason is: "For they cannot die again" (BV), not "they will be sexless like the angels." Only then do we read: "For they are angel-like," which in the light of what follows means that they are *immortal* like the angels.

All this implies that marriage, which in this present age is necessary *inter alia* for the preservation of the human race, can be abolished in the world to come because no one will ever die and thus leave a vacant place to be filled. In that respect redeemed mankind will resemble the realm of the angels, who do not know death and whose number therefore never changes.

It is obvious that the resemblance between the risen saints and the angels, in the light of all the passages discussed, has only two interrelated aspects: there will be no marriage, and no death.[78] We will omit from consideration those further interesting questions regarding the fellowship among the risen saints, especially in connection with family relations, which are raised in this passage. Scripture does not satisfy our curiosity on this point, or on many others.

In conclusion, Matthew 22:30 and parallel passages do not deny that believers will rise in their bodies of flesh, though in a glorified and changed condition. On the contrary, they confirm this scriptural truth.

Not much needs to be said about 1 Corinthians 6:13, which is also often adduced as evidence that the resurrection-body will not be physical. Here Paul declares concerning the belly and food that "one day God will put an end to both" (NEB).

The passage to which this statement belongs has been extensively discussed in the third chapter of this study. There it was shown that in 1 Corinthians 6:12ff. Paul does not distinguish between "body" as *flesh* and "body" as *personality*. In particular, Paul does not say that only the latter will be raised. Throughout this passage "body" denotes the physical body, as is the case whenever Paul uses the word *soma*. It was also pointed out that Paul does not equate *body* with the *belly*. The latter is one specific side or function of the former.

For this reason Paul's statement that God will put an end to the belly and food, cannot possibly mean that God will destroy

[78] G. Kittel, TWNT, I, 87.

our bodies of flesh.   Our present bodies will not be destroyed but *changed,* either through death or, if we are living when Jesus returns, without death, as we found in 1 Corinthians 15:51ff.

The destruction of the belly and food can only mean that the resurrection-body, unlike our present body, will not need any material food.[79]   Not only the sexual but also the digestive function of the human body will cease.   God will sustain our bodies in his wonderful way, which is beyond description or comprehension.

8. ETERNAL EXISTENCE IN SPACE AND TIME

We have found that the passages just discussed do not deny but rather confirm the general teaching of Scripture and of Paul in particular, that the resurrection-body will consist of *flesh,* however great a change our present bodies may undergo at the Parousia.

That this implies a future existence in space and time and also the future existence of a visible cosmos is self-evident.

Many scholars regard time and space on the one hand, and eternity on the other, as mutually exclusive.   At the Parousia, they claim, eternity will replace time and space.[80]

To what consequences this can lead appears from the theories of K. Barth and E. Brunner, to mention only these two theologians.   According to Karl Barth, at the Parousia man will be "eternalized."   There is no continuation of human life beyond death.   Man will eternally "exist," but only "in the sight of God," as "man, who once *has been.*"   This theory amounts to assuming the annihilation of man as an objectively existing being.   It means the denial of any resurrection in the biblical sense of the word.[81]

E. Brunner believes in an individual, spiritual "resurrection" of man at death, but assumes that mankind will "vanish, just as it came into being."[82]

As regards the idea of a transcendent order beyond space and time, R. H. Fuller remarks rightly that this is "a wholly non-

---

[79] So P. Bachmann (ZK), *et al.*

[80] K. Barth, CD, III/2, 455ff., 521, 565; E. Brunner, *Das Ewige als Zukunft und Gegenwart,* pp. 58, 158ff.; C. H. Dodd, *Parables of the Kingdom,* p. 108; *The Apostolic Preaching and its Development,* pp. 84, 96; *The Coming of Christ,* p. 15; and others.

[81] See the Introduction to this study, where reference is also made to works which discuss Barth's conception.

[82] *Op. cit.,* p. 169.

biblical, Platonic conception,"[83] whereas W. Künneth declares that such a "colorless and shapeless conception of eternity" can just as well "be interpreted as Nirvana."[84]

The inseparability of creatureliness and space has already been discussed in connection with the ascension of our Lord. As to time and eternity, O. Cullmann has convincingly shown the contrast between the Greek concept of redemption and that of Scripture. The former requires escape from the time "circle" at the end of this life, whereas the latter is tied to a resurrection that will take place in future "linear" historical time. After the Parousia time will continue. While eternity may imply a *mode* of existence different from that of this age, it is certainly an existence *in* time, in *infinite* time, to be regarded as a succession of moments.[85]

Barth's appeal to 1 Corinthians 15:24 ("Then cometh the end . . .") as evidence for the cessation of time is invalid. The word *telos* (end) may allow for more than one interpretation, yet it is evident from the context that here it has no temporal reference.[86]

No more valid is the appeal sometimes made to Revelation 10:6, where we hear an angel proclaim "that there shall be time no longer." It is generally agreed that the word "time" in this case denotes "delay," *viz.,* delay of the final judgment. NEB renders accordingly: "There shall be no more delay."

The only objection to be raised to Cullmann's conception of eternity as "infinite time" is that he applies this to God also. Here Brunner is right when he declares that if this were true the difference between God's mode of existence and that of his creatures would be merely quantitative.[87] The surprising thing, however, is that Brunner thus implicitly condemns his own theory that man after death will be beyond space and time because in the Parousia God's eternity enters time and replaces it.[88] If that is true, then the difference between God and man becomes merely quantitative after death, an idea which Brunner himself rightly rejects.

[83] *The Mission and Achievement of Jesus,* p. 47.

[84] *Theologie der Auferstehung,* p. 251.

[85] *Christ and Time.* Similarly K. J. Popma, *Inleiding in de Wijsbegeerte,* pp. 59-90; *Eerst de Jood maar ook de Griek,* pp. 121ff.; J. M. Spier, *Tijd en Eeuwigheid, passim.*

[86] Cf. K. Runia, *De Theologische Tijd bij Karl Barth,* p. 242; F. V. Filson, *op. cit.,* p. 66, n. 40; and most commentators.

[87] *Op. cit.,* p. 58.

[88] *Ibid.,* pp. 158ff.

Cullmann is certainly right when he considers eternity infinite time as far as man is concerned, but his theory that God's eternity is of the same nature has to be rejected as not scriptural. In every respect God is essentially different from man, and so is God's eternity in comparison with that of man. The former is absolute, divine, complete, while that of man is partial and derivative.[89]   Divine eternity denotes an existence absolutely beyond and independent of space and time, incomprehensible to the human mind. Creaturely eternity means a *future* existence in infinite time in which man, because he is a creature, is eternally bound to space and time.

Very interesting is the question whether infinite time after the resurrection will be essentially different from time as it is now, especially with regard to the succession of moments.

K. Runia objects to the idea of a succession of moments, which according to him would imply that in eternity there will be a continuous coming-into-being and development. He regards "eternity" and "continuous development" as mutually exclusive conceptions, and suggests that in eternity there will be "duration-without-succession," admitting, however, that this sounds somewhat abstract.[90]

Others, however — and this author would agree with them — regard the conception of a time or a duration in which there is no succession of moments as a *contradictio in terminis*.[91]   Scripture is lacking in evidence that the structure of time will be different in eternity. No doubt the *experience* of time will greatly change. Time will no longer be pressing upon us, as it is now. There will be no impatient waiting for the good to come, neither will there be the nightmarish countdown of minutes before the inevitable comes our way. In eternity we will live in the perfect freedom of God's children.

This difference, however, does not in the least imply that time will cease to be a succession of moments. Already in this life there is a great difference between ten minutes in a lover's arms and ten minutes in the dentist's chair. But the ten minutes as periods of time are the same.

Neither should eternity necessarily exclude continuous development. If eternity brings perfect fellowship not only with God

89 L. Newbigin, *The Household of God,* p. 120.
90 *Op. cit.,* pp. 237-41.
91 So, e.g., K. J. Popma, *Calvinistische Geschiedbeschouwing,* pp. 157ff.; and J. M. Spier, *op. cit.,* pp. 223ff.

and Christ (Rev. 21:1ff.), but also with angels and with the redeemed saints of all ages (Matt. 8:11, Heb. 12:22ff., 1 Thess. 4:17), then the believer may expect a continuous growth in the knowledge of God and of God's wondrous deeds in history and in the lives of the saints.   This continuous growth will lead to ever increasing adoration, thanksgiving, and joy.[92]

Finally, the idea of a "*duration*-without-succession" seems as unacceptable as that of a "*time*-without-succession."   If the word "time," taken as cosmic time, has any reasonable sense, it implies the succession of moments.   But the same is true of "duration."   The moment we use the word we speak of succession. A time and a duration without succession are as unthinkable as a war without combatants, a stream without water, a wedding without a bridal couple.

As has been said, the resurrection of the body of flesh involves also the future existence of *a visible cosmos.*

Scripture teaches us that man is the center of the universe, not in the astronomical but in the theological sense of the word. To man was given dominion over the earth (Gen. 1:26ff., Ps. 8:6).   When man rebelled against God, not only did he become the object of God's punishment but his domain, the earth, was cursed for his sake (Gen. 3:17).   Paul declares that the whole universe became "the victim of frustration" (Rom. 8:20, NEB).

No wonder then that the redemption Christ accomplishes does not stop at man, but includes the whole creation.   Isaiah already prophesied that God will create new heavens and a new earth, and he gave a beautiful description in visionary language of the conditions on the new earth (Isa. 65:17-25; 66:22ff.). Paul proclaims that the whole creation is living in hope of being "delivered from the bondage of corruption into the liberty of the glory of the children of God" and that, while living in hope, the creation "travaileth in pain" (Rom. 8:21ff.).   In Colossians 1:15ff. the same apostle describes the cosmic significance of Christ, whose reconciliation embraces all things "in the heavens and upon the earth."   Then there is John's incomparably beautiful vision of the new heaven and the new earth in Revelation 21 and 22. These chapters, from the day that they were written, have comforted the hearts of numerous believers amid all the sorrows of this present age.

---

[92] Cf. H. B. Swete, *op. cit.,* p. 107; J. M. Spier, *op. cit.,* p. 224; and E. Sauer, *op. cit.,* pp. 180ff.

It is true that the biblical descriptions of this new cosmos are framed in visionary, metaphorical language and must be interpreted accordingly. The world to come is a *new* world, so thoroughly different from the present that any adequate description or conception of it is utterly impossible. It is a world so entirely different from ours that Scripture can say that God will *create* new heavens and a new earth. The creative power of almighty God is needed to bring about this change.

Nevertheless, it is *this* world that will be redeemed. Romans 8:18ff. shows that there is the closest connection between the redemption of creation and that of our bodies. The two will take place simultaneously (vv. 21, 23). The redemption of our bodies, as we have seen, does not mean the annihilation of our present bodies and their replacement by newly created ones, but rather their re-creation, renewal, glorification. In the same way this present creation would not be truly "delivered from the bondage of corruption (v. 21) if it were to be destroyed and replaced by something utterly different, without any material connection with this present world. Here also we may expect re-creation, renewal, glorification.

It is on *this* earth, transformed by God's almighty power into a suitable dwelling place for believers in their glorified bodies, that "God himself shall be with them, and be their God: and he shall wipe away every tear from their eyes; and death shall be no more; neither shall there be mourning, nor crying, nor pain, any more: the first things are passed away" (Rev. 21:3ff.).

It is *this* earth that the meek will inherit, according to the promise of Jesus (Matt. 5:5).

Indeed, in Scripture the resurrection of the body as a glorified body of flesh is inseparably tied to the renewal and glorification of the cosmos.

In contrast to those who would declare this scriptural truth a myth, E. Thurneysen in 1931 expressed his faith in it when he wrote: "The world into which we shall enter in the Parousia of Jesus Christ is therefore not another world; it is this world, this heaven, this earth; both, however, passed away and renewed. It is these forests, these fields, these cities, these streets, these people, that will be the scene of redemption. At present they are battlefields, full of the strife and sorrow of the not yet accomplished consummation; then they will be fields of victory, fields of harvest, where out of seed that was sown with tears the everlasting sheaves will be reaped and brought home."[93]

APPENDIX I

THE IMMORTALITY OF THE SOUL

In order to do justice to the conception "immortality of the soul" we must distinguish carefully between three different connotations of that expression.

There is, first, the Greek conception as it is most beautifully expressed in Plato's *Phaedo*. The Greek regarded man as consisting of two essentially different parts: the one (the soul) is spiritual, divine, and therefore immortal, while the other (the body) is material and as such evil and mortal. The soul dwells in the body as in its prison, out of which it is delivered at death to return to the realm of the divine.

O. Cullmann has criticized this Greek conception in his *Immortality of the Soul or Resurrection of the Dead?* and shown that it is absolutely foreign to Scripture. Man is a unit, and since he sinned he is as such a victim of death. He does not possess an inherent immortality, but becomes immortal as man (in body and soul) only through the resurrection of Christ and through faith in him.

A second conception of the soul's immortality is that of the popular belief of modern times. It is held widely that man's body has no eternal future, but that his soul or spirit will live forever after death, probably in a state of happiness.

Though several specific Greek elements are lacking here, this conception is evidently derived from Greek thought, of which it is a diluted, modernized version. It is equally unbiblical in its denial of the resurrection of the body and its cheap assurance of future happiness for practically everyone.

Wholly different is a third conception, which is found among those who on the ground of Scripture believe that only Christ gives eternal life to his believers, an eternal life which implies the resurrection of the body when Christ comes in glory. Speaking of the immortality of the soul, they express the conviction that after death man continues to exist in a conscious state of either

[93] E. Thurneysen, in his article "Christus und seine Zukunft" in *Zwischen den Zeiten*, 1931, p. 209.

bliss with Christ or misery in hell. In this sense the Westminster Confession of Faith speaks of the souls of men "having an immortal subsistence" (Ch. XXXII).

It is highly questionable, however, whether it is correct to use the term "immortality of the soul" in this connection, despite the fact that the thought behind it is fully biblical.

Scripture never uses the word "immortality" (*athanasia*) to denote the continued bare existence of all men after death. It declares that in the absolute sense of the word God alone possesses immortality (1 Tim. 6:16). He has life in himself and is "life's never failing Fountain."[94] Furthermore, Scripture promises immortality to those that truly believe in Christ (John 3:36; 11:25, 26; 1 Cor. 15:53). This immortality is not inherent in man or in his soul as such, but is the gift of God's grace to the believers. It concerns the whole man, body and soul, and consists in the enjoyment of imperishable life in its fullness, in bliss and glory (Eph. 2:5ff.).

As to men without Christ, Scripture declares emphatically that already during this life they are "dead through their trespasses and sins" (Eph. 2:1,5), that those who reject Christ "shall not see life" (John 3:36), and that at the last day they will die "the second death" — which does not mean their annihilation but their entering into a condition of eternal misery (Rev. 2:11; 20:6, 14; 21:8).[95] This "second death" will affect soul and body (Matt. 10:28).

In the light of all this A. Kuyper was right in declaring that "the expression immortality of the soul is not acceptable in the light of the gospel,"[96] whereas Berkouwer remarks, "The question may well be asked whether the Church by using the terminology "immortal souls" has not darkened the light of revelation."[97]

APPENDIX II

"I BELIEVE ... THE RESURRECTION OF THE FLESH"

As soon as the Christian Church began to confess her faith by means of credal formulations, we find her belief in the resurrection

---

[94] W. Hendriksen, NTC on I and II Timothy and Titus, p. 208.

[95] "Here the miseries of hell are meant" (R. Bultmann, TWNT, *s.v. thanatos*).

[96] Quotation taken from G. C. Berkouwer, *De Mens het Beeld Gods*, p. 298.

[97] *Ibid.*, p. 304.

expressed in the now controversial words: "I believe . . . the resurrection of the flesh."

We see the expression appear already in "quasi-credal scraps" of second century Christian communities.[98] Irenaeus, for example, declares that the Church throughout the world confesses belief in "the resurrection of the flesh," which (he says) belongs to the faith received from the apostles and their disciples.[99] Tertullian also speaks of the resurrection as the "restoration of their [i.e., the dead] flesh," as belonging to the faith taught by Christ.[100]

As J. N. D. Kelly has shown, the expression "resurrection of the flesh" occurred in the (Greek) Roman liturgy of around 200 A.D. as well as in the (Latin) text of the ancient Roman baptismal creed, whereas also in Egypt and Cappadocia the same credal formula was used about the middle of the fourth century.[101]

We may say, therefore, that the entire early Church, in the West and in the East alike, publicly confessed belief in the resurrection of the flesh.

In the Western creeds, under the influence of Rome, this confessional formula has retained its place with hardly any exception. Up to the Reformation there is no exception at all.[102]

The churches of the Reformation retained the expression under discussion in most of their confessions of faith and catechisms as, for instance, Luther's smaller Catechism of 1529; the first Scottish Confession, 1560; the Belgic Confession of 1561; and the Heidelberg Catechism, 1563 (the German text in Question and Answer 57 has *Fleisch*). With a slight variation in the wording the same doctrine is confessed in the Second Helvetic Confession, 1562 (German text: *Fleisch*); Westminster Confession of Faith, 1647; and the Baptismal Liturgy of the Established Kirk in Scotland, 1648.[103]

The Church of England has retained "the resurrection of the flesh" in the Baptismal Service and in the Office for the Visitation of the Sick, whereas in Article 4 of the Thirty-Nine Articles of Religion we have: "Christ did truly rise from the dead and took

---

[98] J. N. D. Kelly, *Early Christian Creeds*, p. 66.

[99] *Against Heresies*, 1; 10, 1 (ANF, I, 330).

[100] *Prescription against Heretics*, Ch. XIII (ANF, III, 249; similarly IV, p. 27).

[101] J. N. D. Kelly, *op. cit.*, pp. 88ff.; 102; 119.

[102] For evidence see Kelly, *op. cit.*, Ch. 12, and H. B. Swete, *The Apostles' Creed*, pp. 102-09.

[103] Cf. P. Schaff, *The Creeds of the Evangelical Protestant Churches, ad loc.*

again His body, with flesh and bones, and all things appertaining
to Man's nature, wherewith He ascended into Heaven, and there
sitteth until he return to judge all men at the last day."

In 1552 for the first time the expression "the resurrection of
the body" was admitted in the Apostles' Creed, but only for popular use in Matins and Evensong; never in the baptismal service of
the Western Church.[104]   Since there is no evidence of any discussion over the change, it may be concluded that the terms "flesh"
and "body" were regarded as equivalent.[105]

The Roman Catholic Church at the Council of Trent authorized
a Manual for Catechists, in which "the resurrection of the flesh"
is explained in fifteen articles, and it is stated that "flesh" in this
connection does not denote complete humanity, but the flesh-
body.[106]

The Churches of the East retained the expression "the resurrection of the flesh" up to the Council of Constantinople in 381.[107]
Then the "Nicaeno-Constantinopolitan Creed" was adopted, in
which Article 11 of the Apostles' Creed reads: "We expect the
resurrection of the dead."[108]   This formulation has since been used
by the whole Eastern Church.

What moved the Fathers of Constantinople to change the traditional expression we do not know.   The Acts or Minutes of the
Council have been lost.   That no change of doctrine was involved
may be concluded from the following facts:

1. The change is not discussed by any contemporary author
now extant.

2. Current teachings in the Eastern Church of those days show
clearly that the resurrection of man in a body of flesh was considered biblical doctrine.   Cyril of Jerusalem in his famous Catechetical Lectures (Ch. 18) writes that God is able "to reconstitute
flesh which has become dust into flesh again."[109]   Gregory of
Naziansum, one of the presidents of the Constantinople Council,

---

[104] J. T. Darragh, *The Resurrection of the Flesh,* pp. 224ff.   Darragh remarks rightly that Art. 4 of the 39 Articles indirectly describes the manner
of the general resurrection, since Christ's resurrection-body is the model
to which our bodies will be conformed.

[105] Cf. J. T. Darragh, *op. cit.,* p. 224; J. Pearson, *op. cit.,* p. 528; and H.
B. Swete, *op. cit.,* pp. 97ff.

[106] Cf. Darragh, *op. cit.,* pp. 243ff.

[107] For evidence see P. Schaff, *The Creeds of the Greek and Latin
Churches,* pp. 31ff., 39, 40.

[108] *Ibid.,* p. 58.

[109] NPNF, VII, 134ff.

declares that in the resurrection the soul receives back from the earth "its kindred flesh."[110]   Similar interpretations are given by Gregory of Nyssa[111] and Basil the Great.[112]   All these prominent leaders of the Eastern Church regard the resurrection-body as the glorified "edition" of this present flesh-body, sharply distinguished from the soul as the immaterial part of human nature.

Later theologians of the Eastern Orthodox Church adhere to the same teachings.[113]

There seems reason to assume that the Eastern Church, without any intention to reject the Western formulations as unscriptural, went her own way in formulating the truth.   The Nicaeno-Constantinopolitan Creed gives ample proof of this.   It is not a revised "Apostles' Creed" but an original Eastern Confession of Faith, drawn up in connection with the Arian controversy.   This explains the use of several non-traditional expressions, among which the one under discussion: "We hope for the resurrection of the dead."

The Western Church adopted the Nicaeno-Constantinopolitan Creed and placed it on a par with the Apostles' Creed, which shows that this Church considered the two formulations of the resurrection truth fully equivalent.

When we ask what moved the early Church to adopt the expression "the resurrection of the *flesh*," which as such does not occur in the New Testament, the answer cannot be that of J. T. Darragh, who says that in the early Church "flesh" was considered to denote "the whole man, complete humanity," and not the flesh-body.[114]

Not only do the later Fathers, whose works have been quoted, distinguish sharply between the soul which they call immortal, and the flesh of the body which dies, but we find the same conception in the writings of the Apostolic Fathers.   None of these earliest Christian writers uses the expression "the resurrection of the flesh," but when they speak of the resurrection their terminology leaves no doubt that the "flesh" to be raised is the flesh-body as distinct from the soul.   This is the case in First Clement[115] and Ignatius.[116]

[110] NPNF, VII, 236ff.
[111] NPNF, V, 466ff.
[112] NPNF, VIII, 100.
[113] Darragh, *op. cit.*, pp. 230ff.
[114] *Op. cit.*, pp. 50, 154.
[115] ANF, I, 12.
[116] ANF, I, 33-44.

The evidence in the works of the Apologists is overwhelmingly against Darragh's interpretation. Justin Martyr in particular uses frequently the expression "the resurrection of the flesh," and explains the word "flesh" as denoting the flesh-body, not the soul.[117] Athenagoras in his treatise on "The Resurrection of the Dead" distinguishes similarly between man's spiritual "part," the soul, and the flesh-body, which dies and is to be raised.[118]

W. Bieder, who recognizes that the early Church laid much emphasis on the substance of the resurrection-body as identical with that of the present flesh-body, suggests that in the Creed the word "flesh" does not necessarily denote "the substance of the body but the *person himself,* who will be raised as man" (without flesh and blood).[119] Bieder claims that this is the meaning of the expression *hujus carnis resurrectionem* (the resurrection *of this flesh*) in the Creed of Aquilea, where Rufinus was a bishop.

Rufinus' own words, however, prove that Bieder misrepresents his doctrine. In his "Commentary on the Apostles' Creed" (Ch. 43) Rufinus declares that "the substance of each individual flesh, though its particles have been variously and diversely scattered . . . to each soul will be restored . . . in order that the flesh together with its soul may . . . either be crowned . . . or punished. . . ." After thus having maintained the traditional doctrine, Rufinus adds that his church, to emphasize the fact that each soul will receive again its *own* flesh-body, has inserted the pronoun "this" ("the resurrection of *this* flesh") and that every person who rehearses the Creed must make the sign of the cross upon his forehead while saying the word "this," in order that every believer may know that "*his* flesh . . . will be a vessel of honour . . ." (*viz.,* in the resurrection).[120]

It is apparent that Rufinus, far from watering down the traditional meaning of the expression "the resurrection of the flesh," rather emphasizes that meaning and wants to safeguard it.

Bieder appeals to another statement by Rufinus, found in the latter's preface to "Pamphilus' Defense of Origen." According to Bieder, Rufinus says here that the expressions "the resurrection of the flesh" and ". . . of the body" are both correct, but the former is the confession of the Creed while the latter is in con-

---

[117] "Dialogue with Trypho" (ANF, I, 87, 197); "Fragments of the lost work of Justin on the Resurrection" (ANF, I, 197ff.).
[118] ANF, II, 148ff., 154, 162.
[119] *Auferstehung des Fleisches oder des Leibes,* pp. 107ff.
[120] NPNF, III, 560.

formity with the apostle (Paul). From this Bieder infers that Rufinus understood the word "flesh" as "person" (apart from flesh and blood), as Paul did.[121]

Taken in their context, however, the words of Rufinus mean precisely the opposite of what Bieder declares them to mean. Rufinus certainly writes that there is a difference in the way the Creed and Paul *express* the doctrine, the one using the word "flesh," the other the word "body." But he emphasizes that there is not the slightest difference in meaning between the two. He declares: ". . . we believe that it is this very flesh in which we are now living which will rise again, not one kind of flesh instead of another, nor another body than the body of this flesh. . . . It is an absurd invention of maliciousness to think that the human body is different from the flesh. . . . On the other [hand] we must not detract from the dignity and glory of the incorruptible and spiritual body. . . ."[122]

Here the modern distinction between "flesh" and "body," or between "flesh" and "person," far from being defended, is refuted.

Our study of some early Christian writers, to whom many could be added who teach the same doctrine, provides the answer to the question, Why did the early Church in her creeds speak of the resurrection of the *flesh*? The answer must be that the early Church wanted to emphasize the identity of this present body with that of the resurrection as regards the *substance* of both, viz., *flesh*.

All the early Fathers, speaking of the resurrection, defend this identity of substance by referring to the statement of the risen Christ that he had a body of "flesh and bones." They reject any spiritualizing conclusion drawn from Paul's statement about the "spiritual body" and about "flesh and blood" which "cannot inherit the kingdom of God." Often they even overemphasize the identity by giving insufficient attention to the change and glorification of the flesh.

And indeed the early Church had more than sufficient reasons to speak so emphatically of the resurrection of the flesh, both in her creeds and by the mouths of her prominent leaders. For in those days pagan philosophers on the one hand and docetic, early gnostic and other heretics on the other, denied the possibility and/or suitability of a resurrection of this body of flesh.

Many opponents were prepared to speak of the resurrection of the *dead,* because they could interpret that as meaning the resur-

[121] Bieder, *op. cit.,* p. 110.
[122] NPNF, III, 421.

rection of dead *souls,* meanwhile denying the resurrection of *dead bodies.*[123]

In all probability it was this misuse of biblical expressions which led the early Church to prefer a formulation, not literally found in Scripture, but, better than any other formulation, designed to safeguard the biblical truth of the believer's resurrection in a body of glorified *flesh.*[124]

From a formal point of view the traditional expression of the Creed may be called a misnomer. The word "flesh" denotes here the substance of the body, whereas it is not the flesh-substance as such, not the crude, unorganized "matter" that will be raised, but *man in his flesh-body.* For this formal reason it would be better to speak of the resurrection "of the body," "of the dead," or "from the dead," as Scripture does.

In our day, however, the older formulation of the Apostles' Creed is under constant fire not for this formal reason, but because the biblical truth of the resurrection in a body of glorified flesh is rejected. The biblical term "resurrection of the *body*" (or "resurrection of the *dead*") is preferred by many because they regard (contrary to Scripture) the *body* as something quite different from the *flesh.* In connection with the resurrection they view the body as "person" or "personality," not as an organism of flesh. *Their appeal to the biblical expression serves the purpose of denying the biblical truth.* Here we may quote E. E. Ellis' statement: "While its advocates speak of Jerusalem, one suspects that the accent is Athenian."[125]

In 1899 H. B. Swete wrote words which have lost nothing of their timeliness: "If in the second century the Gospel of the Resurrection was ridiculed by Pagan philosophers and frittered away by Christian heresy, there are forces at work in these last years of the nineteenth century, which under other names and altered circumstances are tending to the same results. . . ."[126]

It is for this very reason that the Church of our day should continue to confess:

> "*I believe . . . the resurrection of the flesh.*"[127]

---

[123] Tertullian mentions such opponents in "On the Resurrection of the Flesh," Ch. 19 (ANF, III, 558ff.).

[124] Cf. J. N. D. Kelly, *op. cit.,* pp. 97, 165, and H. B. Swete, *op. cit.,* p. 92. Even W. Bieder admits that the word "flesh" was chosen for anti-spiritualizing reasons (*op. cit.,* par. 6).

[125] *Paul and His Recent Interpreters,* p. 48.

[126] *Op. cit.,* p. 98.

[127] For a most able discussion of this article of the Apostles' Creed ref-

erence may be made to L. E. Boliek, *The Resurrection of the Flesh* (A study of a Confessional Phrase), which book reached this present author after the manuscript had been completed. Dr. Boliek defends the confession of the "resurrection of the *flesh*" as "a legitimate expression of the Biblical doctrine of the resurrection" (Proposition I). Other important studies which came to the author's notice when this manuscript was completed are:

M. E. Dahl, *The Resurrection of the Body* (A Study of I Corinthians 15). Though Dr. Dahl rejects the resurrection of the *flesh,* he shows the untenability of all spiritualizing conceptions of the resurrection inherent in what he calls "the accepted exegesis" of I Cor. 15, and claims: "Deficient as the traditional view may be, it does not misunderstand St. Paul any more than the accepted exegesis, and is possibly more faithful to his actual message" (p. 93).

O. Jager, *Het Eeuwige Leven.* Dr. Jager defends the resurrection of the flesh and the eternal existence in space and time.

J. H. Semmelink, "Onsterfelijkheid en Opstanding," Den Haag, 1962 (in *Exegetica*).

SUMMARY OF FINDINGS

Our findings in this study may be briefly summarized as follows.

(1) According to the teachings of Scripture the human body of flesh is God's good creature, the ethically neutral instrument given to man for the glorification of his Creator, before as well as after the fall.

(2) When in Scripture, and particularly in Paul's writings, "body" and "flesh" occur in an ethically loaded sense, as a rule, they do not denote the flesh-body as such but man's sinful nature, concentrated in his heart and expressing itself in and through the flesh-body.

(3) When Paul sometimes speaks of the flesh-body in an unfavorable sense, he does not ascribe any intrinsic evil to it, but refers to the corruption of God's good instrument as the result of man's misusing it in the service of sin.

(4) There is nothing in the human body of flesh as such which makes it unsuitable for or unworthy of an eternal future. As God's good creature it does not need destruction, but rather deliverance through Christ from the results of man's sin: corruption, death, and misery.

(5) According to the unequivocal teachings of the Gospels Christ was raised and appeared to his disciples in the same body in which he died. Since there is no ground for assuming that our Lord abandoned this flesh-body at the ascension, and since the resurrection-body of Christ is the pattern of the body which the believer will receive, the resurrection of the latter in his own body of flesh is guaranteed.

(6) Since Christ is the last Adam, who leads God's creation to the glorified state that Adam would have reached if he had not sinned, not only is Christ's own resurrection-body in a glorified condition, but the believer too will be raised in a completely changed and glorified body of flesh.

(7) That the believer's resurrection-body will be a body of glorified flesh is also clearly promised in the Scriptures, both in the Old and in the New Testament.

228

(8) Whenever the early Church Fathers and Creeds speak of the resurrection "of the flesh," they mean by "flesh" man's flesh-body. The word "flesh" is employed to safeguard the truth against spiritualizing interpretations.

(9) Though the expression "the resurrection of the flesh" is not found in Scripture and does not adequately formulate the biblical truth, it should be retained in view of the spiritualizing tendencies abounding in our modern world.

BIBLIOGRAPHY[1]

Aalders, G. Ch., *A Short Introduction to the Pentateuch,* 1949.
————, *Het Herstel van Israel volgens het Oude Testament,* 1933.
————, *Het Boek Genesis* (KV), 1933-1936.
————, *Het Boek Daniel* (KV), 1928.
————, Daniel (COT), 1962.
————, *Het Boek De Prediker* (COT), 1948.
Aalders, J. G., *Gog en Magog in Ezechiël,* 1951.
Alexander, J. A., *Commentary on the Prophecies of Isaiah,* reprinted in Classic Commentary Library, 1953.
Alford, H., *The Greek New Testament,* 1871.
Allen, E. L., "The Lost Kerugma," in *New Testament Studies,* July 1957.
Allen, W. C., *A Critical and Exegetical Commentary on the Gospel according to St. Matthew* (ICC), 1907.
Althaus, P., *Die Letzten Dinge,* 1933.
————, *Die Christliche Wahrheit,* 1948.
————, *The So-called Kerugma and the Historical Jesus,* 1959.
Andel, J. Van, *Paulus Brief aan de Colossenzen,* 1907.
Andersen, F. I., "We Speak in the Words Which the Holy Spirit Teacheth," in *The Westminster Theological Journal,* May 1960.
Anderson, H., "The Historical Jesus," in *Scottish Journal of Theology,* June 1960.
Athenagoras, *The Resurrection of the Dead* (ANF).
Atkins, G. G., *The Book of Ecclesiastes* (IB), 1956.

Babbage, S. B., "Immortality and Resurrection," in *The Reformed Theological Review,* IX, No. 4, 1950.
Bachmann, P., *Der erster Brief des Paulus an die Korinther* (ZK), 1910.
————, *Der zweiter Brief des Paulus an die Korinther* (ZK), 1918.
Bailey, J. W., *The First and Second Epistles to the Thessalonians* (IB), 1955.
Baillie, D. M., *God Was in Christ,* 1958.
Baillie, J., *And the Life Everlasting,* 1936.
Bakels, H. A., *Circum Sacra,* 1935.
Barclay, W., *The Acts of the Apostles* (DSB), 1955.
————, *The Gospel of Luke* (DSB), 1957.
————, *The Letters to the Corinthians* (DSB), 1957.
————, "The Great Themes of the New Testament," in *Expository Times,* March 1959.
————, *The Mind of St. Paul,* 1958.
————, *The Promise of the Spirit,* 1960.
————, *Crucified and Crowned,* 1961.

[1]The Bibliography contains only books and articles to which reference has been made in this study. The dates are those of the editions consulted.

230

—————, "Hellenistic Thought in New Testament Times," in *Expository Times*, June 1961.

Barnett, A. E., *The Second Epistle of Peter* (IB), 1957.

Barrett, C. K., *A Commentary on the Epistle to the Romans*, 1957.

—————, *The Gospel according to St. John* (IB), 1958.

Barth, K., *Die Auferstehung der Toten*, 1935.

—————, *Church Dogmatics*, 1936ff.

—————, *Credo*, 1936.

—————, *Dogmatik im Grundrisz*, 1947.

—————, *Christ and Adam*, 1956.

—————, *The Faith of the Church*, 1958.

Baruch, *Apocalypse*.

Basil the Great, *The Hexaemeron* (NPNF).

Bauernfeind, O., *"Aselgeia,"* in TWNT, I, 1933.

Baumgärtel, F., *"Kardia,"* in TWNT, III, 1938.

—————, *"Sarx,"* in TWNT, VII, 1960.

Bavinck, H., *Gereformeerde Dogmatiek*, 1918.

Beare, F. W., *The Epistle to the Ephesians* (IB), 1953.

Beek, M., *Inleiding tot de Joodse Apocalyptiek van het O. en N. T. Tijdvak*, 1950.

Beek, M. A., *Das Daniel Buch, sein historischer Hintergrund und seine literarische Entwicklung*, 1935.

Beet, J. A., *St. Paul's Epistle to the Romans*, 1902.

Behm, J., *"Kardia,"* in TWNT, III, 1938.

Berkouwer, G. C., *De Persoon van Christus*, 1952.

—————, *The Triumph of Grace in the Theology of Karl Barth*, 1956.

—————, *De Mens het Beeld Gods*, 1957.

—————, *De Wederkomst van Christus*, I, 1961.

Bernard, J. H., *A Critical and Exegetical Commentary on the Gospel according to St. John* (ICC), 1928.

Betz, O., "Die Geburt der Gemeinde durch den Lehrer," in *New Testament Studies*, July 1957.

Bieder, W., "Auferstehung des Fleisches oder des Leibes," in *Theologische Zeitschrift*, August 1945.

Bigg, Ch., *A Critical and Exegetical Commentary on the Epistles of St. Peter and St. Jude* (ICC), 1961.

Birkeland, H., "The Belief in the Resurrection of the Dead in the Old Testament," in *Studia Theologica*, III, 1950/1.

Blaiklock, E. M., *The Acts of the Apostles* (TNT), 1959.

Blass, F., and A. Debrunner, *Grammatik des neutestamentliches Griechisch*, 1949/50.

Bleeker, L. H. K., *Job* (TU), 1926.

Böhl, F. M. Th., *Genesis* (TU), 1923.

Boliek, L. E., *The Resurrection of the Flesh*, 1962.

Bolkestein, M. H., *Het Verborgen Rijk* (PNT), 1954.

Bondt, A. de, *Wat Leert het Oude Testament aangaande het Leven na dit Leven?*, 1938.

Bonhoeffer, D., *The Cost of Discipleship*, 1959.

Book of Jubilees.

Bornkamm, G., *Jesus of Nazareth*, 1961.

Bouma, C., *De Brieven van den Apostel Paulus aan Timotheus en Titus* (KV), 1937.
Bousset, W., *Kyrios Christos*, 1913.
————, *Die Schriften des Neuen Testaments*, 1917.
Bowie, W. R., *The Book of Genesis* (IB), 1952.
Bowman, J., "The Doctrine of Creation, Fall of Man and Original Sin in Samaritan and Pauline Theology," in *The Reformed Theological Review*, October 1960.
Brandon, O. R., "Heart," in *Baker's Dictionary of Theology*, 1960.
Branscomb, B. H., *The Gospel of Mark* (MNTC), 1937.
Briggs, C. A. and E., *The Book of Psalms* (ICC), 1907/9.
Brown, F., S. R. Driver and C. A. Briggs, *Hebrew and English Lexicon of the Old Testament*, reprinted 1957.
Bruce, F. F., *The Dawn of Christianity*, 1954.
————, *Second Thoughts on the Dead Sea Scrolls*, 1956.
————, *Commentary on the Epistles to the Ephesians and the Colossians* (NIC), 1957.
————, *The New Testament Documents — Are They Reliable?*, 1960.
Brunner, E., *Das Ewige als Zukunft und Gegenwart*, 1953.
Büchsel, F., *"Epithumia,"* in TWNT, III, 1938.
Bultmann, R., *Jesus and the Word*, 1935.
————, *"Thanatos,"* in TWNT, III, 1938.
————, *Theology of the New Testament*, 1952-5.
————, *Kerugma and Myth*, ed. H. W. Bartsch, 1954.
————, *Jesus Christ and Mythology*, 1960.
Buttrick, G. A., *The Gospel according to St. Matthew* (IB), 1951.
Burton, E. de Witt., *Spirit, Soul and Flesh*, 1918.

Caird, G. B., *The First and Second Books of Samuel* (IB), 1953.
Calès, J., *Le Livre des Psaumes*, 1936.
Calkins, R., *The First and Second Book of Kings* (IB), 1954.
Calvin, J., *Commentaries*, reprinted 1948/9.
————, *Institutes of the Christian Religion*, reprinted 1957.
Charles, R. H., *A Critical and Exegetical Commentary on the Book of Daniel* (ICC), 1929.
————, *A Critical and Exegetical Commentary on the Revelation of St. John* (ICC), 1920.
Clavier, H., "Brèves Remarques sur la Notion de Soma Pneumaticon," in *The Background of the New Testament and Its Eschatology*, 1956.
Clement, *First Letter* (ANF).
Cole, R. A., *The Gospel according to Mark* (TNT), 1961.
Cooke, G. A., *A Critical and Exegetical Commentary on the Book of Ezekiel* (ICC), 1936.
Cox, S., *A Commentary on the Book of Job*, 1880.
Cragg, G. R., *The Epistle to the Romans* (IB), 1954.
Craig, C. T., *The First Epistle to the Corinthians* (IB), 1953.
Creed, J. M., *The Gospel according to St. Luke*, 1953.
Cullmann, O., *Christ and Time*, 1951.
————, "Proleptic Deliverance of the Body," in *The Early Church*, 1956.
————, "The Tradition," in *The Early Church*, 1956.
————, *Immortality of the Soul or Resurrection of the Dead?*, 1958.
————, *Early Christian Worship*, 1959.

Curtis, A. H., *The Vision and Mission of Jesus*, 1954.
Cyril of Jerusalem. *Catechetical Lectures* (NPNF).

Dahl, M. E., *The Resurrection of the Body*, 1962.
Darragh, J. T., *The Resurrection of the Flesh*, 1921.
Daube, D. and W. D. Davies, *The Background of the New Testament and Its Eschatology*, 1956.
Davies, J. G., *He Ascended into Heaven*, 1958.
————, "Gospel Origins," in *Expository Times*, December 1961.
Davies, W. D., "Paul on Flesh and Spirit," in *The Scrolls and the New Testament*, ed. K. Stendahl, 1957.
Diessmann, A., *Licht vom Osten*, 1923.
————, *The Religion of Jesus and the Faith of Paul*, 1926.
————, *Paul, A Study in Social and Religious History*, 1957.
Delitzsch, F., *A New Commentary on Genesis*, 1888.
————, *The Psalms* (ZK), reprinted 1955.
————, *The Prophecies of Isaiah* (ZK), reprinted 1954.
————, *The Book of Job* (ZK), reprinted 1956.
Delling, G., *"Lambano,"* in TWNT, IV, 1942.
Denney, J., *The Death of Christ*, reprinted 1950.
Dentler, E., *Die Auferstehung Jesu Christi*, 1910.
Dijk, K., "De Leer der Laatste Dingen," in *Het Dogma der Kerk*, 1949.
————, *Over de Laatste Dingen*, 1951/3.
Dodd, C. H., *Parables of the Kingdom*, 1936.
————, *New Testament Studies*, 1953.
————, *The Coming of Christ*, 1954.
————, "The Appearance of the Risen Lord," in *Studies in the Gospels*, ed. D. E. Nineham, 1955.
————, *The Apostolic Preaching and its Development*, 1956.
————, *The Meaning of Paul for Today*, 1957.
————, *The Epistle of Paul to the Romans*, 1959.
Dooyeweerd, H., *A New Critique of Theoretical Thought*, 1955.
————, Van Peursens Critische Vragen bij "A New Critique of Theoretical Thought," in *Philosophia Reformata*, 1960.
Driver, S. R., *The Book of Daniel*, 1922.
Duhm, F. B., *Das Buch Jesaja*, 1892.

Ebbutt, A. J., *The Life, the Question and the Answer*, 1958.
Edersheim, A., *The Life and Times of Jesus the Messiah*, 1886.
Eichrodt, W., *Man in the Old Testament*, 1957.
Ellis, E. E., *Paul's Use of the Old Testament*, 1957.
————, *Paul and His Recent Interpreters*, 1961.
Enoch, *Ethiopic and Slavonic.*

Feine, P., and J. Behm, *Einleiding in das Neue Testament*, 1956.
Ferris, T. P., *The Acts of the Apostles* (IB), 1954.
Filson, F. V., *The Second Epistle to the Corinthians* (IB), 1953.
————, *The New Testament against Its Environment*, 1956.
Flier, A. Van der, *Jesaja* (TU), 1923, 1926.
Fosdick, H. E., *A Guide to Understanding the Bible*, 1956.
Frey, H., *Das Buch der Anfange* (BAT), 1958.
————, *Das Buch des Werben Gottes um seine Kirche* (BAT), 1961.
Fuller, R. H., *The Mission and Achievement of Jesus*, 1954.

Gaster, Th. H., *The Scriptures of the Dead Sea Sect,* 1957.
Gealey, F. D., *The First and Second Epistles to Timothy* (IB), 1955.
Geldenhuys, N., *Commentary on the Gospel of Luke,* 1950.
Gelderen, C. van, *De Hoofdpunten der Zielsgeschiedenis van Job,* 1905.
————, *De Boeken der Koningen* (KV), 2 Vols., 1926, 1936.
————, *Het Boek Hosea* (COT), 1953.
Gerhardsson, B., *Memory and Manuscript,* 1961.
Gesenius, W., *Hebrew Grammar,* ed. E. Kautzsch and A. E. Cowley, 1956.
————, *Hebräisches and Aramäisches Handwörterbuch über das Alte Testament,* ed. F. Buhl, 1915.
Gilmour, S. M., *The Gospel according to St. Luke* (IB), 1952.
Girdlestone, R. B., *Synonyms of the Old Testament,* reprinted 1956.
Gispen, W. H., *Het Boek Hosea* (COT), 1953.
Godet, F. L., *The Gospel of Luke.*
————, *Gospel of John.*
————, *First Epistle to the Corinthians,* all reprinted in Classic Commentary Library, 1953.
Gollwitzer, H., *Jesu Tod und Auferstehung,* 1956.
Goslinga, C. J., *De Boeken van Samuel,* I (KV), 1948.
Gossip, A. J., *The Gospel according to St. John* (IB), 1952.
Grant, T. C., *The Gospel acording to St. Mark* (IB), 1952.
Gray, G. B., *A Critical and Exegetical Commentary on the Book of Isaiah* (ICC), 1962.
Grayston, K., "Flesh," in *A Theological Wordbook of the Bible,* ed. A. Richardson, 1957.
Green, E. M. B., *2 Peter Reconsidered,* 1961.
Greeven, H., "Proskuneo," in TWNT, VI, 1959.
Gregory of Naziansum, *Panegyric on his Brother S. Caesarius* (NPNF).
Gregory of Nazianzus, *Panegyric on his Brother S. Caesarius* (NPNF).
Greydanus, S., *De Openbaring des Heren aan Johannes* (KNT), 1925.
————, *De Brieven van de Apostelen Petrus en Johannes en de Brief van Judas* (KNT), 1929.
————, *De Brief van den Apostel Paulus aan de Gemeente te Rome* (KNT), 1933.
————, *Is Hand. 9 en 15 in Tegenspraak met Gal. 1 en 2?,* 1935.
————, *Het Heilig Evangelie naar de Beschrijving van Lucas,* 1940/1.
————, *Bijzondere Canoniek van de Boeken van het Nieuwe Testament,* 1949.
Groot, J. de, *De Psalmen, Verstaat gij wat gij leest?,* 1942.
Grosheide, F. W., *Het Heilig Evangelie volgens Mattheüs* (KNT), 1922.
————, *De Brief aan de Hebreën en de Brief van Jacobus* (KNT), 1927.
————, *De Eerste Brief aan Korinthe* (KNT), 1932.
————, *Te Tweede Brief aan Korinthe* (KNT), 1939.
————, *Het Heilig Evangelie volgens Johannes* (KNT), 1950.
————, *De Psalmen Overdacht,* I, 1952.
————, *Commentary on the First Epistle to the Corinthians* (NLC), 1954.
————, *De Brief aan de Hebreën* (CNT), 1955.
————, *De Eerste Brief aan de Kerk van Korinthe* (CNT), 1957.
————, *De Brief van Paulus aan de Epheziërs* (CNT), 1960.
Gutbrod, K., *Das Buch vom König* (BAT), 1959.

Guthrie, D., *The Pastoral Epistles* (TNT), 1957.
————, *New Testament Introduction*, 3 Vols., 1961-3.
Guy, H. A., *The New Testament Doctrine of the Last Things*, 1948.

Hanson, R., *II Corinthians* (TBC), 1954.
Harnack, A., *History of Dogma*, reprinted 1960.
Harrison, E. F., "The New Testament," in *Contemporary Evangelical Thought*, 1957.
Heering, H. J., *De Opstanding van Christus*, 1946.
Hendriksen, H. W., *The Gospel of John*, 2 Vols. (NTC), 1953/4.
————, *I and II Thessalonians* (NTC), 1955.
————, *I-II Timothy and Titus* (NTC), 1957.
————, *Philippians* (NTC), 1962.
————, *More than Conquerors, An Interpretation of the Book of Revelation*, 1961.
Hendry, G. S., *The Holy Spirit in Christian Theology*, 1957.
Henry, C. F. H., "Between Barth and Bultmann," in *Christianity Today*, 1-7, 1962.
Hepp, V., *De Antichrist*, 1919.
Hering, J., *The First Epistle of Saint Paul to the Corinthians*, 1962.
Hewitt, Th., *The Epistle to the Hebrews* (TNT), 1960.
Hijmans, A., "De Androgene," in *Bezinning*, No. 4, 1959.
Hippolytus, *The Refutation of All Heresies* (ANF).
Hodge, C., *The First Epistle to the Corinthians*, reprinted 1959.
————, *The Second Epistle to the Corinthians*, reprinted 1959.
Holtrop, H. H., *De Verschijningen onzes Heeren te Jeruzalem en in Galilea*, 1947.
Holwerda, D. E., *The Holy Spirit and Eschatology in the Gospel of John*, 1959.
Hoon, P. W., *The First, Second and Third Epistles of John* (IB), 1957.
Horst, J., *"Melos,"* in TWNT, IV, 1942.
Hoskyns, E., *The Fourth Gospel*, 1947.
Howard, W. F., *The Gospel according to St. John* (IB), 1952.
Hughes, A., *A New Heaven and a New Earth*, 1958.
Hunter, A. M., *Interpreting Paul's Gospel*, 1955.
————, *The First Epistle of Peter* (IB), 1957.
Hutchison, J., *Lectures, Chiefly Expository, on St. Paul's First and Second Epistles to the Thessalonians*, 1884.

Ignatius, *Epistle to the Smyrnaeans* (ANF).
Irenaeus, *Against Heresies* (ANF).

Jacob, E., *Theology of the Old Testament*, 1958.
Jager, O., *Het Eeuwige Leven*, 1962.
Jeremias, J., *"Adam,"* in TWNT, I, 1933.
————, "Flesh and Blood Cannot Inherit the Kingdom of God," in *New Testament Studies*, February 1956.
Johnson, S. E., *The Gospel according to St. Matthew* (IB), 1951.
Jonker, W. D., *Mystieke Liggaam en Kerk in die Nuwe Rooms-Katholieke Teologie*, 1955.
Josephus, *Antiquitates Judaicae*.
Justin Martyr, *Dialogue with Trypho* (ANF).
————, *Fragments of the Lost Work of Justin on the Resurrection* (ANF).

Käsemann, E., *Leib und Leib Christi,* 1933.
————, *Das Wanderende Gottesvolk,* 1938.
Keil, C. F. and F. Delitzsch, *The Pentateuch* (ZK), 1956.
————, *The Books of Samuel* (ZK), 1956.
————, *The Books of the Kings* (ZK), 1956.
Keil, C. F., *Biblical Commentary on the Book of Daniel* (ZK), 1955.
Kelly, J. N. D., *Early Christian Creeds,* 1952.
Kennedy, H. H. A., *St. Paul's Conceptions of the Last Things,* 1904.
Kenrick B., *The New Humanity,* 1958.
Kittel, G., *Theologisches Wörterbuch zum Neuen Testament,* 7 Vols. to date, 1933-1963.
————, *"Aggelos,"* in TWNT, I, 1933.
————, *"Doxa,"* in TWNT, II, 1935.
————, *"Eikon,"* in TWNT, II, 1935.
Knox, J., *Christ the Lord,* 1941.
————, *The Epistle to the Romans* (IB), 1954.
Koehler, L. and W. Baumgärtner, *A Hebrew and English Lexicon of the Old Testament,* 1958.
Kroeze, J. H., *Het Boek Job* (COT), 1961.
Kuhn, K. G., *"Basileus,"* in TWNT, I, 1933.
————, "Temptation, Sin and Flesh," in *The Scrolls and the New Testament,* ed. K. Stendahl, 1957.
————, "Der Epheserbrief im Lichte der Qumrantexte," in *New Testament Studies,* July 1961.
Kümmel, W., *Das Bild des Menschen im Neuen Testatment,* 1948.
Künneth, W., *Theologie der Auferstehung,* 1934.
Kuyper, A., *De Engelen Gods,* 1923.
————, *Van de Voleinding,* 1929-31.

Lake, K., *The Historical Evidence for the Resurrection of Jesus Christ,* 1907.
Lamparter, H., *Das Buch der Weisheit* (BAT), 1959.
————, *Das Buch der Psalmen* (BAT), 1959-61.
————, *Das Buch der Anfechtung* (BAT), 1961.
Lange, P. J., *The First Epistle of Peter,* in *Commentary on the Holy Scriptures by P. J. Lange* (ed. Ph. Schaff).
Lecerf, A., *Introduction to Reformed Dogmatics,* 1949.
Leeuwen, J. A. C. van, and D. Jacobs, *De Brief aan de Romeinen* (KV), 1932.
Leeuwen, J. A. C. van, *Paulus' Zendbrieven aan Efeze, Colosse, Filemon en Thessalonika* (KNT), 1926.
————, *Het Heilig Evangelie naar de Beschrijving van Markus* (KNT), 1928.
Lenski, R. C. H., *The Interpretation of the New Testament Books,* 12 Vols., 1956/7.
Leupold, H. C., *Exposition of Genesis,* 2 Vols., 1960.
————, *The Psalms,* 1959.
————, *Daniel,* 1949.
Liddell, H. G. and R. Scott, *A Greek-English Lexicon,* reprinted 1953.
Lightfoot, J. B., *Saint Paul's Epistles to the Colossians and to Philemon,* in Classic Commentary Library, reprinted 1953.
Lock, W., *A Critical and Exegetical Commentary on the Pastoral Epistles* (ICC), 1924.

Macgregor, G. H. C., *The Gospel of John* (MNTC), 1942.
————, *The Acts of the Apostles* (IB), 1954.
Machen, J. G., *The Origin of Paul's Religion*, 1947.
Manson, T. W., "The Life of Jesus: Some Tendencies in Present-Day Research," in *The Background of the New Testament and its Eschatology*, ed. D. Daube and W. D. Davies, 1956.
Manson, W., *The Gospel of Luke* (MNTC), 1930.
Martin, R. P., *The Epistle of Paul to the Philippians* (TNT), 1959.
McNabb, V., *The Resurrection of the Body*, 1946.
Mauchline, J., *The Book of Hosea* (IB), 1956.
May, H. G., *The Book of Ezekiel* (IB), 1956.
Michael, J. H., *The Epistle of Paul to the Philippians* (MNTC), 1928.
Milligan, G., *St. Paul's Epistles to the Thessalonians*, 1953.
Milligan, W., *The Resurrection of our Lord*, 1890.
————, *The Resurrection of the Dead*, 1894.
Miskotte, K. H., *De Verborgene*, 1929.
Moffatt, J., *The First Epistle of Paul to the Corinthians* (MNTC), 1938.
————, *The General Epistles* (MNTC), 1928.
Montgomery, J. A., *A Critical and Exegetical Commentary on the Book of Daniel* (ICC), 1959.
Morgan, W., *The Religion and Theology of Paul*, 1923.
Morison, F., *Who Moved the Stone?*, 1930.
Morris, L., *The First Epistle of Paul to the Corinthians* (TNT), 1958.
————, *The Epistles of Paul to the Thessalonians* (TNT), 1956.
Moule, C. F. D., "Jerusalem and Galilee Appearances," in *New Testament Studies*, October 1957.
Moule, H. C. G., *The Epistle to the Romans*.
Mowinckel, S., *He That Cometh*, 1956.
Mulder, E. S., *Die Teologie van die Jesaja-Apokalypse Jes. 24-27*, 1954.
Mulder, H., *Het Synoptische Vraagstuk*, 1952.
Murray, J., *Principles of Conduct*, 1957.
————, *The Epistle to the Romans*, I (NIC), 1960.

Neil, W., *The Epistle of Paul to the Thessalonians* (MNTC), 1950.
Nes, H. M., van, *De Brief aan de Hebreën, de Brief van Jacobus, de Eerste Brief van Petrus* (TU), 1923.
Newbigin, L., *The Household of God*, 1957.
————, *A Faith for This One World*, 1961.
Nineham, D. E., *Studies in the Gospels*, 1955.
Noordtzij, A., *Het Boek der Psalmen* I, II (KV), 1923.
————, *De Profeet Ezechiël* (KV), 1932.
Noordtzij, M., *De Achtenzestigste en de Zestiende Psalm*, 1900.
Nötscher, F., *Daniel*, 1948.
Nygren, A., *Commentary on Romans*, 1958.

Obbink, H. W., *Het Boek Daniël* (TU), 1932.
Oehler, G. F., *Theology of the Old Testament*, 1883.
Oepke, A., "*Anistemi*," in TWNT, I, 1933.
————, "*Egeiro*," in TWNT, II, 1935.
Oesterley, W. O. E., *The Psalms*, 1939.
Olmstead, A. T., *Jesus in the Light of History*, 1942.

Orr, J., *The Resurrection of Jesus*, 1909.
Oyen, H. van, *De Brief aan de Hebreën* (PNT), 1962.

Packer, J. I., *"Fundamentalism" and the Word of God*, 1959.
Pearson, J., *An Exposition of the Creed*, ed. Nichols, 1854.
Philo, *Legum Allegoriae*.
————, *De Opificio Mundi*.
————, *Moses*.
Pickl, J., *Messias-Koning*, 1937.
Pieters, A., *Notes on Genesis*, reprinted 1954.
Plato, *Phaedo*.
Plummer, A., *A Critical and Exegetical Commentary on the Gospel according to Luke* (ICC), 1916.
————, *A Commentary on St. Paul's First Epistle to the Thessalonians*, 1918.
Plumptre, E. H., *The General Epistles of St. Peter and St. Jude* (CBSB), 1899.
Pop, F. J., *Apostolaat in Druk en Vertroosting* (PNT), 1953.
————, *Bijbelse Woorden en Hun Geheim*, 2 Vols., 1956-58.
Popma, K. J., *De Vrijheid der Exegese*, 1944.
————, *Calvinistische Geschiedbeschouwing*, 1945.
————, *Eerst de Jood Maar Ook de Griek*, 1950.
————, *Inleiding in de Wijsbegeerte*, 1956.
Procksch, O., *Jesaja I* (Kommentar zum Alten Testament), 1930.
Purdy, A. C., *The Epistle to the Hebrews* (IB), 1955.

Rad, G. Von, *Genesis, A Commentary*, 1961.
————, *"Zao,"* in TWNT, II, 1935.
Ramsey, A. M., *The Resurrection of Christ*, 1961.
Raven, Ch. E., *St. Paul and the Gospel of Jesus*, 1961.
Rawlinson, A. E. J., *The New Testament Doctrine of Christ*, 1929.
Reid, J., *The Second Epistle to the Corinthians* (IB), 1953.
Rengstorf, K. H., *Das Evangelium nach Lukas* (NTD), 1958.
Richardson, A., *Introduction to the Theology of the New Testament*, 1958.
————, ed., *A Theological Word Book of the Bible*, 1957.
Ridderbos, H. N., *Het Evangelie naar Mattheüs* (KV), I, 1941; II, 1954.
————, *The Epistle of Paul to the Churches of Galatia* (NIC), 1954.
————, *Heilsgeschiedenis en Heilige Schrift*, 1955.
————, *When the Time Had Fully Come*, 1957.
————, *Het Verborgen Koninkrijk*, 1958.
————, *Paul and Jesus*, 1958.
————, *Aan de Romeinen* (CNT), 1959.
————, *Bultman*, 1960.
Ridderbos, J., *Het Godswoord der Profeten*, 1930-41.
————, *De Kleine Profeten*, 3 Vols. (KV), 1932-35.
————, *De Psalmen*, 2 Vols. (COT), 1955-58.
Riesenfeld, H., *The Gospel Tradition and Its Beginning*, 1957.
Robertson, A., and A. Plummer, *A Critical and Exegetical Commentary on the First Epistle of Paul to the Corinthians* (ICC), 1961.
Robinson, C. H., *Studies in the Resurrection of Christ*, 1911.
Robinson, H. W., *The Christian Doctrine of Man*, 1958.
Robinson, J. A. T., *The Body*, 1952.
————, *In the End, God. . . .,* 1958.

Robinson, J. M., *A New Quest of the Historical Jesus,* 1959.
Robinson, T. H., *The Gospel of Matthew* (MNTC), 1937.
Ross, A., *The Epistles of James and John* (NIC), 1954.
Rowley, H. H., *The Faith of Israel,* 1956.
Rufinus, *Commentary on the Apostles' Creed* (NPNF).
————, *Pamphilus' Defence of Origen* (NPNF).
Runia, K., *De Theologische Tijd bij Karl Barth,* 1955.
————, *Karl Barth's Doctrine of Holy Scripture,* 1962.
Russell, B., *History of Western Philosophy,* 1954.
Russell, D. S., *Between the Testaments,* 1960.
Ryle, J. C., *Het Evangelie van Johannes,* 1886.

Saggs, H. W. F., "Some Ancient Semitic Concepts of the Afterlife" in *Faith and Thought,* 1958.
Salmond, S. D. F., *The Epistle of Paul to the Ephesians,* in *The Expositor's Greek Testament,* III, reprinted 1956.
Sanday, W., and A. C. Headlam, *A Critical and Exegetical Commentary on the Epistle to the Romans* (ICC), 1925.
Sasse, H., *This Is My Body,* 1959.
————, "The Second Vatican Council (II)" in *The Reformed Theological Review,* October 1961.
Sauer, E., *The Triumph of the Crucified,* 1957.
Sayers, Dorothy L., *The Man Born to be King,* 1957.
Schaff, Ph., *The Creeds of the Greek and Latin Churches,* 1877.
————, *The Creeds of the Evangelical Protestant Churches,* 1877.
Scherer, P., *The Book of Job* (IB), 1954.
Schilder, K., *Wat Is de Hemel?,* 1935.
Schlatter, A., *Erläuterungen zum Neuen Testament,* 3 Vols., 1936-8.
Schlatter, W., *Biblische Menschkunde,* 1959.
Schneider, J., *"Anabaino,"* in TWNT, I, 1933.
Schniewind, J., *Das Evangelium des Markus,* 1935.
Schweitzer, A., *Die Mystik des Apostels Paulus,* 1930.
Schweizer, E., *"Pneuma,"* in TWNT, VI, 1959.
————, *Lordship and Discipleship,* 1960.
————, *"Sarx,"* in TWNT, VII, 1960.
Scott, E. F., *The Pastoral Epistles* (MNTC), 1936.
————, *The Epistle of Paul to the Philippians* (IB), 1955.
Seesemann, H., *"Opiso,"* in TWNT, V, 1954.
Selwyn, C. G., *The First Epistle of Peter,* 1958.
Semmelink, J. H., *Onsterfelijkheid en Opstanding,* 1962.
Sevenster, G., *De Christologie van het Nieuwe Testament,* 1946.
————, "De Opstanding des Vleses by Tertullianus en in het Nieuwe Testament," in *Nederlands Theologisch Tijdschrift,* 1954-5, pp. 364f.
Shore, T. T., *The First Epistle to the Corinthians,* in The Layman's Handy Commentary Series, ed. C. J. Ellicott, 1957.
Short, J., *The First Epistle to the Corinthians* (IB), 1953.
Simon, W. G., *The First Epistle to the Corinthians* (TBC), 1959.
Simpson, C. A., *The Book of Genesis* (IB), 1952.
Simpson, E. K., *Commentary on the Epistles to the Ephesians and the Colossians,* 1957.
————, *The Pastoral Epistles,* 1954.
Sjöberg, E., *"Pneuma,"* in TWNT, VI, 1959.

Skinner, J., *A Critical and Exegetical Commentary on Genesis* (ICC), 1910.

Smedes, L. B., *The Incarnation: Trends in Modern Anglican Thought,* 1953.

Smelik, E. L., *De Weg van het Woord, het Evangelie naar Johannes* (PNT), 1956.

——————, *De Brieven van Paulus aan Timotheus, Titus en Filemon* (PNT), 1961.

Smith, W., *Therefore Stand,* 1945.

——————, "Resurrection," in *Baker's Dictionary of Theology,* 1960.

Snaith, N. H., *The First and Second Books of Kings* (IB), 1954.

Spier, J. M., *Tijd en Eeuwigheid,* 1953.

——————, *An Introduction to Christian Philosophy,* 1954.

Stacey, W. D., *The Pauline View of Man,* 1956.

Stam, C., *De Hemelvaart des Heren in de Godsopenbaring van het Nieuwe Testament,* 1950.

Stauffer, E., *Jesus and His Story,* 1960.

Stempvoort, P. A. van, "De Opstanding des Vleses in 1 Kor. 15, in *Vox Theologica,* 1939, p. 176f.

Stendahl, K., ed., *The Scrolls and the New Testament,* 1957.

Stibbs, A. M., *The First Epistle General of Peter* (TNT), 1959.

Stonehouse, N. B., *The Witness of Luke to Christ,* 1951.

——————, *Paul Before the Areopagus,* 1957.

Strack, H. L., and P. Billerbeck, *Kommentar zum Neuen Testament,* 5 Vols., 1922-28.

Strauss, D. F., *Das Leben Jesu kritisch bearbeitet,* 1864.

Strawson, W., *Jesus and the Future Life,* 1959.

Streeder, G. J., *De Prediking van de Opstanding der Doden in het Oude Testament,* 1956.

——————, *Een Beoordeling van Barth's Exegese van 1 Corinthen 15,* 1938.

Swete, H. B., *The Life of the World to Come,* 1918.

——————, *The Apostles' Creed,* 1899.

Tasker, R. V. G., *The Gospel in the Epistle to the Hebrews,* 1956.

——————, *The Second Epistle of Paul to the Corinthians* (TNT), 1958.

——————, *The Gospel according to St. Matthew* (TNT), 1961.

Taylor, V., *The Life and Ministry of Jesus,* 1955.

——————, *The Gospel according to St. Mark,* 1952.

Taylor, W. R., *The Book of Psalms* (IB), 1955.

Telder, B., *Sterven en Dan?,* 1960.

Tertullian, *On the Resurrection of the Flesh* (ANF).

——————, *Prescription against Heretics* (ANF).

Thomas, W. H. Griffith, *Genesis,* reprinted 1957.

Thurneysen, Ed., "Christus und seine Zukunft," in *Zwischen den Zeiten,* 1931.

Tillich, P., *Systematic Theology,* 1958.

Traub, H., *"Ouranos,"* in TWNT, V, 1954.

Trench, R. C., *Synonyms of the New Testament,* 1953.

Tresmontant, C., *Saint Paul and the Mysteries of Christ,* 1958.

Uitman, J. E., *Christus het Hoofd, De Brief aan de Colossenzen* (PNT), 1955.

Unnik, W. C. van, "Jesus the Christ," in *New Testament Studies,* January 1962.

Ursinus, Zacharias, *Commentary on the Heidelberg Catechism,* 1958.

Valeton, J. J., *De Psalmen*, 2 Vols., 1913.

Verhoef, P. A., *Die Vraagstuk van die Onvervulde Voorsegginge in Verband met Jesaja 1-39*, 1950.

Vincent, M. R., *Word Studies in the New Testament*, reprinted 1946.

Vos, G., *The Pauline Eschatology*, reprinted 1953.

————, *The Teaching of the Epistle to the Hebrews*, reprinted 1956.

Waaning, N. H., *Onderzoek naar het Gebruik van* pneuma *bij Paulus*, 1939.

Walton, F. R., "After-Life," in *The Oxford Classical Dictionary*, 1950.

Weatherhead, L., *After Death*, 1930.

Wedel, T. O., *The Epistle to the Ephesians* (IB), 1953.

Weiss, B., *Kritisch-exegetisches Handbuch über die Evangelien des Markus und Lukas*, 1878.

Weiss, J., *Earliest Christianity*, 1959.

Wendland, H. D., *Die Briefe an die Korinther* (NTD), 1954.

Westcott, B. F., *The Gospel of the Resurrection*, 1906.

————, *The Revelation of the Risen Lord*, 1907.

White, E., *St. Paul, the Man and His Mind*, 1958.

Wilder, A. N., *The First, Second and Third Epistles of John* (IB), 1957.

Willemze, J., *De Tweede Brief van Petrus, de Brieven van Johannes, de Brief van Judas* (TU), 1924.

Windisch, H., *Die katholischen Briefe*, 1930.

Wohlenberg, G., *Der erster und zweiter Thessalonischerbrief* (ZK), 1909.

————, *Der erster und zweiter Petrusbrief und der Judasbrief* (ZK), 1911.

Wren-Lewis, J., "When Did the Fall Occur?" in *Expository Times*, October 1960.

Wright, J. S., *Man in the Process of Time*, 1956.

Young, E. J., *The Prophecy of Daniel*, 1953.

Zahn, Th., *Das Evangelium des Matthäus* (ZK), 1910.

————, *Das Evangelium des Lukas* (ZK), 1913.

————, *Die Apostelgeschichte des Lukas* (ZK), 2 Vols., 1919-21.

————, *Der Brief des Paulus an die Römer* (ZK), 1910.

INDEX OF AUTHORS

242

INDEX OF SUBJECTS

247

INDEX OF BIBLICAL REFERENCES